John Eliot and the Praying Indians of Massachusetts Bay

John Eliot and the Praying Indians of Massachusetts Bay

Communities and Connections in Puritan New England

Kathryn N. Gray

Lewisburg
BUCKNELL UNIVERSITY PRESS

Published by Bucknell University Press
Co-published with The Rowman & Littlefield Publishing Group, Inc.
4501 Forbes Boulevard, Suite 200, Lanham, Maryland 20706
www.rowman.com

10 Thornbury Road, Plymouth PL6 7PP, United Kingdom

British Library Cataloguing in Publication Information Available

Library of Congress Cataloging-in-Publication Data
Gray, Kathryn N., 1975–
John Eliot and the praying indians of Massachusetts Bay : communities and connections in Puritan
New England / Kathryn N. Gray.
p. cm.
Includes bibliographical references and index.
ISBN 978-1-61148-503-5 (cloth : alk. paper) — ISBN 978-1-61148-504-2
1. Eliot, John, 1604-1690. 2. Indians of North America—Missions—Massachusetts. 3. Missionar-
ies—Massachusetts—Biography. 4. Puritans—Massachusetts—Biography. I. Title.
E78.M4E5265 2013
266'.58092—dc23
[B] 2013023883
ISBN 978-1-6114-8691-9 (pbk : alk. paper)

♾™ The paper used in this publication meets the minimum requirements of American
National Standard for Information Sciences Permanence of Paper for Printed Library
Materials, ANSI/NISO Z39.48-1992.

Printed in the United States of America

For Scott

Contents

Introduction

Two prevailing images of John Eliot, missionary and minister, have endured since visual artists of the nineteenth century memorialized his life and work: Eliot is either depicted as a youngish man standing with his arm raised heavenward preaching amid a group of Native American tribesmen, or he is portrayed as a much older man in his declining years sitting at a desk with a prominently placed copy of his own translation of the Algonquian bible, *Mamusse Wunneetupanatamwe Up-Biblum God.*[1] One image remembers Eliot's gift for oratory and the other his work as an ambitious and successful linguist. In each of these images Eliot's relationship with Algonquian people and their language is prioritized as we witness them receiving religious instruction aurally from Eliot's sermons or in textual form from his biblical translation.

It is perhaps unsurprising that artists chose to remember Eliot through the value he placed on the power of the spoken word: after all, as a preacher and missionary he was first and foremost an orator who privileged public speech in the form of sermons and prayers in his day-to-day ecclesiastical life. These artists have followed Cotton Mather's lead when he referred to Eliot as "Moses in America," then likened him to "John the Baptist"[2] and coined his lasting title, "Apostle to the Indians,"[3] modeling him on the great orators of the New Testament. In each of Mather's descriptions and the visual depictions of Eliot as a young man preaching in the wilderness, Eliot's verbal eloquence and his gift for powerful oratory remained central components to his success as a missionary. The alternative image of Eliot as an older man with his hand resting on a copy of the Algonquian bible brings to the fore the value Eliot placed on the written word as an equally valuable communicative tool which would continue to bring God's word to Algonquian Christian readers for generations to come.[4] These images highlight the fact that John

Eliot more than any other individual in colonial New England believed that Native languages, in this case Massachusett, a dialect of Algonquian, could be and should be a language of Christianity. The purpose of this study is to examine Eliot's relationship with Algonquian people and their language and consider the processes and circumstances of Native American conversion to Christianity.

From Mather's depiction of Eliot and the visual memorials which have evolved from the nineteenth century it would be easy to assume that Eliot's verbal and written encounters with Algonquian people of Massachusetts existed in isolation from the religious and political upheaval of life in seventeenth-century England. In fact nothing could be further from the truth. During his long career as a minister and a missionary Eliot made numerous contributions to missionary narratives which were published in London (commonly referred to as the Eliot Tracts), and engaged fervently in millennial debates over England's political and religious trials during the 1650s. Through spoken and written communications Eliot created a network of individuals and communities in Native and colonial New England as well as in England, both in the metropolitan center, London, and in regional parts of England. By demonstrating the ways in which each of these geographically distinct audiences coalesce into communities of readers or communities of gathered listeners in relation to Eliot's mission, the political and religious motivations of the New England mission are, I hope, revealed with a new inclusiveness. For a very long period, from his arrival in 1631 until his death in 1690, Eliot consciously situated his New England mission within a tapestry of contesting, transatlantic political and religious forces.[5]

The written communications and spoken utterances that circulated in this charged transatlantic space were of many kinds. There were private letters, published correspondence, public declarations of faith, narrative accounts of native conversion, language primers, the Algonquian bible itself, religious instruction manuals, records of religious utterances (catechism, examination and prayer, for example), dying speeches and fictional dialogues. By paying attention to the various English, colonial, and Native communities with whom Eliot interacted and the influences at work in their expressions of religious utterance, I believe it is possible to examine many of the configurations of collective and individual identity available to speakers, listeners, and readers of all communities, as they use the mission to redefine their political and religious identities in a century defined by comprehensive social and political upheaval. We should remember that this upheaval was differently configured in England, colonial New England, and the territories of the Southern Algonquian people on the Eastern seaboard.

In summary, by focusing on John Eliot's interactions with correspondents and communities in England, as well as his interactions with communities of Algonquian penitents, we can better understand the political and religious impulses that allowed first-generation colonial New Englanders like Eliot to establish a culture of spiritual renewal in a difficult and unpredictable environment. When the Puritans set sail for the New World the civil and political necessity of establishing a community was driven by their religious fervor, and racialized when they confronted communities of Natives whose lives and appearances were very different from their own. They were also tested to the very limits as they endured a harsh and at times unforgiving landscape. In part, this study traces the lines and patterns of communication within these communities and considers the impact that these local and transatlantic connections had in the "contact zone"[6] of colonial New England, as well as in the hearts and minds of armchair missionaries in England. The composition of the different communities with whom Eliot engaged ranged from Indian listeners and speakers in the immediate space of the local native settlements and praying towns in the colony, to a transatlantic community made up of personal correspondents and official exchanges with the London-based Corporation for the Propagation of the Gospel and, in the last years, the Royal Society.

The programs and effects of Eliot's communications have been studied before, and Sandra Gustafson, for example, has fairly recently made a significant contribution to the field in her study, *Eloquence is Power*, which establishes a new set of parameters for the study of speech and speech acts in colonial North America, in which Eliot and praying Indians of Massachusetts Bay play a key and prominent role. In *Dry Bones and Indian Sermons*, Kristina Bross covers similar terrain but within a transatlantic framework. Also, in *Allegories of Desire*, Thomas Scanlan has considered the literary resonances of Eliot's work in an educated and elitist colonial environment, with specific reference to *Indian Dialogues*.[7] The present study, however, aims to build on these important publications by developing a keener understanding of the *communities* in which Eliot and the praying Indians of Massachusetts Bay interacted in order to achieve a fuller understanding of the power relationships and cultural negotiations which took place in Eliot's seventeenth-century mission.

Such a methodology puts particular emphasis on the idea of community, much discussed in recent scholarship. In their introduction to *Communities in Early Modern England*, Phil Withington and Alexandra Shepard trace the development of the term *community* and conclude that the term underwent continual refashioning as technologies developed, nations coalesced and empires expanded. They even go so far as to state that in the sixteenth and seventeenth century, "communities were present, so to speak, in the turmoil of their own refashioning."[8] It is useful, therefore, to consider the changing meanings and functions of communities and how this fits with Eliot's understanding of the term.

communis?n The roots of the term community have been traced back to the fourteenth century where the term identified "the commons or common people" as opposed to those of "rank."[9] Since then, sociologists have argued that the contemporary understanding of a community has its roots in the Puritan's sense of the commonwealth, referred to both in England and New England as the ideological union of civil and theological concerns.[10] From its very beginnings, colonial New England aspired to establish its status as a gathered civil community, first with the Mayflower Compact, closely followed by the lay preachings of John Winthrop and his vision of an isolated city on a hill. When Eliot finally set sail from Southampton in 1631 on board the *Lyon* he was following in Bradford's and Winthrop's footsteps to take his place in a geographically isolated community of educated and devout Puritans in New England. This was a far cry from the sheltered intellectual communities of his early education in Hertfordshire and later at Cambridge under the inspirational and influential Thomas Hooker. In the apparent wilderness of New England, new congregations and communities were forged and Eliot took his place as minister of Congregationalists in Roxbury, Massachusetts.

As print culture replaced manuscripts, as monarchs and governments redefined their civil and ecclesiastical structures, and as the flow of letters from colonial settlers replaced the day-to-day conversations with their families back home, different kinds of people utilized new forms of communication either to increase their collective audiences or to maintain precious, personal connections. In this context, John Eliot's networks of communication cut across racial, cultural, and geographical boundaries. He participated in meetings, prayers, sermons, and confessions in praying towns and in traditional tribal homes and when he was able to he communicated in Algonquian. He also maintained significant connections with key correspondents in England, thus establishing further communities of reception as the successes and challenges of the mission were transmitted to a diverse group of ordinary and influential English readers. Further, when Indian speeches were translated and transcribed for the benefit of an English audience, the oral performances of praying Indians came into close, virtual contact with a larger community of religious and missionary sympathizers thousands of miles away. Communities had been bridged across spatial, cultural, and linguistic difference. In an effort to map these cross-currents, this study takes as its organizing principle what sociologists have called an "ego-centered" or "personal" approach to community.[11] That is, Eliot is deliberately positioned as conduit through which disparate and, sometimes, fragile communities are connected.

Finally, with regard to ideas of community, some acknowledgement of Stanley Fish's contribution to the complexities of a community's power and function is appropriate with regard to the effort to remain sensitive to the subtle nuances of colonial and transatlantic communications. With reference to his term "interpretive communities" he suggests that in the midst of a conflict between authorial and textual autonomy, the meaning or meanings of a text are properly understood to be located within a community of readers who collectively negotiate the meaning(s) of the text. [12] In this study communities respond to a large variety of texts in both spoken or written forms, and these texts include letters, narratives, dialogues, speeches, confessions, prayer, sermons, the Bible, an act of worship, or funeral rites. The ways in which different communities negotiate the meanings of these texts is at the heart of our understanding of Eliot's mission. The interpretive strategies and conclusions of contesting communities can differ substantially, and by remembering that different communities from radically different cultures will interpret the same text in radically different ways we can more fully understand the negotiations of faith which evolve from Eliot's mission. This analytical framework allows full consideration of the interpretive strategies of Algonquian communities who received religious sermons and texts from Eliot and negotiated a new identity in the new colonial landscape. It also allows for a fuller understanding of seventeenth-century Puritans and the ways in which the performance of praying Indians was mediated to accommodate concerns of New England's errand into the wilderness, as well as England's revolutionary spirit and its attempt to dominate the New World. All the reception communities in this study coalesce into interpretive communities as they negotiate the impact of Eliot's mission in the context of their own circumstances.

The wilderness, religious conversion, and spiritual renewal are all alive and well in the figure of Eliot: as a self-defined "shrub" [13] in the wilderness, his powerful oratory swayed Native listeners to believe in the Christian God, and through his intellectual commitment to biblical translations he provided a literary legacy for Algonquian praying Indians. In England the written accounts of a successful religious conversion, and the materiality of the Algonquian bible in print, provided England with a religious foundation on which to rebuild and reshape her reputation as a dominant player in the Atlantic world, as well as providing England and her colonists with what was quickly interpreted as a stamp of providential authority over the colonial landscape. Within a complex network of performances where the praying Indian enacts everything England has lost and will become again, the New Englander emerges as both the actor and the architect of this design. Missionary success in the colony is certainly dependent on England for financial survival, but, by wielding significant religious and rhetorical sovereignty, the colonizers manage to disconnect themselves from their English heritage and establish themselves as morally superior and spiritually renewed. Significantly, this is achieved without ever promoting themselves directly. In these publications the canny New England Puritans bask only in reflected glory and New Englishness begins to emerge from its English roots by successfully communicating this new cultural type, the praying Indian, to an English audience.

In the chapters that follow I have organized my analysis on the basis of community types and their engagement with Eliot either through speech acts or literary speech acts. In each chapter a different community of speakers, readers or listeners is defined in relation to the ways in which they coalesce around Eliot's spoken or written utterances. In chapter 1, I consider Eliot's private correspondence with his English supporters and patrons in an effort to situate Eliot and his mission in the political and religious tensions which helped define the seventeenth century Atlantic world. Specifically, this chapter considers the ways in which Eliot adapts the immediacy of conversation in the implied intimacy of the private epistle and also considers the methods by which the privacy of these letters and manuscripts forged a select community of private readers with common concerns regarding Eliot's mission and England's place in the race to dominate the colonial landscape. Eliot's correspondence spanned sixty years, which allows conceptual mapping of Eliot's attempts to respond to changing political and religious impulses in England as they impact on colonial New England.

Chapter 2 considers narrative accounts of the mission intended for public readers in metropolitan and rural England. This analysis involves the transformation of speech acts, primarily the confessions of the praying Indian, into literary speech acts, specifically through the transcription of these confessions to communities of private readers and gathered listeners in England. I explore literary speech acts to demonstrate the effects of the disunity between the experience and the narration of a community's internal cohesion as it occurs at the point of reception. As Pratt also suggests, "in any case where communication between a speaker and intended addressee is dependent on a mediator, the speaker's utterance exists in a kind of limbo until the mediation is completed."[14] It is through this necessary limbo and mediation, when letters and narratives containing speech acts travel across the Atlantic to their intended audiences, that interesting readings and misreadings can be detected, serving to highlight the large differences of interpretation between English and Algonquian interlocutors. Through these performances, colonial scribes set out to prove the success of the mission but, as I will go on to demonstrate, they are also intent on redefining their cultural identity in relation to the new world environment and against old world values.

Negotiations of faith through spoken utterances are explored in chapter 3. The spaces of religious utterances and the turn-taking dynamics of speech acts, as speakers and listeners give and take their access to the floor, are mapped in order to account for the negotiations of faith in a charged and volatile colonial environment. In this part of the discussion, I argue that spaces of education, politics, wigwams, and praying towns must be delineated before the nuances of the power balances at work in the "total speech situations"[15] of praying Indians with missionary colonizers can be productively assessed. My understanding of the term, "total speech situation," is taken from Judith Butler's critique of J. L. Austin's speech act theory. Austin's theory, detailed in *How To Do Things With Words*, distinguishes between words that report an event (constative utterances) and words that enact the event (performative utterances). Austin restricts his analysis of performative language to the spoken word since, he argues: "written utterances are not tethered to their origin in the same way spoken ones are."[16] That is, as Judith Butler states in her critique of the problem, the force of the speaker and speaker's bodily gestures cannot be known so the "total speech situation" is incomplete.[17] Jacques Derrida, however, expands the limits of speech act theory to account for the performative possibilities of written text when he asserts that "(w)riting is thus a modality of language and marks a continual progression in an essentially linguistic communication."[18] Finally, as Della Pollock has argued, and as I wish to demonstrate in relation to Eliot's work generally, "(w)riting that takes up the performativity in language is meant to make a difference, 'to make things happen.'"[19] This assessment of speech act and literary speech acts, provides a suitable category through which Eliot's letters, missionary narratives, dialogues, speeches, and promotional tracts may be analyzed.

Chapter 4 considers forms of speech similar to those of chapter 3 but instead focuses exclusively on Native Christian women. Women have been largely neglected in studies of Eliot's mission, yet, as I will argue, they were the key to its success; on many occasions it is nameless mothers and wives who have responded to Eliot's teachings and it is they who make possible the conversion of whole families to Christianity. This chapter considers Christian Indian women as a category separate from Christian Indian men because the expectations on them appear to be different from those of their husbands and sons. It is my contention that amid the racial and gendered complexities of colonial New England, Christian Indian women coalesced into a unique community of believers which was predicated on expectations placed on women through tribal traditions, as well as the expectations placed on them by white colonial society in seventeenth century New England.

The final chapter of this study attends to communities of Native readers. This chapter explores levels of literacy, and what constitutes literacy, among indigenous people of New England, focusing on the contesting values of oral and written traditions of communication. It also accounts for the negotiation of faith in Native communities, specifically through their relationship with the written word. This negotiation of faith was made possible by Eliot's orthography, language primers and *Indian Grammar Begun*, his biblical translations, and his religious instruction manuals, which allowed communities of Native readers to adapt oral traditions and written text into a new hybrid form of communication, one which sustained their desire to control their own voices and identities.

Overall, in the first two chapters, my analysis considers communities of private readers and gathered listeners in England, as a way of foregrounding the significance of the transatlantic debates in which Eliot operated throughout his career as a missionary-colonizer. These debates had a huge impact on the ways in which Native American identities were shaped, controlled, and contested. The final three chapters focus on Native reception communities: as communities of penitent Indians of speaking subjects as they utter words of conversion; as communities of Christian Indian women who quietly, for the most part, hold the fabric of Christian Indian communities together; and as communities of Indian readers, who adapt textual strategies into their oral traditions. This framework has also allowed me to begin with an analysis of the private epistle and manuscript culture in England, and end with a very different kind of scribal culture in Native New England, allowing the trajectory of this study to reflect the enduring negotiation of oral Native traditions with western textual forms.

NOTES

1. *See* "Eliot and the Indians," memorial panel on Congregational Association Building, 14, Beacon Street, Boston; "John Eliot Preaching to the Indians," Mural by Henry Oliver Walker, 1903, Massachusetts State House, Boston; "Portrait of John Eliot," Headmaster of Roxbury Latin School, Roxbury, Massachusetts, U.S.A., from the frontispiece to F. Washington Jarvis, *Schola Illustris: The Roxbury Latin School, 1645–1995* (Boston: D. R. Godine, 1995).

2. Cotton Mather, *Magnalia Christi Americana, Or, the Ecclesiastical History of New-England, from the First Planting in the Year 1620 unto the Year of our Lord, 1698.* (Printed for Thomas Parkhurst, London, 1702.) *Eighteenth Century Collections Online* at, www.jischistoricbooks.ac.uk (accessed April 8, 2013), Book 3, 172, 180. In this original and unabridged version, Mather goes on to state: "He that will write of *Eliot*, must write of *Charity*, or say nothing. His *Charity* was a star of the *First Magnitude* in the bright Constellation of his Vertues; and the Rays of it were wonderfully various and extensive" (Ibid., 181).

3. Mather endorses Eliot's status as "Apostle to the American Indians" when he incorporates a letter from his father, Increase Mather, to Dr John Leusden, Professor of Hebrew at the University of Utrecht, into his narrative, *see*: "A Letter concerning the success of the Gospel, Amongst the Indians of New England," Boston, July 12 1687 (Mather, *Magnalia*, (1702) 194–95). For a more recent, abridged edition, *see*: account Cotton Mather, *Magnalia Christi Americana, Or, The Ecclesiastical History of New England. Edited by Raymond J. Cunningham* (New York: Frederick Ungar Publishing, 1970).

4. For analysis of New England Puritans and their relationship with speech and text for example, see Jane Kamensky, *Governing the Tongue: The Politics of Speech in Early New England* (Oxford: Oxford University Press, 1999); Sandra M. Gustafson, *Eloquence is Power: Oratory and Performance in Early America,* (London and Chapel Hill: Published for the Omohundro Institute of Early American History and Culture, Williamsburg, Virginia, by the University of North Carolina Press, 2000); James Axtell, "The Power of Print in the Eastern Woodlands," *William and Mary Quarterly* 44, no. 2 (April 1987): 300–9; and his *The Invasion Within: The Contest of Cultures in Colonial North America,* (New York: Oxford University Press, 1985); Jill Lepore, "Dead Men Tell No Tales: John Sassamon and the Fatal Consequences of Literacy," *American Quarterly* 46, no. 4 (December 1994): 479–512; David Murray, *Forked Tongues: Speech, Writing and Representation in North American Indian Texts* (Bloomington: Indiana University Press, 1991); Craig White, "The Praying Indians Speeches

as Texts of Massachusett Oral Culture," *Early American Literature* 38, no. 3 (Fall 2003): 437–67. For analysis of how this relationship developed in the eighteenth century, *see* Jay Fliegelman, *Declaring Independence: Jefferson, Natural Language & the Culture of Performance* (Stanford, CA: Stanford University Press, 1993).

    5. For an introduction to some general themes in the Atlantic world not mentioned elsewhere in this study, see *The British Atlantic World 1500–1800*, ed. David Armitage and Michael J. Braddick (New York: Palgrave MacMillan, 2002); Bernard Bailyn, *Atlantic History, Concepts and Contours* (Cambridge, MA.: Harvard University Press, 2005); *Soundings in Atlantic History, Latent Structures and Intellectual Currents, 1500–1830*, ed. Bernard Bailyn and Patricia L Denault (Cambridge, MA: Harvard University Press, 2009); Thomas Benjamin *The Atlantic World: Europeans, Africans, Indians and Their Shared History* (New York: Cambridge University Press 2009); John Huxtable Elliot, *The Old World and the New 1492–1650* (Cambridge: Canto, Cambridge University Press, 1970. Reprint 1992); Mary C. Fuller, *Voyages in Print: English Travel to America, 1576–1624* (Cambridge: Cambridge University Press, 1995); Alison Games, *Migration and the Origins of the English Atlantic World* (Cambridge, MA: Harvard University Press, 1999); Stephen Greenblatt, *Marvellous Possessions: The Wonder of the New World* (Chicago: University of Chicago Press, 1991); *Colonial British America: Essays in the New History of the Early Modern Era*, ed. Jack P. Greene and J. R. Pole (London and Baltimore: Johns Hopkins University Press, 1984); Andrew Hadfield, *Literature, Travel, and Colonial Writing in the English Renaissance 1545–1625* (Oxford: Oxford University Press, 1998); *America in European Consciousness, 1493–1750*, ed. Karen Ordahl Kupperman (Chapel Hill: University of North Carolina Press, 1995); and *Transatlantic Literary Studies: A Reader*, ed. Susan Manning and Andrew Taylor (Edinburgh: Edinburgh University Press, 2007).

    6. I am using this term in the same spirit as the term was originally coined by Mary Louise Pratt in, *Imperial Eyes: Travel Writing and Transculturation* (London and New York: Routledge, 1992), 4.

    7. Gustafson, *Eloquence is Power*; Kristina Bross, *Dry Bones and Indian Sermons: Praying Indians in Colonial America* (London and Ithaca, NY: Cornell University Press, 2004); Thomas Scanlan, *Colonial Writing and the New World 1583–1671: Allegories of Desire* (Cambridge: Cambridge University Press, 1999); John Eliot, *Indian Dialogues: A Study in Cultural Interaction*, ed. Henry W Bowden and James P Rhonda (Westport, CT.: Greenwood Press, 1980).

    8. *Communities in Early Modern England: Networks, Place, Rhetoric*, ed. Alexandra Shepard and Phil Withington (Manchester: Manchester University Press, 2000), 1–15, 7.

    9. Raymond Williams, *Keywords: A Vocabulary of Culture and Society* (London: Croom Helm, 1976), 65–66.

    10. C. J. Calhoun, "Community: Toward a Variable Conceptualization for Comparative Research," *Social History* 5, no. 1 (1980): 105.

    11. Alan MacFarlane, "History, Anthropology and the Study of Communities," *Social History* 2, no. 5 (May 1977): 637.

    12. Stanley Fish, *Is there a Text in this Class? The Authority of Interpretive Communities* (London and Cambridge, MA: Harvard University Press, 1980, rpt. 2003), 15.

    13. "John Eliot to Robert Boyle, 26 August 1664," *The Correspondence of Robert Boyle*, ed. Michael Hunter, Antonio Clericuzio and Lawrence M. Principe (London and Burlington, VT: Pickering and Chatto, 2001) 2:1662–65, 305–6.

    14. Mary Louise Pratt, *Toward a Speech Act Theory of Literary Discourse* (London and Bloomington: Indiana University Press, 1977) 121.

    15. Judith Butler, *Excitable Speech: A Politics of the Performative* (New York: Routledge, 1997) 3.

    16. J. L. Austin, *How to Do Things with Words*, ed. J. O. Urmson and Marina Sbisà, 2nd ed. (Oxford: Clarendon Press, 1975) 6.

    17. Butler, *Excitable Speech*, 2-3.

    18. Jacques Derrida, "Signature, Event, Context," *Limited Inc.* (Evanston, IL: Northwestern University Press, 1997) 4.

19. Della Pollock, "Performing Writing," in *The Ends of Performance*, ed. Peggy Phelan and Jill Lane (New York and London: New York University Press, 1998) 94–95.

Abbreviations

MHSC Massachusetts Historical Society Collections

NEGHR *New England Genealogical and Historical Register*

RPC1 *Records of the Plymouth Colony , Acts of the Commissioners of the United Colonies in New England, 1643–1651*, ed. David Pulsifer, vol. 1 (New York: AMS Press, 1968).

RPC2 *Records of the Plymouth Colony, Acts of the Commissioners of the United Colonies in New England, 1653–1678/9*, ed. David Pulsifer, vol. 2 (New York: AMS Press, 1968).

Chapter One

Private Petitions and Transatlantic Discursive Communities

John Eliot's correspondence with English friends, acquaintances, and donors began at least as early as 1633, only two years after he arrived in New England. From 1633 until his death in 1690, Eliot corresponded with many named recipients including significant theologians and intellectuals in London, such as Richard Baxter, Robert Boyle, and the antiquarian Sir Simonds D'Ewes, as well as regional supporters in Devon, including Reverend Jonathan Hanmer and Reverend John Nicholls. In more than sixty years as a minister and missionary, Eliot established a network of supporters across England through the regular transmission of letters and manuscripts. Eliot's correspondence represents a small proportion of what David Cressy has calculated as several hundred surviving letters which made the journey from New England to metropolitan centers and provincial parts of England.[1]

Eliot also had official correspondence with the Corporation for the Propagation of the Gospel, or the New England Company, as it came to be known, demonstrating an equal interest in maintaining open dialogue with the metropolitan center in London. The large majority of this correspondence which highlights Eliot's missionary success can be found in the eleven Tracts published by the Corporation and, in the following chapters of this study, I deal with the nature of published correspondence and narrative accounts more fully. By contrast, this chapter adapts Roger Chartier's observation that letter-writing is a type of "'ordinary,' everyday and private writing" which "maintain(s) and extend(s) the bonds of social life and solidarity," of familial or political ties.[2] Through a focus on these personal bonds, this chapter considers the ways in which Eliot's private petitions to named recipients formed a network of missionary fundraisers, as well as a transatlantic discursive community which debated matters of ecclesiastical government and church order.

In this chapter, Eliot is situated in a transatlantic context as an observer of and contributor to the religious and political debates of the seventeenth-century Atlantic world. Eliot's private correspondence provides a fair account of his political and religious concerns, concerns which mirrored the religious and political forces that shaped the colony and the Atlantic world at the time.

A RHETORIC OF INTIMACY AND SPEECH

John Eliot composed the first of many transatlantic private petitions in September 1633. Unusually for Eliot, this letter, which was addressed to Sir Simonds D'Ewes, carries very little information about the Algonquian and barely a hint of the missionary endeavor that would seal his reputation as Apostle to the Indians. All mention and discussion of "natives" is dispensed with in one sentence:

> We are at good peace with the natives, and they do gladly entertain us and give us possession, for we are as walls to them from their bloody enemies, and they are sensible of it and also they have many more comforts by us, and, I trust, in God's time they shall learn Christ.[3]

This letter pays lip service to the original charter granted by Charles I, the "principle end" of which was to "incite the Natives of country, to the Knowledg and Obedience of the onlie true God and Saulor of Mankinde,"[4] and does little to persuade us that John Eliot would be a leading participant in that endeavor in the decades which followed. Instead, Eliot begins the letter by describing the form of colonial government which the "young commonwealth" has installed, he details the building of substantial and suitable homes, and promises hundreds of acres of land for everyone "though ten thousand more should come."[5] In this sense, Eliot's letter has much in common with promotional correspondence and promotional narratives leaving North America at that time. David Cressy and Catherine Armstrong, for example, have convincingly demonstrated that despite rumors of religious persecution by the Puritan authorities, compounded by stories of supposedly war-mongering natives and failed harvests, attention was more often paid to the peaceful and harmonious relationships between colonial communities and native communities.[6] The more positive letters and pamphlets also emphasized the supposedly vast empty acreage, with all the agricultural and trading opportunities, which that implies.

The most obvious promotional aspects of Eliot's letter include his aim to promote the idyllic circumstances of colonial life. Land is apparently free and aplenty, and the agricultural economy is said to be thriving: "Cattle do much increase in every kind. Ploughs begin to cut the ground, and one hath reaped a rich harvest."[7] Eliot's observations on land and cattle are, of course, contrary to those of men who were involved in trade: William Hammond's letter written in the same year to the same recipient paints a picture where cattle are scarce and prices are rising.[8] Eliot's letter fits in well with the rhetorical optimism of some of the major promotional pamphlets and permissible private epistles of the time, where abundant utopias belied the rather more challenging reality of early colonial life.[9]

Despite his erring on the details of colonial life, the promotional *agenda* of Eliot's earliest surviving letter reveals something of the man who would go on to spend around fifty years of his life tirelessly promoting his missionary cause by petitioning friends, clergymen, and patrons in England for sufficient money and goods to allow him to devote his time to the conversion of Algonquians to Christianity. In this early letter, his fundraising efforts take the form of a passionate appeal for the creation of an educational establishment for New England's younger generation. He would do this again in *New England's First Fruits* (1643), ten years later, and in this later publication he matches this enthusiasm for learning with accounts of the very beginnings of Native American religious conversion.[10] By contrast, this earlier piece of private correspondence has a more singular purpose: "if we nourish not learning, both church and commonwealth will sink."[11] Eliot's appeal rests on the vanity of his correspondent whom he supposes desires his good work to be publicly recognized and held in perpetuity: "the commemoration of the first founder of the means of learning would be a perpetuating of your name and honor among us."[12] Further, by suggesting that the fledgling colony may not survive without D'Ewes' financial help of around five hundred pounds, he adds a further layer of urgency to the cause.

The impression Eliot gives of the young colony in this letter is a malleable one. Certainly, the predominant image is one that shows that the colony has laid down forms of governance which are carefully and effectively maintaining a stable society: "we have sweet and glorious justice and judgment among us" and "(f)or our churches, we walk in all things as near to the revealed will of God as we can."[13] But Eliot modifies this idyllic description by asserting the colony's inherent vulnerability. This vulnerability is not in the form of the usual threats of Indian attacks, or even the harsh circumstances of living in such a new and at times unforgiving landscape, indeed both of these concerns are countered in the letter: Eliot maintains that they are living side by side with peaceful natives, and the "air is temperate, and both heat and cold is comfortably tolerable by the weakest, having warm houses."[14] Rather, in this exchange, the colony rises or falls on the generosity of wealthy individuals who might support the colony's educational establishment.[15] Far from an established, resilient community of saints, the New

England colony is also a "poor commonwealth" and on the verge of "sink-ing," but for the knowledge of governance and justice which an able lawyer and politician like Sir Simonds D'Ewes would bring.[16]

In later correspondence with Rev. Jonathan Hanmer, Mr. Edward Win-slow and Rev. Richard Baxter, it is the educational welfare of indigenous people that concerns Eliot most: he variously asks them for books, ink, paper and linen, as well as the funds to continue his publication of religious works in the Algonquian language. These petitions will be considered below, fol-lowing an examination of the rhetorical strategies which Eliot employs with D'Ewes since these remain constant throughout his sixty years of transatlan-tic communication.

One particular and commonly used strategy is Eliot's appeal to a much wider audience when he prevails upon D'Ewes to "stir up" other "worthy gentlemen which are favorers of learning"[17] to contribute to the colony's future. As a substitute for face-to-face dialogue with coteries of like-minded individuals, Eliot invites D'Ewes to circulate his letter around wealthy indi-viduals who could be persuaded to support his cause. As recent studies of seventeenth-century letter writing have indicated, friends and family mem-bers who could not read or write would also be incorporated into the *conver-sation* of the letter, extending the number of interlocutors beyond the writer and the named recipient and replacing the face-to-face conversations many of them craved.[18] Even in more learned circles, the act of writing became inter-linked with the spontaneity and intimacy of conversational speech. Thomas Shepard, a minister and contemporary of John Eliot, illustrates this tendency to imitate speech in text in a cover letter he wrote from a New England dockside: "Sir, I had ended these relations once or twice, but the stay of the Vessell increaseth new matter; which because 'tis new and fresh, you shall have it as I heard it from a faithfull hand."[19] Similarly, in his letter to Richard Floyd and other "Gentlemen of the Corporation," John Endicott writes: "the Ship being ready to set sayle I have made bold to write these few lines unto you"[20]

The replacement of face-to-face conversation, the spontaneity of spoken conversation, and the considered prose of the letter, are skillfully brought together in many examples of seventeenth-century transatlantic correspon-dence, and Eliot is not slow to pick up on the intimacy fashioned by this type of rhetorical gesture.[21] Therefore, in an attempt to overcome his own geo-graphical distance from his audience whom he might well have met and spoken with directly, had circumstances been different, Eliot asks D'Ewes to "stir up" their emotions on his behalf. Eliot's rhetorical gesture is fascinating in its duality: he either expects the very physicality of the letter to substitute for his own voice and be circulated in manuscript form to a community of private readers or, by focusing on the performative implications of his use of "stir up," he may have intended that D'Ewes become his mouthpiece to a gathered listening audience of the wealthy and worthy of London. In either circumstance, D'Ewes is in a privileged position: he is the named recipient and he receives firsthand accounts of the opportunities for trade, agriculture and education, but he is also the gateway to a selected wider audience. In this way Eliot harnesses the tone of personal intimacy and extends his reach beyond the limits of the designated recipient to a much wider audience. This dual aspect of private intimacy and public reception is a significant feature of Eliot's letter-writing, and it became particularly valuable in later years when his fundraising for praying towns and Algonquian publications began in earnest.

FUNDING THE MISSION AND THE PERSONAL TOUCH

Over the course of many years Eliot was successful in his fundraising efforts and spent a significant amount of time courting donors in the way he had courted D'Ewes. For example, Lady Mary Armyne gave fifty pounds annually, to cover Eliot's salary; Theodore Heminge of York left 50 pounds to the Corporation in his will when he died in 1657; and, in 1657, the death of Mr. Jesse (Jessy) occasioned a parcel of goods worth eleven pounds to be sent from England to Eliot in Massachusetts Bay. [22] In response to this generosity, Eliot was keen to reward his patrons with details of his work: Eliot advised the Corporation's treasurer, Richard Lloyd, that he has distributed Jessy's gift as he had intended and, in 1671, he asks William Ashhurst to allow Lady Armyne, Mr. Henley, and his cousin Postlethwait "a sight of" his letters and writings which account for the past year's missionary endeavors. [23] The circulation of Eliot's letters and manuscripts around his patrons was not uncommon and, in 1676, when Katherine Jones, Vicountess Ranelagh, writes to Eliot offering her support for praying Indians and their sufferings and "distress" on Deer Island, it is testament to the sharing of manuscripts that she has some understanding of the situation for praying Indians in Massachusetts Bay at the time of King Philip's War. She wonders at the plight of the praying Indians, knowledge she claims to have "heard" from the "ye letter read yu (Eliot) writ to my bro. Boyle of the tryals and sufferings of yr poore praying Indians." And, thanks to Eliot's correspondence, she now has the opportunity to "cast" her contribution "into yt Treasury of God." [24] As well as sharing letters and manuscripts between readers, on this occasion it seems that Boyle has read the letter aloud to an audience of interested individuals and with the inclusion of his sister in this audience, we might assume that they were not all members of the Corporation or the Royal Society. [25]

Some of these contributions, and others, including Mr. Mowche's gift of 350 pounds, were obtained and distributed through the centralized body of the Corporation for the Propagation of the Gospel, but not all contributions took this route. Indeed, Eliot spends a significant amount of time tending to the private and, importantly, direct donors to his missionary cause. He was "master of the begging letter,"[26] as William Kellaway rightly contends, and he was also able to capture the powerful intimacy of private correspondence and extend it to a far wider reception community. In the many private letters which followed throughout his life, key aspects of his very early letter to D'Ewes remain constant. Petitions to private individuals for prayers, goods, and money were sustained and were as important to Eliot as the centralized missionary fundraising of the Corporation. The controlled extension of audience, through Eliot's request and at the discretion of the recipient, is also a common feature in later work and it confirms Eliot's desire to interact with a manuscript-reading community in England.

TRANSPORTATION, PRIVATE CORRESPONDENCE, AND THE MISSION

The makeup and targeting of various reception communities aside, the transportation of letters and goods was fraught with difficulties, notwithstanding the deliberate tactics of interception and surveillance during the uncertain times of Revolution and Restoration. John Winthrop fell afoul of this during the 1630s and comments on the practice of making private letters public in his *Journal*: in 1633 the private letters of so-called "indiscreet" individuals who had "written against the church government" were opened when their caretaker, Captain Levett, died on board the ship carrying them.[27] David Cressy further stresses the methods of surveillance and reprimand which individuals suffered at the hands of the Massachusetts Court for communicating negative impressions of the colony to their families and friends in England: he cites examples of individuals being whipped and banished for what they wrote in their private letters.[28]

Eliot's awareness of these political sensitivities is at times a little suspect, as I will outline principally in relation to Baxter's correspondence below, but he is certainly aware of the precarious physical conditions which accompany transatlantic correspondence when he comments that letters must pass through "so many hands before they can come at you," accounting for the repetition of largely the same letter written to Jonathan Hanmer twice in 1652.[29] In these two letters, Eliot responds to a previous appeal for books, which the Rev. Jonathan Hanmer appears to have taken up, by noting that his request has been fulfilled, firstly by the Corporation, who provided the means to purchase the libraries of Reverend Thomas Weld and Reverend Thomas Jenner, and, secondly, by the "reverend elders, ministers of Exon"[30] who regularly send books, *Annotations Upon All the Books of the Old and New Testament* (London, 1651, 2nd edition) being the most recent.[31]

Private donations and central funding by the Corporation sat together very easily for Eliot, and he does not miss an opportunity to demonstrate how Hanmer, the private individual, might take his place in this wider fundraising network. Hanmer has secured a gift of 50 pounds from Mr. Speacot and asks Eliot in what way it might best be spent. Eliot instructs Hanmer on the types of cloth he should buy and how it should be transported to Massachusetts Bay, offering several networks of secure passage, through Barnstaple or Mr. Bulcher in London, to Massachusetts Bay or to the Reverend John Brock in the Isle of Shoals.[32] Despite anxieties about the potential loss of letters as they travel through "many hands" or, the very real possibility of ship-wreck,[33] Eliot invokes a transatlantic network of trust and reliability to se- \
cure Hanmer's help and by doing so demonstrates to him that he is an integral part of the missionary network. Hanmer could easily have directed the money to the Corporation, who could then allocate it centrally, but in a letter written at about the same time to Mr. Winslow, another "respected friend," Eliot explains the time delays which official channels incur. He begins by suggesting that the "remoteness of the Court," through which goods and money from the Corporation flow, "doth much retard the improvem^t of what is sent," and, more specifically, he concludes his letter by requesting: "if you send bibles &c. I request y^t a few for psent use may bee sent to my hand directly, on account, because if Mr. Rawson have them I shall not have them till next Court of Comissioners wch would loose time."[34] For obvious reasons, then, Eliot wants to take immediate control of the money and uses the intimacy of personal correspondence to secure this outcome.

When the delivery is finally made, Hanmer's management of the money and the goods is fully recognized in the itemized invoice in the landing bill, as well as in Eliot's subsequent letter: "That Liberal gift that Christian gentleman Mr. Speacot and his religious familie, with your owne exceeding great love, care, paines and travaile about the same, I did by blessing of the Lord receive, safe and in good condition, in the end of the yeare 1653."[35] As further reward, Eliot provides Hanmer with a brief account of the success of the mission:

> Religion is on the gaineing hand (I blesse the Lord) though in church estate, and affaires of ecclesiastical polity, they come but slowly. . . . This yeare 1654, we have had another meeting about it, viz: for the examination of the Indian in poynt of knowledge in the doctrinal part of religion. . . . In conclusion wheroff the elders did give testimony of theire good satisfaction in what they had received from them. But a more particular relation of the dayes meeting, I have sent over to the Corporation to be published, together with the present state we stand in, touching our further proceeding, in gathering them into a church estate and covenant, unto which I must make bold to refer you fuller information.[36]

Eliot privileges Hanmer and Speacot by offering them the first glimpse of the kind of difference their contributions have made, and then promises further reward in a fuller account in the official pamphlet, soon to be published in London by the Corporation.

A similar use of personal intimacy and friendship occurs in Eliot's letters to Mr. Winslow and Hugh Peters during the early phase of native settlement into praying towns, where he asks for goods including bibles, inkhorns and paper for school use, as well as tools and glass to complete important building work. In Winslow's case, Eliot mentions Winslow's son, who has newly arrived in the colony and is establishing a good reputation. He also mentions mutual friends, Lord and Lady Armyne, who have supported the mission financially, and he makes very brief mention of Winslow's help in communicating to the Corporation the work being undertaken in the colony. Eliot is at pains to encourage Winslow to bypass the Corporation in London and the Commissioners in New England and with a deft sleight-of-hand he uses the example of Lady Armyne's gift donated through a Brother Bell (perhaps John Bell, Dean of Christ's Church, Oxford) in order to initiate another transatlantic link in the missionary network. The fact that Armyne's gift was transferred through the Corporation is, for Eliot, largely beside the point.

Hugh Peters is also asked by Eliot to send goods through Bristol in another trusted trading route. In this letter Eliot appeals to Peters personally, by offering his support at a time when his radical religious fervor made him a notable and controversial figure in revolutionary England. Peters was present at the execution of Charles I and responsible for his funeral sermon and Eliot lends his support to Peters' religious zeal without equivocation. As well as expressing his ecstasy over Peters' part in the "opportunity" that Parliament now has "to bring in Christ to rule in England," Eliot's letter uses the great distance between both interlocutors to draw attention to the continuance and strength of their friendship: "I cannot wish you in New England so long as you are of such great use and service in the Old; not because I love you not, but because I love you and the cause of God, which you do *totis viribus* pursue and prosper in."[37] Once this friendship has been reconstituted Eliot's support gives way to more practical matters, as he embarks on his request to Peters to help his missionary endeavor.

The background of Cromwellian military action deliberately haunts the request: Eliot is aware that criticisms against Peters extended to his part in military action where he led sections of Crowellian forces in battle. It was considered unseemly that a clergyman and minister for the army could unite religion and military action in such a visceral and successful way. In his correspondence with Peters, Eliot commends his logistical success in sourcing a "Magazine of Provisions"[38] for the army at Pembroke and he uses this military rhetoric, in the first instance to flatter Peters into sourcing and sending similar tools and "instruments of husbandry" to Massachusetts to help him with the building of the first praying towns. In the most practical terms, Eliot asks Peters to help build a new Christian Commonwealth and in doing so rhetorically aligns New and Old England in a common holy and military cause.[39]

In Eliot's private petitions we see him appeal to the conscience of the individuals whose opinion he clearly values and whose generosity is already accepted. We also see Eliot's concern with different kinds of reception communities become more specific than the very generalized "worthy gentlemen" mentioned in the Simonds D'Ewes letter. In the private correspondence between Eliot, Hanmer, Winslow, Baxter, and Boyle, different types of reception communities are addressed: the named recipient, communities of manuscript readers, and a local church congregation in Exeter. In each of these correspondences, Eliot uses the intimate nature of the private epistle to ensure that the individual recipient sees himself as a privileged and significant link in a network of individuals that work toward the same missionary goal. In all cases, Eliot asks his private correspondents to see themselves as a crucial part of a transatlantic network: he convinces them that their actions will make a more direct difference to the lives of the "poore Indians,"[40] than the slow bureaucracy of the Corporation and the Commissioners of the United Colonies. In conjunction with these concerns, Eliot also used his network of correspondents to navigate the theological and ecclesiastical concerns which helped shape New England's evolving religious identity.

DISCURSIVE COMMUNITIES: *THE CHRISTIAN COMMONWEALTH* (1659) AND *COMMUNION OF CHURCHES* (1665)

Within the intimacy of the private letter, Eliot's most controversial and radical separatist views were transmitted and debated within a transatlantic discursive community. The evolution of two of Eliot's pamphlets on church order, *The Christian Commonwealth*[41] and *Communion of Churches*[42] can be traced through the epistolary exchanges between Eliot and his correspondents, Jonathan Hanmer, Ferdinando Nicolls, and Richard Baxter. These exchanges provide some insight into the ways in which transatlantic discursive communities helped Eliot to hone and temper his religious views. Hanmer and Nicolls are involved in discussions about *The Christian Commonwealth* and Baxter, *Communion of Churches*.

Despite its late publication in 1659, Eliot sent *The Christian Commonwealth* to England as early as 1652 (or even 1651) when he asked Jonathan Hanmer and Ferdinando Nicolls for their comments on the manuscript and, from the accompanying letter, it becomes clear that Eliot links his thoughts on ideal church government with the conversion of Algonquians at Natick:

> In the yeare 1651 in a day of fasting and prayre, they (Indian penitents) entered
> into a covenant with God, and each other, to be ruled by the Lord in all thiere
> affaires civilie, making the Word of God theire only magna charta, for govern-
> ment, laws, and all conversation. And choose rulers of tennes, fifties, and of an
> hundred. The Platforme of which holy government of Gods owne institution, I
> have sent over this yeare unto Mr. Nicols with the reverend elders in Exon.
> And if the Lord give you opertunity, I should gladly wish your selfe might also
> have a sight of it, that I might receive your animadversions on it. [43]

Aside from providing evidence of his missionary success, and Eliot's pre-
ferred module of church governance with rulers of tens, fifties, and hundreds,
this exchange also demonstrates that Eliot was part of a transatlantic discursive community. How Nicolls, Hanmer and the Exeter Elders responded to
Eliot's ecclesiastical treatise remains speculative as their replies are not extant, but what we can recover from this evidence is that Eliot was part of a
community of readers who were in the habit of sharing manuscripts and
letters. This exchange also supposes that Eliot places significant importance
on the intellectual support given by his friends and acquaintances in this
regional community of readers in Devon.

In his preface to *The Christian Commonwealth*, Eliot notes that his treatise is, in part, a response to a book he recently read, *Plea for Non-subscrib-
ers*. It was also a response to "the grounds and reason of many Ministers of
Cheshire and Lancashire"[44] who, he believes, are too reticent in their response to Charles I's execution: "my heart bled to see such precious holy
men, pleading (as they believe) for God, with a pure and sincere Conscience,
and yet in so doing strongly to speak against the glorious work of the Lord
Jesus, in casting down Antichrist, and setting up his own Kingdom foretold
in Scripture."[45] Within this discursive community, where the printed text as
well as public declarations of religious concerns over the civil unrest and
upheaval are acknowledged, Eliot begins his transatlantic dialogue on the
issue of church order and civil organization with Hanmer, Nicolls, and the
Exeter brethren.

In his treatise, Eliot prescribes without equivocation his vision of an ideal
society, one which would prepare the way for the new millennium. In the
opening chapter he sets out his vision of an ideal commonwealth with direct
reference to Old and New Testament sources; the role of Moses as a civil and
religious leader and Daniel's prophetic visions are established as Old Testament types which unite biblical time and earthly time through the lens of
typological analysis. Further, John, in the Book of Revelation, becomes a
New Testament antitype to justify England's violent revolution and acts of
regicide. [46] Through this typological allegory, Eliot explains and justifies the
present state of England and in particular the death of Charles I. [47] In his
lengthy *Preface* he also asks his readers to

consider the times, and compare the Prophecies of Scripture, with the present providences; and see if you finde not all things to come to pass, according as it is written; and that these wonderful providences are not without Scripture-authority, and much to be regarded by the people of God. Nor be they the executions of Divine wrath upon either Church or World, by profane hands, who act their own wills and lusts, though they accomplish Gods ends; but they be the pouring out of the wrath of God upon Antichrist, for his destruction and overthrow of his Kingdom, by the hands of holy Saints; according to the command of Christ; Christ himself riding forth Victoriously among them, and performing his great works, written and foretold in the holy Scriptures.[48]

In this context, Eliot's tract has much in common with the Fifth Monarchist, William Aspinwall, and his 1653 tract, *A Brief Description of the Fifth Monarchy*. Both writers justify the execution of Charles I through direct reference to the Books of Daniel and Revelation. On the execution of the Antichrist, which Eliot implies is synonymous with the execution of Charles I, Eliot refers to Daniel, stating: "The means of execution of that judgement, is by the Wars of the Lamb, the Lord Jesus, as appears in the Book of *Revelation*."[49] Aspinwall, however, is far more direct and refers to Charles as a "Tyrant and persecuter of the Saints" and becomes "(T)he Beast or chief Soveraign" who was "slain or beheaded,"[50] which in 1649, according to Aspinwall, directly fulfilled the prophecy of Daniel 7 and signaled that the end of the Antichrist's dominion would be 1673. By insisting on specific times and dates, Aspinwall links biblical prophecy with historical time and establishes a linear trajectory of Christian fulfillment which coincides with regicidal and revolutionary England. Eliot and Aspinwall have in common a reliance on biblical sources, which are used to explain current events in England and, further, justify them as pre-ordained acts. The typological performance, that is the enactment of biblical prophecy on English soil, is one which holds promise for both Eliot and Aspinwall. For each writer, the New Jerusalem and the second-coming are at least a step closer to realization, if not directly immanent.

The body of Eliot's text becomes much more practical and far less prophetic as it focuses on the ecclesiastical and civil structures which might form the platform of this new Christian Commonwealth. Eliot explains that the people should be governed by a continuous hierarchy of rulers in charge of ten, fifty, one hundred, or one thousand people, and the remainder of the treatise goes on to outline the workings of the courts and the hierarchy of judicial authority.

With the benefit of hindsight and in the context of Eliot's 1652 letter to Jonathan Hanmer, we can see Eliot's treatise is, or should have been, part of a debate which took place in reading communities and church congregations across New and Old England in the early 1650s. Eliot's millennial treatise takes its place in transatlantic disagreements about toleration and separatism and as such sits in dialogue with other equally radical voices in England, Aspinwall's Fifth-monarchism, John Cotton's and Roger Williams's debates on religious toleration,[51] as well as striking a chord with Gerard Winstanley's Digger tract *Law of Freedom* (1652). Both treatises by Eliot and Winstanley, as noted by James Holstun, seek to "offer themselves as patterns for social organization that can be applied immediately, with little or no concern for the inertial authority of pre-existing social and political forms."[52] Although their propositions are inherently different, still there is an emerging image of England becoming the place of change and opportunity.[53]

Eliot's manuscript, however, was not published until 1659. Other commonwealth treatises also published in London that year include Milton's *The Readie and Easie Way to a Free Commonwealth*, which was characterized as a lament at a missed opportunity, and Richard Baxter's *The Holy Commonwealth*, which again laments what the Republic might have been.[54] Both are very much of their time and in keeping with the overwhelming sense in the late 1650s that the Stuart monarchy was ready to return to the throne.[55] In contrast, Eliot's treatise strikes a bold and controversial note, wholly due to the fact that it was written several years earlier for audiences in both New and Old England who were still acclimatizing to the theological and constitutional consequences of regicide and revolution.

More than ten years after the initial manuscript reached England, it is still possible to trace Eliot's continued revolutionary fervor and his persistent, reformist agenda through his private correspondence with Richard Baxter. In particular, in an exchange of letters in 1663 Eliot rather bullishly asserts

> it may please the Lord to direct his People into a Divine Form of Civil Government, of such a Constitution, as that the Godly, Learned in all Places, may be in all Places of Power and Rule, this would so much the more advance all Learning, and Religion, and good Government; so that all the World would become a Divine Colledge. And *Lastly*, when Antichrist is over-thrown, and a divine Form of Church-Government is put in practice in all Places; then all the World would become Divine: or at least, all the World would become very Divine or very Prophane, *Rev.* 22.11, 15.[56]

This kind of discourse may have been permissible in the late 1640s through the 1650s but in 1663, three years after Charles II assumed his place on the throne, such talk was at the very least indiscreet and at worst treasonous. We might remember that two years earlier Eliot was forced to withdraw his controversial treatise, *The Christian Commonwealth*, by the order of the Massachusetts court.[57] He was also asked to publicly disown the tract and its contents by supporting the incumbent monarch and parliament, describing them as an "eminent form of government."[58] By recasting the radical and controversial aspects of his treatise on ecclesiastical government in a letter to Baxter, he was risking his own censure and that of Baxter.

Aware of the potential consequences, Baxter ameliorates the provocative nature of Eliot's letter by suggesting: "As for the divine Government by the Saints which you mention, I dare not expect such great Matters upon Earth, lest I encroach upon the Priviledge of Heaven, and tempt my own Affection downwards, and forget that our Kingdom is not of this World. . . . We shall have as we would, but not in this World."[59] Given the sensitive nature of the topic, this letter certainly signals the private and intimate relationship that had developed between the two men: Eliot trusts Baxter with his apparently dangerous sentiments and Baxter is able to guide him away from such controversy, towards a place of co-operation and exchange.

Eliot's respect for Baxter's work is also manifest in his calls for him to think again about a "composition of meditations," a request which began in the first of the extant letters, written in October, 1656. Eliot writes: "Now resp(ec)ted and dear S^r, the sense and savor wch the Lord hath impressd on my spirit by these your holy labors, doth imbolden me to make a motion to you, and a request, y^t you would spend the rest of your life in writing practical meditations." Eliot admits to the boldness of the request, as he duly admits, "I am a stranger to you by face," but this doesn't deter him from telling Baxter precisely how this might be achieved in a busy working day.[60]

Richard Baxter's correspondence with Eliot is an important part of evolving ecclesiastical and theological debates, not least because of the longevity of the correspondence. The friendship, as it has recently been described, began as early as 1656 and lasted until 1691 when news of Eliot's death reached Baxter.[61] Eliot's relationship with Baxter was predicated on issues of church government, defense of the New England way, and more general theological issues. While discussion of Eliot's mission was often part of this correspondence, it was not the central feature. Not until the 1680s did Eliot began to petition Baxter in earnest about donations to the cause. When he finally did begin to ask for help with fundraising, the wealth of intimacy generated in over twenty-five years of this transatlantic exchange was easily brought to bear.

By the early 1660s Eliot and Baxter had developed a free and candid discourse and from these exchanges Eliot's second treatise on church governance, *Communion of Churches*, emerged. Just as Hanmer, Nicolls, and the Exeter elders were asked to send animadversions on *The Christian Commonwealth*, in the early 1660s Baxter is asked to do the same for *Communion of Churches*.

It is not too much of an exaggeration to say that Eliot's second tract on ecclesiastical governance grew from correspondence between Baxter and Eliot and through these transatlantic exchanges Eliot's ecclesiastical church model was reshaped. The model of church governance proposed in the *Communion of Churches* is a unification of Presbyterian and Congregational models of church order into one single framework: "Uniting those two Holy and Eminent PARTIES, The *Presbyterians* and *Congregationals.*"[62] In this treatise, Eliot insists on four levels of church organization: local churches, provincial councils, a national council or synod, and an Ecumenical council. Each level is linked as each church or council sends representatives to the next hierarchical level.[63] At each level, the churches and councils send one teaching elder and one ruling elder forward into this pyramidal structure, until the "eminent lights"[64] of the church communities are creamed-off to sit on the Ecumenical council.

This is a perfunctory treatise which considers the duties of each council and even calculates the costs incurred in such a model: after due collections are taken from each parish to maintain itself, Eliot suggests that the remaining councils will cost the average State with twenty ecclesiastical provinces one thousand pounds per annum.[65] One might presume that the National council, who are most closely linked with the state's civil authority (a Monarch or Parliament), would be instrumental in maintaining this grant. Notwithstanding this focus on practicalities, Eliot cannot resist an opportunity to compare this cost with what he perceives as the extravagancies of unreformed religious practices: "[T]his charge will be less then the revenues of some one Bishoprick. The design of *Antichrist* was to *pamper the flesh*; the design of Christ is to mort[...]ie it, and to honour *Grace.*"[66] Eliot's plan is ambitious and certainly utopian, but Baxter's initial response to the document was a positive one. This might well have been expected since Baxter's influence on this treatise is apparent from the outset:

> [W]ere it not an excellent worke for ye Pastors of yor Ch^h to joyne in an earnest p(er)swasive to union, to ye Presbyterian and Congregationall Brethern in England, and to be p(ro)pounded ye termes in certain Propositions.? Sure it might doe abundance of good. Yo^r Authority is yet great with ye godly of both Partyes: If it prevailed not with all, it would with many. What hath ye Church and Christian cause suffered by o^r breach![67]

Before committing his ideas to a treatise, Eliot fully engages with the sentiments which Baxter has communicated and responds by observing that it is a "weighty and good matter but hard to be done by us at this distance. They y^t are neare the mark may better tell how to aime at, and hit, the spirit of the times."[68]

By the 1660s, Eliot finally overcomes the practical difficulties of his distance from the center of reform in England, and begins writing this treatise with this sentiment of union and hierarchical forms of church order fully in mind. Baxter's correspondence was integral to the inception of Eliot's treatise and his later correspondence demonstrates his continued involvement in its refinement; between 1657 and 1671 Eliot's ecumenical design occupied a large part of their correspondence. By 1667 Baxter had read the treatise and compiled a very precise and formal set of corrections and points of debate titled: "Animadversions of Mr. Eliot's Book for Stated counsels."[69] Baxter's concerns ranged from relatively straightforward semantics to more complex matters of the balance between civil and ecclesiastical judicial authority. He begins his corrections by observing that "[with one heart] should not be in the definition of a visible church," and also notes that the numbers twelve and twenty-four, which Eliot frames his structure on, are "handsome" but not, as Eliot would have them, divinely sanctioned.[70] He also welcomes news of the Boston synod in 1662 where the Half Way Covenant was established, easing the relationship between Presbyterians and Congregationalists further.[71] More seriously, however, Baxter takes issue with the powers of national councils: perhaps with the Quakers in mind, Baxter argues that when a "Nationall Council is sinfully disobeyed, and ye magistrate too, yet Death may be too great a punishment."[72] An open and frank dialogue develops and included in this is Eliot's eight point defence of the decision to execute blasphemous Quakers in New England.[73]

The printed text of the treatise evolves through this dialogue and continues to evolve even after printing since the preface invites corrections and amendments from those "Godly and Able hands" to whom the printed text was entrusted:

> Although a few Copies of this small Script are Printed; yet it is not published, onely committed privately to some Godly and Able hands, to be Viewed Corrected, Amended, or Rejected, as it shall be found to hold wright in the Sanctuary Ballance, or not. And it is the humble Request of the Author, That whatever Objections; Rectification, or Emendati[...]ns may occure[...], they may be conveyed unto him; who desireth nothing may be accepted in the churches, but what is according to the Will and Minde of God, and tendeth to Holiness, Peace, and Promotion of the holy Kingdome of Iesus Christ.[74]

In this framework, the printed text is being used in the same way as a manuscript which might be circulated, discussed and then amended in response to this discursive process. Eliot comments that it is only through convenience that the text was printed rather than written: "The procuring of half so many Copies Written and Corrected, would be more difficult and chargeable, then the Printing of these few."[75] More specifically, in relation to his theological exchanges with Baxter, Eliot sends a second copy of his book and asks Baxter to commit his own hand to further amend the script: "I also sent you another of the same booke corrected, and in it a Schedule aded in the page 5, in wch Schedule in the first pag(e) of it—lin(e) 37—I desire you to blot out these words (be mixt, &). Enough is said wthout these words and these words are lyable to an objection beyond my intent and meaning."[76] Baxter's annotated copy of the *Communion of Churches* [77] has insertions and corrections in the margins and it is almost certainly the case that large majority of these are Eliot's changes; the tone and phrasing of the marginal notes are very much in keeping with the rest of the treatise and Eliot's prose style more generally. An intended addition to page seventeen is a case in point:

> When Christ shall rule all the World, both and religious in Civil and Ecclesiastical affairs, by the *Word of his mouth* managed by the hands of his Saints, even holy *Kings, Princes* and *chief Rulers*). Oh that the Lord would put it into the heart of some of his Religious and Learned servants, to take such pains about the holy *Hebrew Language*, as to fit it for *Universal glorious use*![78]

In another lengthy note there is a warning against sliding into chaos or simply mirroring the catholic hierarchy and establishing a different kind of "pope" in the process of establishing a new ecclesiastical and civil order: "we must beware of falling into an anarchy in the communion of churches" and that "while we pull down one Pope for usurping dominion of many churches, (we do) not set up a pope."[79] These amendments do not challenge the text. Instead, they extend and exemplify ideas already present confirming that this is most likely to be the second copy of *Communion of Churches* which Eliot refers to in his correspondence and that the amendments are most likely in Eliot's own handwriting. In its annotated state, this printed document evolved through a lengthy and intense debate, encompassing theological, ecclesiastical, and civil matters. Importantly, this process of spiritual renewal and ecclesiastical reform took place within a transatlantic epistolary and discursive space, emphasizing the breadth and depth of influence Eliot courted in his endeavor to shape religious identity in New England.

Besides Baxter's role in the evolution of the text, Eliot also demands knowledge of the book's reception from a much larger discursive community: concretely, he wants to know "how it is reputed among God's people."[80] Unfortunately for Eliot there is little evidence that the text was read or even discussed, far less appreciated, in any significant way. Rather, by 1671 when Baxter was still pressing Eliot to push for synods, which are "needful for mutuall assistance & concord,"[81] and their debates were as lively and intricate as before, John Woodbridge writes to Baxter from Connecticut, offering an abrasive account of the churches there and roundly dismisses Eliot's ecclesiastical policy: his "booke about Councells" was "better tooke with himself that with any of his Bretheren."[82] By mid-1671 the issue of church policy and church unity seemed to be on the wane in Eliot's correspondence and in its place are concerns relating to Eliot's work with Native penitents and Algonquian language texts.

ELIOT, THE CORPORATION, AND THE NEW ENGLAND COMMISSIONERS

Despite Eliot's failed attempts to impress his transatlantic readership with plans for church reform, he maintained his correspondence with Baxter and developed a keen correspondence with Robert Boyle when he became president of the Corporation, or New England Company, especially in relation to the financing of his mission. Indeed, Richard Baxter's first correspondence with Boyle in October 1660 unites all three individuals in a common purpose: "Having some speciall use for your favourable assistance in the worke of propagating the Gospell among poore barbarous infidels, I intreate you by this messenger to send me word when I may find you at home."[83] In addition to developing his own relationship with Boyle which was based on a shared interest in current theological debate, Baxter would spend time and energy promoting the value of Eliot's Algonquian translations in person to Boyle and this common cause briefly unites Eliot, Baxter, and Boyle in transatlantic discussion.[84] The very fact that Baxter made a personal visit to Boyle, on the basis of Eliot's cause, without ever having met Eliot, is testament to the effectiveness of Eliot's personal correspondence with Baxter. Compared to his relationship with Baxter, Eliot's relationship with Boyle would develop in an equally friendly manner, with one very important difference: as president of the New England Company, Boyle was in a position to fund and sustain the mission, which included Eliot's ambitions to publish his translations, primers, catechisms and other religious texts.

Exchanges between both men are, therefore, always part of *official* correspondence between the colony and the company and vice versa, despite the often personal tone. This personal tone is cast in a much clearer light when compared with the correspondence between Boyle and the commissioners in New England, the official body who managed the finances at the company's behest. Eliot casts himself very deliberately as a lone operator: initially he does this to bypass the lengthy and time-consuming fact of the commissioner's bureaucracy, but latterly his distance from the commissioners of New England becomes politically expedient when relations between the New England colony and the restored Stuart monarchy falter.

From one of the very first of Eliot's letters to Boyle, the image of Eliot as a lone operator is confirmed:

> I am but a shrub in the wildernesse, & have not yet had the boldnesse to looke upon, or speake unto those Cedars, who have undertaken an honourable protection of us. but for sundry reasons, I have now broke out, & have taken upon me the boldnesse to write unto your selfe, Right honourable Sir, because I doe sufficiently understand how learning & honour doe rendezvous in your Noble brest: & what a true friend you are to all learning, & also to this good work of

the Lord, in promoting religion, & the knowledg of Christ among our pore Indians.[85]

Eliot addresses Boyle as "Noble Governour" and extends his address to the society as a whole, acknowledging the official nature of the letter. However, we cannot afford to miss Eliot's typically personal tone and humble veneer. When Eliot employed this rhetoric with previous correspondents, Hanmer and Nicolls, for example, he was deliberately developing personal relationships as a way to circumvent the mechanisms and delays implicit in the bureaucracy which linked the colony's and the Corporation's financial dealings. Despite the fact that Boyle was the figurehead of the Corporation, and part of the bureaucracy which Eliot was trying to avoid, he used the rhetoric of personal intimacy to exactly the same purpose. Even in official letters to the president of the Corporation, Eliot seeks to bypass the commissioners in New England and deal directly with Boyle. Eliot's motivations are based partly on the fact that the commissioners only meet twice annually and can only process and settle financial gifts and salaries at these meetings, so there are definite financial benefits in operating outside of this forum. However, it is largely their reluctance to bankroll the publication of Algonquian language texts, including the bibles, primers, and catechisms that caused Eliot to approach Boyle directly.

Before approaching Boyle for money, in his initial letter he mentions his current translation of Lewis Bayly's *Practice of Piety*, as well as the development of his Algonquian grammar, a project still in its infancy.[86] Eliot styles himself as an individual hard at work at the Corporation's bidding: not only is he a "shrub in the wilderness" in relation to the vast distance between him and the "cedars" of the mother country, his language also suggests that he is a lone preacher, translator, and linguist who works independently in response to God's call for him to convert Algonquians of Massachusetts to Christianity. As is well known, he was not the only missionary in the area: Thomas Mayhew, Richard Bourne, and John Cotton Jr. were all active in a similar way in other parts of New England. Therefore, this is a deliberate tactic to prioritize his own mission above others and gain the ear of the president of the Corporation for this own personal petitions.

Notably, in this first letter there is no mention of financial need; rather, Eliot establishes a rhetorical framework which prioritizes trust through a demonstration of personal experience in this *holy* endeavor. Letters on the progress of the mission follow, particularly in 1669, when Eliot and Richard Bourne are asked to submit a progress report to the Corporation via the commission. Coincidently, Eliot's report would arrive independently of the Commission's official letter to the Corporation. Richard Bourne's report, on the other hand, was included in the official documentation. No reason has been given as to why this is the case, but it does appear to be symptomatic of

Eliot's desire to be perceived as a lone operator, writing separately from official channels of transatlantic communications. The rhetoric of the report bears this out, especially when compared with Bourne's narrative of New Plymouth praying Indians.

Bourne's narrative has only four brief points and is less than one page, providing only basic facts about his mission: for example, among the Mashpee and Wakoquet he calculates that there are approximately two hundred praying Indians who have been allowed to establish a church state with six or seven of them appointed as rulers in civil affairs.[87] Further, two individuals, Pompumit and Kanoonus, who appear to be native instructors or lay-preachers, require books and catechism that they might further their work. In fundamental terms, this is very similar to Eliot's narrative account of Massachusetts: Eliot identifies the praying towns, the number of praying Indians, and provides details of individuals, including Waban, who have become rulers and instructors to other praying Indians, demonstrating the successful implementation of civil and church order. The significant difference is that Eliot's narrative is more fulsome in its account of individual success stories: Waban, ruler at Natick, Captain Gookins, Habbakuk Glover, and Eliot's recently deceased son, are noted for their contribution to the maintenance of civil order and education at Natick; Job is identified as a scholar at Harvard; James, who helped with the translation and printing of the Bible, is duly praised, as is George, a teacher at Wamesut. The narrative concludes with an account of an inter-tribal battle where many non-Christian Indians were killed, and according to Eliot, it is this "hand of God, the Indians take notice of."[88]

In comparison to Bourne, Eliot celebrates his success much more effectively and, while he incorporates the work done by many other individuals, including that of his late son, this piece of official public record sets him up as an authority and lynchpin of the mission as a whole. As a consequence, when the time comes for Eliot to ask the authorities for funds to finance the second imprint of his Algonquian bible, he feels emboldened and even justified in bypassing the commissioners of New England entirely and writes to Boyle, both as the president of the Corporation and, by this time, as a trusted, personal supporter of his work.

In 1680 Eliot's petitions to Boyle for financial backing begin in earnest: in the wake of the destruction caused by King Philip's War in 1675, Eliot insists that "Praying Indians, both in the Ilands, & on the maine are (considered together) numerous, <thousands of Soules, of whom some true believers, some learners, & some are still Infant.> & all of them, beg, cry intreat for bibles."[89] Boyle, who is not convinced of the need for so many more Algonquian bibles, has already directed Eliot to the commissioners suggesting that they need to be more involved in the venture and that production should be organized on an official basis not through this personalized correspondence which Eliot prefers.[90] This doesn't distract Eliot from his own method of personal petitioning, and he challenges Boyle that a "word" from him "will raise a contribution to such a work."[91] That is to say, with Boyle's sanction, the money might be raised easily, quickly and without challenge. When Boyle still does not respond in Eliot's favor, he falls back on his network of supporters in England and petitions Richard Baxter to plead on his behalf.[92] With all available means of petitioning exhausted, Eliot begins the print run from his own funds only to be surprised to find that six days after he has confirmed his own personal financial stake to Boyle, the Corporation released four hundred pounds for the project. Having overstepped the mark, Eliot offers a personal apology for his haste and for pre-empting their decision.[93]

Among other things, this episode highlights Eliot's continued desire to work outside the parameters of the official bureaucracy of the colonial authorities and the London-based company which financed his mission. This proved to be an advantageous position for Eliot and for the colony, in the end, when relations between the restored Stuart monarchy and the colony faltered.

This faltering relationship became apparent in April 1664 when Robert Boyle wrote to John Winthrop Jr. detailing Charles II's response to Eliot's Algonquian bible. After looking on it a "pretty while" he is soon distracted by other invited guests and Boyle soon turns his attention to the Lord Chancellor's position on the colonial charters.[94] Boyle assures Winthrop that their "sivile Government" and their "liberty" shall not be infringed by the newly restored Monarch but he also suggests that the colonial authorities need to demonstrate "loyalty" and "affection" rather than bare "obedience."[95] This private correspondence soon becomes part of a much wider transatlantic discursive community when the Commissioners for the United Colonies are given the letter and send a fulsome response to Boyle in their own defense.

John Endecott is the first to respond to Boyle, appealing for his help in recalling the royal commissioners who had travelled to the colonies ostensibly to witness the development of educational establishments, the justice system, and freedom of religion. The royal commissioners had some unofficial duties which New England authorities were wise to be concerned about: these unofficial duties included a reassessment of the original charters, the colonial community's attitude toward Monarchical rule and, in particular, an assessment of their reception in Massachusetts.[96] A standoff was induced: Charles was determined to bring the colonies back under his control, and the colonies, especially Massachusetts, were determined to maintain their religious and civil independence.

Within this framework a certain strand of the transatlantic discursive community came alive: Boyle's initial warning letter makes its way to Endecott via the meeting of the United Colonies in Connecticut that year. Boyle's surprise at the wide readership of his private letter to Winthrop Jr. is detailed in his response to Endecott's plea to act as a negotiator in London in support of New England's independence: "I did not imagine that what I occasionally writt to Mr. Winthrop . . . should have ben taken notice of by so considerable an assembly as yours." He goes on to comment that he will not be able to act on their behalf because, as he diplomatically suggests, some passages of their communication with the King and the Lord Chancellor were "more unexpected then welcome."[97]

Boyle had already noted to Henry Ashurst that it was the Massachusetts court which presented most problems and resistance to the royal commissioners,[98] which was later proven with "The Humble Supplication of the General Court of Massachusetts Colony in New England to the King," wherein the Massachusetts authorities pledged allegiance to the King only as it fitted with their own liberty of conscience.[99] The supplication goes on to demand that they be left to their own civil and religious authorities, else they will be forced into a "great unhappiness" which will "reduce" them "to so hard a case as to have no other testimony of our subjection and loyalty offered us but this, viz. To destroy our own being, which nature teacheth us to preserve, or to yield up liberties, which are far dearer to us than our lives."[100] Boyle's rebuke is most certainly in relation to this petition, and it is compounded when the Lord Chancellor allows him access to the correspondence sent to the colonies. Boyle can find no evidence of England's intention to deny liberty of conscience in New England. Quite ironically, and perhaps unknown to Boyle, Charles's "Secret instructions for the Commissioners," which included an instruction to "gain the good opinion of the principal inhabitants, so as to lead them to desire a renewal of their charter,"[101] meant that the Massachusetts court had plenty to fear.

To summarize the epistolary connections and discursive communities in this case: Boyle notes that his letter has been shared, quite to his unwelcome surprise, and he also notes that the Lord Chancellor has shared copies of "instructions" and "all th'other papers" with him. By invoking both public and private correspondence, Boyle uses the framework of established networks of communication to persuade Endecott that the Massachusetts court is stepping out of line and that they might soon find themselves excluded from the established discursive space which they currently enjoy, noting that he and many of their "friends" in England will be "much discouraged" to speak on their behalf if current tensions continue to dominate their correspondence. As I have noted, Eliot plays no part in this particular transatlantic debate, which may be due to sensitivities surrounding his recent retraction of *The Christian Commonwealth*, but his missionary work is what draws him back into the frame. Boyle's letter notes the good work of the "conversion of the natives" on which the strength of the colony's reputation now lies.[102] In the final words of this epistolary reprimand, it is Eliot's missionary work which is used to restore the reputation of this unpopular and outspoken colony.

By emphasizing the circulation of Eliot's private correspondence and manuscripts within a transatlantic framework, it becomes easier to appreciate the fact that his mission and his engagement with Algonquian peoples are inextricably linked with the contesting political and religious forces that shaped the seventeenth century Atlantic world. The "ego-centred" approach to community, which prioritizes Eliot as a conduit through which information is sent and transmitted, is crucial to our understanding of the role which praying Indian communities would play in the Atlantic politics of religious renewal and colonial dominance. Through his private correspondence and, as will be demonstrated in the following chapters, through published treatises and narrative accounts, Eliot believed himself to be, and asked that his Native, colonial and English reception communities believe him to be, the influential center around which the mission rotated.

The influential and lasting effects of Eliot's correspondence might be best demonstrated by a letter written on March 19, 1683, and signed by sixteen praying Indians from Natick. The letter was received by the Corporation, and in this letter they are asked to support Daniel Gookin as he continues to do the work which the aging Eliot can no longer provide. By adopting written forms of communication, praying Indians play an active role in this transatlantic discursive community and as such begin to present and perform their own identities in literary form. This will be considered in more depth in the final chapter, but in the context of private petitions and the shaping of a transatlantic epistolary and manuscript community, it is clear that John Eliot casts a long shadow over the transatlantic politics of missionary funding and support throughout the seventeenth century.

More so than in his private petitions, in his published letters and narrative accounts, Eliot creates the praying Indian, a new cultural type, through his transatlantic communications, in an effort to boost the reputation of New England colony as a place of spiritual renewal. The following chapter explores the public dimension of Eliot's transatlantic correspondence and the mediation of Native conversion to Christianity to an English reception community. As the New Englander emerges in the seventeenth century Atlantic community, he does so in relation to the religious and political upheavals in England and, importantly, in relation to the successful presentation of Native American conversion to Christianity.

NOTES

1. David Cressy, *Coming Over: Migration and Communication Between England and New England in the Seventeenth Century* (Cambridge: Cambridge University Press, 1995), 213–14.

2. Roger Chartier, Alain Borneau, and Cecile Dauphin, *Correspondence: Models of Letter-Writing from the Middle Ages to the Nineteenth Century.* 1991, trans. Christopher Woodall (Oxford: Polity Press, 1997), 2, 15.

3. "John Eliot to Sir Simonds D'Ewes, September 18, 1633," in *Letters from New England: The Massachusetts Bay Colony, 1629–1638,* ed. Everett Emerson (Amherst: University of Massachusetts Press, 1976), 106.

4. More fully, the original charter states that with the good behavior and example of English settlers they "maie wynn and incite the Natives of Country, to the Knowledg and Obedience of the onlie true God and Saulor of Mankinde, and the Christian Fayth, which in our Royall Intencon, and the Adventurers free Profession, is the principall Ende of this Plantacion." "The Charter of Massachusetts Bay," *The Avalon Project at the Yale School of Law.* 1629, at http://avalon.law.yale.edu/17th_century/mass03.asp (accessed March 23, 2013), n.p.

5. "John Eliot to Sir Simonds D'Ewes, September 18, 1633," in Emerson, *Letters from New England,* 106.

6. Cressy, *Coming Over*; Catherine Armstrong, *Writing North America in the Seventeenth Century: English Representations in Print and Manuscript* (Aldershot: Ashgate, 2007). For further comment and analysis on the rhetorical means of transcribing the New England experience, see also Virginia DeJohn Anderson, *New England's Generation: The Great Migration and the Formation of Society and Culture in the Seventeenth Century* (Cambridge: Cambridge University Press, 1991); Stephen Carl Arch, *Authorizing the Past: The Rhetoric of History in Seventeenth-Century New England* (Dekalb: Northern Illinois University Press, 1994); Anthony Pagden, *European Encounters with the New World: From Renaissance to Romanticism* (New Haven, CT: Yale University Press, 1993); Mary Louise Pratt, *Imperial Eyes: Travel Writing and Transculturation* (London: Routledge, 1992); Phillip H. Round, *By Nature and By Custom Cursed: Transatlantic Civil Discourse and New England Cultural Production, 1620–1660* (London and Hanover, NH: University Press of New England, 1999); David S. Shields, *Civil Tongues & Polite Letters in British America* (Chapel Hill: Published for the Institute of Early American History and Culture, Williamsburg, VA, by University of North Carolina Press, 1997).

7. "John Eliot to Sir Simonds D'Ewes, September 18, 1633," in Emerson, *Letters from New England,* 106.

8. "William Hammond to Sir Simonds D'Ewes, September 26, 1633," in Emerson, *Letters from New England,* 110–12.

9. Some well-known promotional pamphlets include: Thomas Hariot's "A Brief and True Report of the New found Land of Virginia, 1588," in *The English Literature of America 1500–1800,* ed. Myra Jehlen and Michael Warner (New York: Routledge, 1997), 64–89; Edward Johnson's, *Johnson's Wonder Working Providence, 1628–1651,* ed. Franklin Jameson, Original Narratives of Early American History Series (New York: Charles Scribner's Sons, 1910); Lochinvar's *Encouragements for New Galloway in America* (Edinburgh: Printed for John Wreittoun, 1625); In *Narratives of Early Maryland, 1633–1684,* ed. Clayton Colman Hall (New York: Charles Scribner's Sons, 1910) *see* reprints of Father Andrew White, *Briefe Relation of Maryland* (1634), John Hammond's *Leah and Rachel, Or, The Two Fruitful Sisters Virginia and Maryland* (London: Printed by T. Maab, 1656), and George Alsop's *A Character of the Province of Maryland.* London 1666; John Smith, *A Map of Virginia* (London 1612), in *Narratives of Early Virginia 1606–1625,* ed. Lyon Gardiner Tyler (New York: Charles Scribner's Son, 1907); and his *A Description of New England . . .* (London: R. Clerke, 1616); Edward Waterhouse's "A Declaration of the State of the Colony in Virginia (London 1622)," in *The English Literature of America 1500–1800,* ed. Myra Jehlen and Michael Warner (New York: Routledge, 1997), 129–46; Edward Winslow, *Good News From New England* (1624) (London: Printed by Matthew Simmons, 1648), printed in *Massachusetts Historical Society Collections* 2nd ser., vol. 9, 1832 (hereafter cited *MHSC*).

10. William Kellaway notes that in response to this tract Lady Ann Mowlson donated a gift of £100 to the Colleges first scholarship in *The New England Company 1649–1776: Missionary Society to the American Indians* (Westport, CT: Greenwood Press, 1975), 10.

11. "John Eliot to Sir Simonds, September 18, 1633," in Emerson, *Letters from New England,* 106.

12. Ibid., 106.

13. Ibid., 105.

14. Ibid., 106.

15. Eliot writes: "had we a place fitted for we should have our terms and seasons for disputations and lectures, not only in divinity but in other arts and sciences and in law also, for that would be very material for the welfare of our commonwealth." ("John Eliot to Sir Simonds D'Ewes, September 18, 1633," Emerson, *Letters from New England*, 109).

16. Ibid., 109.

17. Ibid., 108.

18. David Cressy, *Coming Over*; William Merrill Decker, *Epistolary Practices: Letter Writing in America before Telecommunications* (London and Chapel Hill: University of North Carolina Press, 1998); Round, *By Nature and By Custom Cursed*; Phillip H. Round, "Neither Here nor There: Transatlantic Epistolarity in Early America," in *A Companion to the Literatures of Colonial America*, ed. Ivy Schweitzer and Susan Castillo (Oxford: Blackwell Publishing, 2005), 426–79; Shields, *Civil Tongues and Polite Letters*.

19. Thomas Shepard, *The Clear Sun-shine of the Gospel*, in *The Eliot Tracts: With Letters from John Eliot to Thomas Thorowgood and Richard Baxter*, ed. Michael P. Clark (London and Westport, CT: Paeger, 2003), 137. Cressy indicates that this strategy of commenting on the act of writing and issues over transport is common to letters of the seventeenth century. Cressy, *Coming Over*, chap. 9.

20. John Eliot, *A Further Account of the Progress of the Gospel Amongst the Indians in New-England* (1659), in Clark, *Eliot Tracts*, 331.

21. For a paradigmatic analysis of the spoken and written word in early American literature and culture, see Sandra M. Gustafson, *Eloquence is Power: Oratory and Performance in Early America* (London and Chapel Hill: University of North Carolina Press, 2000).

22. J. D. *A Sermon Preached at the Funeral of that incomparable lady the Honourable the Lady Mary Armyne*, in *Early English Books 1641–1700*, University of Michigan, microform, wing 1381:09; and Company for Propagation of the Gospel in New England and the Parts Adjacent in America, London, Experience Mayhew, and John W. Ford, in *Some Correspondence between the Governors and Treasurer of the New England Company in London and the Commissioners of the United Colonies in America the missionaries of the colony and others between 1657-1712* (London: E. Stock 1897), 1–2.

23. Company for Propagation, *Some Correspondence*, 49-51.

24. Katherine Jones, "Katherine Jones, Viscountess Ranelagh to John Eliot," August 13, 1676. Royal Society Archives, London, RB/3/5/9. Previous numbers, BL 5, fols. 17–18.

25. This was, presumably, on one of the occasions where the Corporation met at Ranelagh's house in Pall Mall. *See* Kellaway, *New England Company*, 51.

26. Kellaway, *New England Company,* 32.

27. This information was used against Winthrop and the colony by Sir Ferdinand Georges and Captain Mason in a petition to the Privy Council. John Winthrop, "A Journal of the Transactions and Occurrences in the Settlement of Massachusetts and the other New England Colonies from the year 1630–1644," (Hartford: Elisha Babcock, 1790). Also available online at http://archive.org/stream/journaloftransac00wint#page/n7/mode/2up (accessed October 20, 2009), 48.

28. Cressy, *Coming Over*, 22.

29. "Roxbury July 19, 1652," and "Roxbury, October 7, 1652," in *John Eliot and the Indians 1652–1657: Being letters addressed to Rev. Jonathan Hanmer of Barnstaple, England*, ed. Wilberforce Eames (New York: The Adams and Grace Press, 1915) 11.

30. "Roxbury July 19, 1652," *John Eliot and the Indians 1652–1657,* 8.

31. Eames, *John Eliot and the Indians 1652–1657,* 15.

32. Ibid., 15–16.

33. "John Eliot to Mr. Winslow, Roxbury 20th 8 1651," New England Genealogical and Historical Register (hereafter cited *NEHGR*), July 1882, 291-94. For the costs incurred salvaging this wreck, *see* "Documents of the Society for Promoting and Propagating the Gospel in New England," *NEHGR*, July 1882, 371-76. In this case, the cost of labor and equipment came to over £12.

34. "John Eliot to Mr. Winslow, Roxbury 20th 8 1651," *NEHGR* 36 July 1882, 291–94.

35. "Jon Eliot to Rev. Jonathan Hanmer, Roxbury, 29th August 1654," in Eames, *John Eliot and the Indians 1652–1657*, 21.

36. Ibid., 21–22.

37. Address dated October 12 1649, Hugh Peters, *A Memoir or Defence of Hugh Peters.* Boston: C. C. P. Moody, 1851. *Early English Books Online* at http://eebo.chadwyck.com/home (accessed March 26, 2013), 39.

38. Ibid., 39.

39. Ibid., 40.

40. Ibid., 39.

41. John Eliot, *The Christian Commonwealth, Or, The civil Policy of the Rising Kingdom of Jesus Christ* (London: Printed for Livewell Chapman, 1659), available in *MHSC*, Boston, 1846–1849.

42. John Eliot, *Communion of Churches, Or, The Divine Management of Gospel-Churches* (Cambridge, MA: Printed by Marmaduke Johnson, 1665). *Early English Books Online* at http://eebo.chadwyck.com/home (accessed April 2, 2013).

43. "Eliot to Jonathan Hanmer, Roxbury, 19th July 1652," in Eames, *John Eliot and the Indians 1652–1657*, 7.

44. Eliot, *Christian Commonwealth*, 129.

45. Ibid., 129.

46. "The means of execution of that judgement (God's last judgement), is by the Wars of the Lamb, the Lord Jesus, as appears in the Book of *Revelation* and the people executing those Wars, by this text seem to be a people ruled by this order of Government: which if it be so, may it not give some light to find out the ten Kings which shall hate the Whore, make her desolate and naked, eat her flesh, and burn her with fire?" Eliot, *Christian Commonwealth,* 138.

47. For commentaries concerned with New English Puritanism and typology in seventeenth-century not considered elsewhere, *see* Sacvan Bercovitch ed., *Typology and Early American Literature* (Massachusetts: The University of Massachusetts Press, 1972); Sacvan Bercovitch, "Typology in Puritan New England: The Williams-Cotton Controversy Reassessed," *American Quarterly* 19, no. 2 (Summer 1967): 166–91; and *Horologicals to Chronometricals: The Rhetoric of the Jeremiad,* ed. Eric Rothstein, 3rd ed. (Madison: The University of Wisconsin Press, 1970); Thomas M. Davis, "The Traditions of Puritan Typology," in *Typology and Early American Literature*, ed. Sacvan Bercovitch. (Massachusetts: The University of Massachusetts Press, 1972); David D. Hall, "Religion and Society: Problems and Reconsiderations," in *Colonial British America: Essays in the New History of the Early Modern Era,* ed. Jack P. Greene and J. R. Pole (London and Baltimore: Johns Hopkins University Press, 1984); and "Toward a History of Popular Religion in Early New England," *William and Mary Quarterly.* 41, no. 1 (1984): 49–55; Mason I. Lowance Jr., "Typology and the New England Way: Cotton Mather and the Exegesis of Biblical Types," *Early American Literature* 4, no. 1 (Spring 1969): 15–37; Janice Knight *Orthodoxies in Massachusetts: Rereading American Puritanism* (Cambridge, MA: Harvard University Press, 1994; rpt. 1997).

48. Eliot, *Christian Commonwealth*, 140.

49. Ibid., 138.

50. William Aspinwall, *A Brief Description of the Fifth Monarchy, Or, Kingdom.* (London: Printed by M. Simmons and are to be sold by Livewell Chapman, 1653), 1. For an account of the Fifth-monarchist agenda, see B. S. Capp, *The Fifth Monarchy Men: A Study in Seventeenth-Century English Millenarianism* (London: Faber, 1972).

51. In the contest to capture the public imagination in the 1650s, Gura suggests that Roger Williams (New Englander) and John Milton (English) who supported toleration were the winners, and John Cotton (New Englander) and Thomas Hooker (New Englander) the losers. The public battle between Williams and Cotton began with Williams's "The Bloudy Tenant of Persecution. London, 1644." *Early English Books, 1641-1700,* microform, 228:E.1, no. 2. n.d.; and Cotton's rebuttal "The Bloudy Tenent, Washed, and Made White in the Bloud of the Lambe," London: Printed by Matthew Symons for Hannah Allen, 1647. Early English Books 1641–1700 Series, microform, 136:14; followed by Williams's "The Bloody Tenant of Persecution yet more Bloody, London, 1652." *American Culture Series,* 57:6. n.d. This battle was

played out between London and the colony and Williams was supported in London with John Clarke's *Ill Newes from New-England, Or, A Narrative of New-England's persecution* (London: Printed by Henry Hills, 1652).

52. James Holstun, *A Rational Millennium: Puritan Utopias of Seventeenth Century England and America* (New York: Oxford University Press, 1987) 35.

53. In recent years this perception of England as a kind of "tabula rasa" on which to build a new civil polity has been situated within a transatlantic dynamic of radical Puritan thought. Philip F. Gura, *A Glimpse of Sion's Glory: Puritan Radicalism in New England, 1620–1660* (Middleton, CT: Wesleyan University Press, 1984), 204. Gura focuses on the religious writing of radical Puritan individuals in New England as they influence, and are incorporated into, orthodox Puritan theocracy in the New World. For some of the best analysis of religious writings and commonwealth treatises concerned with ecclesiastical reform in seventeenth-century England and New England, see Holstun's *A Rational Millennium*. For further comment Eliot's treatise on church governance in relation to other treatises, *see* Theodore Dwight Bozeman, "John Eliot and the Civil Part of the Kingdom of Christ," in *To Live Ancient Lives: The Primitivist Dimension in Puritanism* (Chapel Hill: University of North Carolina Press, 1988), 263–86.

54. At the very beginning of this second edition, Milton outlines his general purpose: "Although, since the writing of this treatise, the face of things hath had some change, writs for new elections have been recalled, and the members at first chosen re-admitted from exclusion; yet not a little rejoicing to hear declared the resolution of those who are in power, tending to the establishment of a free commonwealth, and to remove, if it be possible, this noxious humour of returning bondage, instilled of late by some deceivers, and nourished from bad principles and false apprehensions among too many of the people; I thought best not to suppress what I had written." John Milton, "The Ready and Easy Way to Establish a Free Commonwealth (1660)," in *The Prose Works of John Milton*, vol. 2 (London: Henry G. Bohn, 1853) 108–9. William Lamont says that Baxter's *A Holy Commonwealth* was a kind of love letter to Richard Cromwell and, "everything in the treatise hinges upon the support that Richard Cromwell's Protectorate could give clergyman like Baxter." Richard Baxter, *A Holy Commonwealth*, ed. William Lamont (Cambridge: Cambridge University Press, 1994), ix-x.

55. For an account of the colonial response to the Restoration, *see* Jack M. Sosin, *English America and the Restoration Monarchy of Charles II: Transatlantic Politics, Commerce, and Kingship* (London and Lincoln: University of Nebraska Press, 1980).

56. "John Eliot, Roxbury, 6th July 1663," in *Calendar of the Correspondence of Richard Baxter, 1660–1669*, ed. N. H. Keeble and Geoffrey Nuttall (Oxford: Clarendon Press, 1991), 2:40.

57. Although *The Christian Commonwealth* was not printed in New England it was certainly in circulation, since the General Court demanded that each copy be returned when Charles II returned to the throne. At a session on May 22, 1661, the General Court decreed: "all persons whatsoever in this Jurisdiction (Massachusetts Bay), that haue any of the said Bookes in theire Custody shall on theire perrills within fowerteene dayes after publication hereof either cancel and deface the same or deliuer them vnto the next Magistrate or to the Secretary, whereby all farther divulgation and improovement of the said offensiue Booke may be prevented," (*Records of the General Court*, 4:370.) An excerpt of this session is appended to *The Christian Commonwealth*, and has been reprinted in the *MHSC*, Boston, 1846-1849, 27–164.

58. *Records of the General Court*, 4:370, see *The Christian Commonwealth*, in *MHSC*, Boston, 1846–1849, 27–164.

59. "John Eliot to Richard Baxter, Roxbury, 6th July 1663," in Keeble and Nuttall, *Calendar of the Correspondence of Richard Baxter*, 2:41.

60. "John Eliot to Richard Baxter, October 16, 1656," in *Some Unpublished Correspondence of the Rev. Richard Baxter and the Rev. John Eliot, "The Apostle to the American Indians," 1656–1682*, ed. F. J. Powicke, The John Rylands Library (Manchester: Manchester University Press, 1931), 138–76; 442-66; 154–55.

61. For an account of this acquaintance, see Alison Searle, "'Though I am a Stranger to You by Face, yet in Neere Bonds by Faith': A Transatlantic Republic of Letters," *Early American Literature* 43, no. 2 (June 2008): 277–308.

62. Eliot, *Communion of Churches*, title page, n.p.
63. It is structured so that twelve churches will gather together in communion and establish a "society of churches" by electing two individuals to represent them. Subsequently, the "society of churches" which has twenty-four members, will agree to elect twelve of their number to establish a provincial council. In a community of twelve provincial councils, each will send two representatives to the national council, and from there twelve national synods will send two representatives to an Ecumenical council. (Eliot, *Communion of Churches*, 7)
64. Eliot, *Communion of Churches,* 8.
65. Ibid., 38.
66. Ibid., 38.
67. "Baxter to Eliot, January 20th 1656/7," in Powicke, *Some Unpublished Correspondence*, 156.
68. Ibid,, 159.
69. "Animadversions of Mr. Eliot's Book for Stated counsels, 1667," in Powicke, *Some Unpublished Correspondence*, 160–63.
70. . Ibid., 160.
71. Williston Walker ed., *The Creeds and Platforms of Congregationalism* (New York: Charles Scribner's Sons, 1893), 194–237. In the years leading up to 1662, the diminishing number of first generation church members resulted in ever decreasing congregations and this proved to be one of the deciding factors in establishing a Half-Way covenant, where children of existing church members could be baptized without the public confession which was usually demanded for church membership.
72. "Animadversions, 1667," in Powicke, *Some Unpublished Correspondence*, 162.
73. Ibid., 163.
74. Eliot, *Communion of Churches*, preface, n.p.
75. Ibid., preface, n.p.
76. "Eliot to Baxter, 22 January 1667/8," in Powicke, *Some Unpublished Correspondence*, 166.
77. This copy is one of only two copies and it is held at the Bodleian Library, Oxford: Eliot, *Communion of Churches*, pamphlet E 122, 13, hereafter cited Baxter copy. The other copy is held at Harvard.
78. Eliot, *Communion of Churches*, 17 (Baxter copy). Another lengthy amendment fills the margins on the right side and the foot of the page:

for the Lord will in his last period of the world pouer out his grace most frequently upon the mountains of the earth. The stone cut out of the mountain (Jon or Ian). 2. 45. is Christ in search of his Saints who sit upon the mountains. Ten such Kings or (Principality) shall be at or about the beginning of this work. (&c.) 17.16 & n/y plane that become a great mountain filling this whole earth. (Jon) 2.35. n/y war of (affliction?)will cause in all the (...) nations (esay) 2.4. the mountains shall bring (praer?) unto the people. ps.72.3. all z/y forces shall combine against the common (in...) of Christ as of the churches.wch wrk finished all shall attend to the building the glorious city (& Temple) viz. To mould both church and & (...) to the holy (p...) town in the Scriptures. wh will be a new heaven and a new earth in (compison) of wt hath been already (esay 65.17) & 66.22. pas 3.13. And n/y z/y wrk will be to spread this (iO) (glorious) glory of Christ all the world about (..) 11.15. e(ls)ay 62.2. mat .24.31. both unto the (known) or [as yet] unknown(.....) ps 67.2. esay 66.18 ps 2.8. And if we may (...) further times by fortune, how will we wrk enough for the churches for a thousand years) I say in (...) to these thousand kinds. Oh that & c. (17)

79. Eliot, *Communion of Churches*, 3 (Baxter copy).
80. "Eliot to Baxter, 10 January 1667/8," in Powicke, *Some Unpublished Correspondence*, 166.
81. "Baxter to Eliot, September 2, 1671," in Powicke, *Some Unpublished Correspondence*, 465.

82. "John Woodbridge to Baxter, 31 March 1671," in Keeble and Nuttall, *Calendar of the Correspondence of Richard Baxter*, 2: 110.

83. "Richard Baxter to Boyle, 20 October 1660," *The Correspondence of Robert Boyle*, ed. Michael Hunter, Antonio Clericuzio and Lawrence M. Principe (London and Burlington, VT: Pickering and Chatto, 2001), 1:1636–661, 435.

84. See "Richard Baxter to Robert Boyle, 14th June 1665," in Hunter, Clericuzio, and Principe, *Correspondence of Robert Boyle*, 2: 473–78.

85. "John Eliot to Robert Boyle, 26 August 1664," in Hunter, Clericuzio, and Principe, *Correspondence of Robert Boyle*, 2: 305–6, 305.

86. Ibid., 306.

87. "Richard Bourne to The Commissioners of the United Colonies in New England, appended to, Commissioners of the United Colonies in New England to Robert Boyle, 8th September 1669," in Hunter, Clericuzio, and Principe, *Correspondence of Robert Boyle*, 4: 149.

88. "John Eliot to Robert Boyle, 6 July 1669," in Hunter, Clericuzio, and Principe, *Correspondence of Robert Boyle*, 4: 140.

89. "John Eliot to Robert Boyle, 4 November 1680," in Hunter, Clericuzio, and Principe, *Correspondence of Robert Boyle*, 5: 223.

90. Ibid., 224–25.

91. "John Eliot to Robert Boyle, 17 June 1681," in Hunter, Clericuzio, and Principe, *Correspondence of Robert Boyle* 5: 255–56.

92. "Richard Baxter to Robert Boyle, 29 August 1682," in Hunter, Clericuzio, and Principe, *Correspondence of Robert Boyle* 5: 332–33.

93. "John Eliot to Robert Boyle, 27 November 1683," in Hunter, Clericuzio, and Principe, *Correspondence of Robert Boyle*, 5: 434–35.

94. "Robert Boyle to John Winthrop Jr., 21 April 1664," in Hunter, Clericuzio, and Principe, *Correspondence of Robert Boyle*, 2: 267.

95. Ibid., 267–8.

96. *Calendar of State Papers, Colonial Series, America and the West Indies 1661–1668*, ed. W. Noel Sainsbury (London: Her Majesty's Stationary Office, 1880), 200–1. http://archive.org/stream/1964colonialrecordsc05greauoft/1964colonialrecordsc05greauoft_djvu.txt (accessed April 2, 2013).

97. "Boyle to Endecott, 17th March 1665," in Hunter, Clericuzio, and Principe, *Correspondence of Robert Boyle*, 2: 459–61.

98. "Boyle to Henry Ashurst, March 1665," in Hunter, Clericuzio, and Principe, *Correspondence of Robert Boyle*, 2: 458–59.

99. "The Humble Supplication," October 1665, in Sainsbury, *Calendar of State Papers*, 247-49.

100. . Sainsbury, *Calendar of State Papers*, 247–49.

101. "Secret instructions for the Commissioners," in Sainsbury, *Calendar of State Papers*, 200–1.

102. "Boyle to Endecott, 17th March 1665," in Hunter, Clericuzio, and Principe, *Correspondence of Robert Boyle*, 2: 459–61.

Chapter Two

Dedicated Dignitaries and the Christian Reader

Reading the Mission in England

In 1653, Eliot dedicated his account of some of the first extensive and extemporaneous confessions of Native Americans to Oliver Cromwell: "Envy it self cannot deny that the Lord hath raised and improved You in an Eminent manner to over throw Antichrist, and to accomplish, in part, the Prophesies and Promises of the Churches Deliverance from that Bondage."[1] Ten years later, in 1663, and in different political circumstances, the Commissioners of the colony appended a dedicatory epistle to about twenty copies of the complete translation of the Indian bible for distribution in England: "To the high and Mighty Prince, Charles the Second, by the grace of god King of England, Scotland, France and Ireland, defender of the faith, &c."[2] Both dedications capture the sensitive relationship between New and Old England during the mid-seventeenth century. Careful negotiation of the political and religious affiliations of the writers of the Tracts was necessary during the revolution, restoration and beyond, so there is a shift from Cromwell as key patron in the 1650s to Charles II in the 1660s.

From the dedications and addresses of Eliot and the Commissioners it is clear that they were keen political operators: while Eliot maneuvered to meet his own spiritual ends, the Commissioners used claims of the colony's spiritual success to derive political bargaining power to enhance the colony's standing in England. This chapter locates Eliot as a central figure in a network of individuals and organizations who promoted the New England mission to English audiences, either to enhance financial patronage, as was Eliot's main goal, or to advance the dominance of England's claim to the

New World over competing claims from France and Spain. Eliot's transatlantic dialogue with his English reception community is in fact part of a larger Atlantic framework in which the politics of Europe's claim to the New World are contested.

The spiritual and political motivations of the colony and mission had already been forged before Eliot set sail for New England. The colony's charter had already declared that Native conversion to Christianity would be the driving force of the colony's purpose. Furthermore, the famous company seal imposes on a solitary Indian the words—"Come over and help us!"— invoking the plea of the Macedonians to St Paul. The performance of faith, particularly of penitent Indians, is a defining feature in the reputation of the colony in England from the day the charter is signed, and this idea of the mission was conveyed to armchair missionaries through dedicatory epistles and notes and letters to the putative Reader.

The Eliot Tracts were edited and published in London, and Eliot's dedicatory address to Cromwell was appended to *Tears of Repentance*, the seventh of eleven tracts. As well as sales in London there was wide distribution of the tracts across parishes in England. In considering their publication history William Kellaway suggests that something between one thousand and one thousand five hundred was considered to be an appropriate print run.[3] The Algonquian bibles did not have the same popular reach but they were also distributed around England to significant patrons and members of the Corporation. Generally, Eliot's mission addressed English reception communities so as to give a growing sense of cultural autonomy in the New England religious and social elite, and it was the key exemplary figure of the penitent Indian that enabled the distinctions between New and Old England to emerge in their fullest forms.

This chapter continues to consider the "truth-telling" rhetoric of transatlantic correspondence, but it does so through the open letters and narratives sent from New England clergy and governors to the Corporation for the Propagation of the Gospel in England.[4] The letters and narratives were published in London for the purpose of raising funds for the mission, but they were also part of a larger impulse to promote the religious and civil distance between England and colonial settlements. Eliot's *Indian Dialogues,* in which native speakers act as missionaries to willing native penitents, were also sent to England. Although they were never published in England, it is my contention that they too continued the work of promoting the colony through the performances of praying Indian speakers.[5]

In each of these texts, the tracts and *Indian Dialogues,* the growing confidence of Puritan New Englanders in developing a distinct identity in the midst of political upheaval in England is apparent through their control over the ways in which direct speech is incorporated in written text. The texts include dedicatory prefaces, dedicatory letters and narratives containing the transcription of spoken Indian confessions, literary speech acts encapsulating the New Englander's desire to control the performative representation of the self and others. First and foremost, it was the New Englander's transcription of his firsthand accounts, and his eye- and ear-witness testimony that distinguished his account of the New World from all other English commentators.

ADDRESSING THE AUDIENCE AND FRAMING THE MISSION

English readers interested in colonial affairs in the seventeenth century could have seen a lot of positive and negative accounts of colonial life. The earliest promotional pamphlets to reach England from the New World colonies include Thomas Hariot's *A Briefe and True Report of the New Found Land of Virginia, 1588*, and Edward Waterhouse's *A Declaration of the State of the Colony in Virginia, 1622*. Several years later, in 1643, *Good News from New England* encouraged preachers, scholars, merchants, seamen, husbandmen, and manual laborers to transport themselves to the Massachusetts Bay colony to benefit from the abundance of work and wealth which they could hope to acquire.[6] The letters and narratives contained in Eliot's Indian Tracts are certainly part of the drive to attract new settlers, but the promotional campaign funded by the Corporation for the Propagation of the Gospel had a slightly different agenda. By focusing on the missionary experiences with Algonquians of the Massachusetts Bay area, the writers of the tracts tried to encourage financial contributions from wealthy patrons and parishes in England and to counter the bad press from those disillusioned by their experience of the New World.

In part, the tracts responded to pamphlets like Thomas Morton's famously derisory account of New England Puritan fervor in "New English Canaan" (1637), John Clarke's bitter account of his trial and corporal punishment in *Ill News from New England* (1652), and Roger Williams's embattled theological exchange with John Cotton in *The Bloudy Tenent of Persecution* (1644) and *The Bloody Tenent yet more Bloody* (1652). Although Morton vividly describes the beauty of the colony, "New English Canaan" is remembered for its humorous criticism of the Puritan reaction to his revelry and the Maypole celebration.[7] John Clarke's more visceral response to his New England experience focuses on the harsh nature of the judicial system and the equally savage and dangerous Natives. A Baptist, Clarke was found guilty of preaching and baptizing without authority and refusing to remove his hat in the presence of a Congregationalist preacher. He likens his punishment to that endured by those guilty of "whoredome" or "forcing a little Child" and challenges the excessive force of this penalty.[8] Clarke also refers to the threat of Native tribes and fear of their rituals, a perception that Edward Waterhouse in particular had taken great pains to overcome in the early years of settlement. Roger Williams, who had been persecuted and banished for his separatist religious beliefs in 1635, was also perceived by New England to be a serious threat to the reputation of the Massachusetts Bay Colony. In 1643 he travelled to London and obtained his own charter from Charles I, successfully retaining this by appealing in person to Parliament in 1651 and 1654, and then appealing again to Charles II in 1663. He had been one of their own ministers but sensationally rejected their offer of John Wilson's ministry at the First Boston Church because of his dismay at his Congregationalist brethren and their continued links with the Church of England.[9] Another influential publication was the translation of Bartolome Las Casas's *Brevísima relación de la destrucción de las* Indias (1542), titled in English as *A Short Account of the Destruction of the Indies or, Tears of the Indians*. This narrative perpetuated the myth of the Black Legend and tales of Spanish torture and devastation. Although this pamphlet first appeared in the sixteenth century, it was re-printed throughout the seventeenth century, and *Tears of Repentance*, the seventh of the Eliot's Indian tracts introducing its English audience to the first, extensive public confessions of praying Indians, is an obvious attempt to match and counter *Tears of the Indians*.[10]

In an anti-New English, anti-native and anti-Spanish climate, Eliot and his fellow contributors set out to reshape the impression of Puritan New England in the minds of their English reception community. In response, William Steele, president of the Corporation, articulated the dual motivation of the tracts by identifying the writers' attempts to encourage financial generosity from English patrons for missionary work, as well as their attempts to disparage negative impressions of the colony and its spiritual endeavors. In his appendix to the sixth tract in the series, *Strength out of Weakness* (1652), Steele states "we of the Corporation" felt bound to publish it:

> [L]ooking upon it as one meanes to advance the work in the hearts of Gods people, and to stirre them up thereby to contribute more freely towards the carrying on the same: The reason wherefore we have published so many testimonialls, and shall insert more, is because too many that come from thence labour to blast the worke, by reporting here that there is no such worke afoote in the Countrey.[11]

The main "laborers" in this work were John Eliot, Thomas Mayhew Jr., and Thomas Mayhew Sr., and their contribution to the pamphlets is extensive, including letters as well as transcriptions of Indian narratives. The letters of other important New Englanders must also be noted, including Thomas Shepard, minister at Cambridge, Richard Mather, minister at Dorchester, theologian, and coauthor of *The Bay Psalm Book*, 1640 (together with Thomas Weld and John Eliot), William Leverich, a member of the Sandwich government at New Plymouth, and John Endicott, governor of Massachusetts. In arranging the publication of the tracts, the Corporation also added their own gloss by asking an excolonial or another interested individual to unite the fragmented and multivocal nature of each pamphlet in their dedicatory epistle. George Parker Winship and William Kellaway suggest that the names of a variety of contributors were highlighted on the title pages so as to give the impression that more men than Eliot were involved in the mission in New England.[12] Both refer to the committee meeting on March 19 to illustrate the involvement of the Corporation in the selection and editing process of the tracts:

> [A]ttend Dr. Reynolds & let him understand that the Corporation doe not think fitt to print Mr Mahews Manuscript & to give him thankes in the Corporations name for his panes.
>
> That ye title [the word "Page" is cancelled] of the booke bee referred to Dr. Reynolds & that one of the last bookes bee presented unto him. That ye Dedecacon of the new booke bee accordinge to ye effect of the last book. That there bee a Postscript att the End of the booke now to bee printed to intimate that the bible is now alsoe about to be printed in the Indian Language.[13]

The editors attend both to contents and to the dedication and the postscript: the dedication was to be similar to the last pamphlet, and the postscript was to contain further notable information about forthcoming successes. Indeed, over the course of the eleven pamphlets, the appearance became more coherent and consistent. In 1643, when *New England's First Fruits* was published, it appeared without an author's name or a dedicatory address, but by 1647, with the publication of *The Day Breaking,* we see efforts to gloss the publication and to engage more directly with the general reader. Six lines of text introducing the tract, the narrative of which concerns a series of meetings with Waban, offer the "Reader" assurances of the truth and veracity of the account by emphasizing Eliot's credentials as a minister, whilst his position "as an eye or an ear witnesse" "is not to be questioned."[14] This short introduction lays the groundwork for future publications by showing the importance of framing the text for a general readership and pointing to the rhetorical means by which colonial encounters of any sort were relayed to armchair enthusiasts in England.

These pamphlets were subject to similar tests of truth and veracity as the many kinds of travel narratives analyzed by Anthony Pagden, by means of what he calls a discourse of "autopsy."[15] The authenticity and value of colonial travel narratives and histories of the New World relied on the recitation of "intricate detail" by the observer's firsthand experience.[16] He also notes that in the writing of history and travel narratives autopsy replaces the authority of Church Fathers and the Bible.[17] However, in the case of these tracts the New England observer, who is the authoritative observer and the "I" who allows the reader to "see" the New World, situates his responses within the rhetoric of religious authority. The discourse of "autopsy" and religious authority are both used throughout the tracts. An early example of this appears in *New England's First Fruits* where the author constructs a dialogue of objections and rebuttals, with an imagined but typical English interlocutor, in order to encourage prospective settlers to New England:

> 1. Your ground is barren,
> Answ: 1. If you should see our goodly Corne-fields, neere harvest you would answer this your selfe . . .
>
> . . .
>
> 7. Many speak evill of the place.
> Answ: Did not some doe so of the Land of *Canaan* it selfe yet *Canaan* was never the worse and themselves smarted for so doing.[18]

As well as insisting on the need to *see* in order to believe the wealth and abundance of New England's soil, the anonymous New Englander invokes the rhetoric of biblical authority by suggesting that the New World might be comparable with Canaan, thus further strengthening his authority.

In the thirteen years which followed, up until the tenth and penultimate tract of 1660, both framing dedications and the emphasis on eye- and ear-witness accounts become more elaborate, particularly when the Native confessions became an ever more conscious topic of concern between the Corporation, New English writers, and their English community of readers. By 1648 and the publication of *The Clear Sun-shine*, a format of dedications was established which included addresses to English authorities, in this case Parliament, as well as to the general "Christian" reader. By 1653 *Tears of Repentance* incorporates five different dedications and introductions to the main body of the text, signaling perhaps the importance that the Corporation, commissioners, and missionaries placed on the first extensive report of substantial confessional narratives from penitent Indians. The dedications are a mixed bag, but all with the same public audience in mind. William Steele's address demonstrates unsurprising and unflagging support for Cromwell; Mayhew's public letter to the Corporation provides extensive details of his successes on Martha's Vineyard; Eliot addresses Cromwell and the reader in two separate dedicatory addresses; and Richard Mather, a much respected intellect and colonial voice, addresses the reader and guides him or her as to how the contents of the main account might be interpreted. These dedications seek a relationship of trust between writer and reader and foster a strong and interdependent relationship between the colony and England. In Eliot's and Mather's addresses in particular the dialogue with the reader is strengthened by much biblical typology. Eliot likens the missionary endeavor in the New World to Israel's return from Babylon and further asserts that it is the Reader who turns the "wheel" of conversion and is the key to the mission's success.[19] Mather also uses Israel as a biblical comparison but strikes a far more aggressive tone toward his English reader when he suggests that just as God took his Kingdom from Israel when they faltered so he might do the same to England.[20] While Eliot's dialogue with the reader highlights the importance of England's contribution to the colony's religious success, Mather separates Old England from New by chastising the former's lax commitment to spiritual renewal.[21]

This small but distinct difference in tone is symptomatic of the larger difficulties encountered by New Englanders in forging a close relationship with the English readership, and the unsettled political situation between England and New England presented a particular dilemma for New Englanders. When Charles I was executed many Massachusetts Puritans were interested in a political realignment. Even earlier, between 1642 and 1646, when English Puritans began to wield significantly more power than in previous years, Phillip H. Round notes that along with Increase Mather, John Leverett, and Edward Winslow, one-third of Harvard graduates returned to England from the colony.[22] Nathaniel Mather also comments on the general social benefits of being "a New English man" in England.[23] One might imagine that by 1660, *New Englishness* in England may have become more crippling than enabling, but the terms of Mather's self-representation as a "New English man," are telling. As early as the second tract, *The Day-Breaking if not the Sun-Rising of the Gospel* (1647), Thomas Shepard refers to the "New English" as a separate cultural category. Invoking the authority of the Bible, New England settlers perceive themselves as legally and spiritually justified: "God had carried us safe to *New England*," and, "In sweeping away great multitudes of the Natives by the small Pox; a little before we went thither, that he (God) might make room for us there."[24] Their errand separates them from their Brethren in England and, from the beginning, there is a distinction in the mind of the Puritan settlers as to who they were and who they are becoming. In 1649 when England was in the throes of revolution and the possibilities of social, political, and constitutional change, Eliot imagines these changes in England as separate from his own reality: "Oh that blessed day in *England* when the Word of God shall be their *Magna Charta* and chief Law Book."[25] The use of "their" rather than "our" is telling as a mark of cultural separation.

Tensions between New and Old England are fairly well entrenched, particularly in the earlier tracts. In the epistle to the Reader, from *The Clear Sunshine of the Gospel*, severe warnings characterize the situation in which England finds itself: "*if he cannot have an* England *here, he can have an* England *there; &* baptize *& adopt them into those* privileges, *which wee have* looked *upon as our burthens. We have* sad decayes *upon us, we are a* revolting *Nation, a people* guilty *of great* defection *from God*."[26] Pressing the growing differences between New and Old England further, Whitfield, who had returned from the colony, makes a five-point comparison explaining the positive changes in New England against the backsliding prevalent in

England: where Indians receive the truth and the rules of Christ, England "*wrangle(s)*" the truth and as a result, "*peace*" is "*lost*"; Indians are "*industrious and pursue the things of their salvation*," while in England people are defined by their "*bed-rid dispositions, sunk down into a sottish and sensuall way*"; when Indians weep for their sins, the English, "*live with dry eyes and hard hearts.*"[27] The strongest attack on England comes in the fourth tract, when it concludes: "The *converted Heathens* in *New-England*, goe beyond you, O ye *Apostate Christians* in *England*!"[28] It is to be noted that the opposition is constructed between the English and the praying Indian, not with the Puritan New Englander. In that way the praying Indian emerges as a symbol of what England once was and may become again, and the confessional performances of the Indian convert become, in this respect, a tool to distinguish New English Protestantism from Old.

Despite all this posturing, Eliot and others knew that it was English reception communities, political leaders, religious dignitaries, and implied Christian readers, on which the success or failure of the colony rested. The collective address from the Corporation to Parliament in *The Clear Sun-shine of the Gospel* demonstrates the Corporation's keen understanding of audience, both in terms of the addressee and the general reader of this open letter:

> In *order* to do this what doth God *require* of us (English), but that we should *strengthen* the hands, *incourage* the hearts of those who are at *work* for him, *conflicting* with difficulties, *wrestling* with discouragements, to *spread* the Gospel, & in that, the *fame* and honor of this Nation, to the *utmost* ends of the earth? It was the *design* of your *enemies* to make them *little*, let it be your *endevor* to *make* them *great*, their *greatnesse* is your strength.[29]

The letter flatters and entices the addressee and the general reader while also laying out the recipient's responsibilities to conscience, faith, and country. The interlinking of religious fervor with colonial dominance allows the English Parliament and the English reader to imagine itself as a nation doing God's work and, by implication, competing with the colonial advances of their Catholic European enemies, specifically France and Spain. The Corporation constructed a reciprocal relationship between Puritans of New and Old England: while England provided financial security, New England offered a way for Protestant England to renew itself spiritually and imagine itself as a stronger nation.[30]

Some tracts included postscripts, which provided additional success stories and more practical information about the administration of the mission's financial dealings. For example, the education of two Native students, Caleb and Joel, and the work of printing and distributing the Algonquian bible appear as short appendices. Sometimes postscripts were used by the Corporation editors to pre-empt criticisms of the management of the mission. It was hard work to persuade readers that the mission was a success and individual donors that their money was being well spent. Claims of misspending were plentiful. The Corporation had embarked on some bad investments of land and property, and the reputations of some individuals with financial responsibility, specifically Hugh Peters and Thomas Weld, came under fire, because of accusations of misappropriating funds.[31] Accordingly, in a dedicatory address Henry Whitfield sets out his defense of the colony and his desire to "undeceive" the "Christian Reader" concerning rumors about the ill-use of their donations.[32] In postscripts a few years later, also on behalf of the Corporation, William Steele was keen to dismiss these claims by offering metropolitan readers the chance to peruse the "original Copies" for themselves.[33] The availability of a manuscript in the hand of one actually engaged in the work of the gospel in the colony, and already having a trusted relationship with the community of readers, makes for a very useful rhetorical device. A few years later, with finances still under scrutiny, readers *"such as desired to be satisfied how the moneys Collected, are disposed of,"* were again encouraged to come along to the Corporation's next meeting.[34]

The framing format of dedications and postscripts was more or less followed up until and including the publication of *A Further Account of the Gospel*, 1660. It is worth noting that the final tract, *A Brief Narrative of the Progress of the Gospel*, published in 1670, did not have any of the framing devices used in previous years. Instead, the tract was simply a letter, sent by Eliot and published as a single item. Use of the letter form maintained the accepted understanding of epistolary truth-telling claims, as did the rhetoric of eyewitness reportage, but the reasons for the lack of any presentational framing are not clear. It could simply be that after the restoration of the Stuart monarchy, the millennial potential surrounding the mission had been lost.

While the relationship between England and New England changed in the years following Charles II's restoration, the dedications appended to the Algonquian bible in the 1660s demonstrate that English reception communities continued to be crucial to the survival of the mission and the colony. At a time when Charles II was trying to restake a claim on Massachusetts's apparently freewheeling independence from the Crown, the commissioners of the United Colonies were more eager than they might otherwise have been to append a dedication to Charles II highlighting the importance of the colony as a site of England's spiritual renewal. The dedicatory epistle of the 1663 Indian bible states: "Religion is the End and Glory of Mankinde. and as it was the Professed End of this Plantation; so we d[e]sire ever to keep it in our main Design (both as to our selves, and the Natives about us) and that our Products may be answerable thereunto."[35] It is fair to say that this really was Eliot's motivation.[36] However, it is unlikely that the commissioners of the United Colonies who prefaced the bibles with this dedicatory address had similar intentions. A far larger portion of the address is taken up with flattering the King and playing on the rivalry felt between English and Spanish interests, particularly in the New World. The commissioners assert that royal patronage for this project will "stand among the Marks of Lasting Honour in the eyes of all that are Considerate, even unto After-Generations."[37] The most important feature of the dedication is the appeal it makes to England's, and by extension Charles II's, reputation as a world power:

> The Southern Colonies of the *Spanish Nation* have sent home from this *American Continent*, much Gold and Silver, as the Fruit and end of their Discoveries and Transplantations: That (we confess) is a scarce commodity in this Colder Climate. But (sutable to the Ends of our Undertaking) we Present this, and other Concomitant Fruits of our poor Endeavours to Plant and Propagate the Gospel here; which, upon a true account, is as much better than Gold, as the Souls of man are of more worth than the whole World.[38]

The colony is presented with an abject modesty, but England's moral and religious superiority is asserted over avaricious Spain and the Indian bible is characterized as an object of English national pride. As for other English readers, or perhaps more accurately, English owners, the Indian bible was presented as a gift in thanks for generous financial contributions to the mission. For Lady Mary Armyne, and other owners like her, including Richard Baxter, Robert Boyle, Ralph Frecke, ancestors of William Pole from Devon, as well as members of the Corporation, the bible could only be a linguistic oddity and cultural artifact, a symbol and a gesture, not a book to be read.[39] It may also have been as politically motivated as English translations traced by Christopher Hill in *The English Bible and the Seventeenth Century Revolution.*[40] It is important to note that in the first run of the New Testament, 1661, around forty copies were sent to England and of the first edition of the complete bible, 1663, twenty were sent to England, each with a dedication to Charles II, the newly restored King.[41] These dedications are significant as they explain, in part, the reasons for such an extravagant and costly publication, which, in truth, could be read by very few people. The Indian bible had become objectified, so as to provide England with a textual symbol of itself as a leading European power, or to allow its English owner, as an armchair missionary, to feel part of the "Errand" in the New World.

GATHERED LISTENERS IN ENGLAND

Dissemination of the Tracts was not limited to private readership, although private readers were the primary target audience. Rather, as Richard Mather indicates in his dedication to *Tears of Repentance* when he addresses the "godly Christian, who shall read or hear this ensuing Relation," people might gather to "hear" the tracts read aloud.[42] Indeed, it was the Corporation's intention to circulate the tracts to parishes across England to extend the national endeavor to support the mission beyond the metropolitan reader. When the Corporation for Propagating the Gospel was created by an act of Parliament in 1649, the scope of its fundraising and consciousness-raising efforts was clear. Linda Gregerson notes that after reading the act to parishioners, ministers were expected to visit each household and collect donations.[43]

Not only the Act but also the tracts themselves may have been read to doubtless bemused local church-goers across England. Two letters from ministers in Cheshire and Dauntsey confirm the importance of local ministers in this far-reaching promotional campaign. Henry Newcome writes:

> There came now orders for a collection for the Indians. A large narrative came with it, and letters, well penned, from both the universities. I was taken with design; and receiving but the papers on Saturday morning, turned off my ordinary subject and preached two sermons purposely, about Feb. 27th on I Chr. xxix. 3. And the Lord did humble me mightily after evening sermon when I called up the people to subscribe, and they did it so slenderly and acted in it as if I had not said one word about it. But afterwards the Lord moved upon some of them to help me; and I went up and down from house to house, and making every servant and child that had anything to give, I raised it to a pretty sum for that little place, seven pounds odd money.[44]

While Henry Newcome records the eventual success of his collection, Richard Bigge, minister of Winterbourne, Dauntsey, reads the "bookes and papers" to his congregation, but somewhat apologetically relates: "Sir, of my selfe I am not able any way to promote soe religiouse a worke, having but thirty shilling yearely settled on me for my cure. I went with both ye Churchwardens & desired gratuityes at every mans house; But could force noe man nor persuade any man or woeman to be soe charitable as to give one peny."[45] I assume that the "bookes"[46] and large narratives referred to are in fact the tracts of the early 1650s, possibly including *Tears of Repentance*; the publication date, around March 1653, corresponds closely with the date of Bigge's letter, May 1653. As has been noted, some congregations were not wealthy or generous enough to freely contribute. Nonetheless, the Corporation realized: "it was upon them (the ministers) that the ultimate success or failure of the collection rested."[47] New England Company receipt books demonstrate, however, that numerous ordinary men and women across England donated small amounts in response to these pleas from the pulpit.[48] In the knowledge that the tracts might be, or at least should be, read aloud to groups of parishioners, the contributors to the tracts were keen to use conventions of oratory for the benefit of this particular reception community. From the euphoric rhetoric of J. D., a contributor to the tracts, the spiritual and financial intentions of tracts are abundantly clear, but so too is the intention to engage a gathered, listening audience:

2. *Rouze up your selves my Brethern: ye Preachers of the Gospel*, this work concernes you. Contrive and plot, preach for and presse the advancement hereof. Its cleare you may do much: Let not this be your condemnation, that you did nothing.

3. *Come forth ye Masters of money*, part with your Gold to promote the Gospel; Let the gift of God in temporal things make way, for the Indians receipt of spiritualls. [49]

Preachers and rich merchants are to be mobilized, and the rousing tone of J. D. also points towards the importance of oratory in the delivery of the tracts to gathered listeners. The importance of the voice in the pulpit, from ministers like Newcome and Bigge, was crucial to the success of the Corporation and implicitly, the continuation of Eliot and Mayhew's missionary endeavors. Through their publication and oration the tracts also acquired the weight and authority of proclamations from Parliament and the pulpit. This manipulation of speech and oratory is further complicated and significantly heightened when the substance of Algonquian spoken confessional narratives is translated and transcribed for metropolitan readers and regional congregations alike.

FROM SPEECH TO TEXT: THE "ELOQUENCE" OF PRAYING INDIANS[50]

Parliament had endorsed the literary transcription of praying Indian speech acts for readers of the tracts across England, and a ministerial voice from the pulpit re-stated the narratives to a congregation of gathered listeners. Through a process of translating speech into text and back again into speech, Eliot and his missionary supporters in England and New England manipulated the inherent forces of written and spoken utterances to support their spiritual errand in the wilderness. The power of both epistolary conventions and conventions of oratory is brought together quite subtly in these tracts.

Such a combination may also attract theoretical analysis. In *Eloquence is Power*, Sandra M. Gustafson outlines the features of text and voice and the ideological implications of their uses, in her comprehensive account of oratory and performance:

A four-term set of oppositions structures Western ideas and images of language: the dead letter mirrors and disrupts stable text while demonic speech mocks the living voice. These four terms can be construed as two opposed pairs. Text that is privileged for its permanence and stability is set against the ruptures effected by demonic speech. When the powers of the living voice are celebrated, they are imagined triumphing over the dead letter. In performance, this doubled dynamic of language both emerges as a set of mutually constitut-

ing symbolic categories and produces speech and text as performatives that
signify through the very choice of medium. [51]

The prioritized uses of text over speech, and vice versa, are significant features of the Tracts, and the participants were aware of the manipulative
possibilities. By way of endorsing the authenticity of the texts, for example,
William Leverich comments: "Sir, you have a naked Narration of our proceedings." [52] For rhetorical purposes a pure unadulterated account is presented in pure unadulterated prose. For his part, Thomas Shepard hopes that with
his "rent and ragged relation," "no mans Spectacles may deceive him." [53] The
fragmentary nature of Shepard's pamphlet then testifies to the authenticity of
the writer and the text. Developing this truth-telling device, he uses a conversational register as he describes the consequences of a ship leaving late: "Sir,
I had ended these relations once or twice, but the stay of the Vessell increaseth new matter; which because 'tis new and fresh, you shall have it as I heard
it from a faithfull hand." [54] The intimacy and immediacy of speech are in-
voked, even if it will be some time before the words reach the recipient. The
process of articulating what they see and hear into a supposedly stable written format has its political considerations.

Their own ideological motives are often thinly veiled by their apparent
objectivism, and the written words become part of a cultural performance.
With the inclusion of direct speech from praying and non-praying Indians, as
well as the transcription of public confessional narratives from Indian converts, the move from speech to text via "epistolary truth-telling" [55] shows
how the "four-term set of oppositions" is deployed in the Tracts. Eliot tends
to gloss over the complexities of translation and transcription, stating "let the
work it selfe speake," while he remains "silent," giving the illusion of the
transparency which he believes direct speech offers. Yet, it is through the
management of transcribing this speech that a specific image of the praying
Indian is constructed for the English reader. [56]

One of the first penitent Indians whose words were re-constructed in
textual form was Wequash. Eliot describes him as the "Captaine" of the
Pequot tribe, but his words are presented in a voice suggesting a lesser status
in English convention: *"Wequash, no God, Wequash no know Christ."* [57] He
may be an accomplished warrior, but he refers to himself in the third person.
The clumsy speech pattern would have given the impression that he was
uneducated and implied that he was from a more 'primitive' race. In other
words, Eliot uses what he claims are Wequash's own words to give the
impression of early version of the noble savage, who, far from threatening
the colonizer, is waiting for the colonizer to educate and civilize him. Wequash is perceived to be at the beginning of a developmental process, and his
speech patterns seem to accord with the notion of a natural man as set out in
Locke's considerations of language and its controlling influence on social

development.[58] Eliot constructs a racial and cultural continuum, in which, as Holstun argues, Native Americans can be imagined as a pre-Christian and pre-civil people.[59] In Eliot's logic, and the ethnocentric logic of Europeans generally, this will eventually lead Wequash to develop a more literate Christian and, ultimately, more English sense of self.

As Eliot's presentation continues, Wequash gradually sheds his image as the supposedly *barbarous heathen* familiar to English audiences. This was important if a metropolitan audience was to overcome its doubts about whether the conversion of the so-called savages was possible. The Pequot War, although over in 1637, several years before the first tract was printed, remained in the transatlantic cultural formation of the colony and its inhabitants.[60] Wequash, the savage Pequot Indian, therefore, becomes the most productive site of conversion:

> This man (Captain Wequash) a few years since, feeing and beholding the mighty power of God in our English Forces, how they fell upon the *Peqans*, where divers hundreds of then were slaine in an houre: The Lord, as a God of glory in great terrour did appeare into the Soule and Conscience of this poore Wretch, that very act; and though before that time he had low apprehensions of our God, having conceived hime to be (as he said) but a *Muskett* God, or a God unto a flye; and as meane thoughts of the English that served this God, that they were silly weake men; yet from that time he was convinced and per-swaded that our God was a most dreadfull God; and that one *English* man by the help of his God was able to slay and put to flight an hundred *Indians*.[61]

He understands the English God in terms of his success in battle—fittingly for a tribal warrior—but goes on to grow "greatly in the knowledge of Christ, and in the Principles of Religion and became thorowly reformed according to his light"[62] and thus becomes the praying Indian, key to the new image of New England being promoted in England.[63]

When these words were collated in England the direct or reported speech of Wequash and other praying and non-praying Indians became an integral part of a communicative exchange between New and Old England. Editorial interjections in many of the later tracts also give details of penitents' earnest contrition and their tears of sorrow. Within the bounds of these mutually acknowledged assurances between the writer and reader, Eliot's transcription of Indian voices aims to confirm the authenticity seemingly guaranteed by the "living voice," which Gustafson describes. In this context, Judith Butler's analysis of interpellation is also useful in understanding the Puritan uses of Wequash's speech. Butler argues that:

> Language sustains the body not by bringing it into being or feeding it in a literal way; rather, it is by being interpellated within the terms of language that a certain social existence of the body first becomes possible. To understand this, one must imagine an impossible scene, that of a body that has not yet

been given social definition, a body that is, strictly speaking, not accessible to us, that nevertheless becomes accessible on the occasion of an address, a call, an interpellation that does not "discover" this body, but constitutes it fundamentally.[64]

One might imagine the emerging identity of Wequash to be the "impossible scene" which Butler describes.

Within this emergence and propagandist performance, however, still lies the possibility of disruption, and "impossible scene" may still be the right phrase. Wequash understands the English God as a powerful warrior, responsible for overpowering "an hundred Indians." He is still able to accommodate Christian beliefs into his own worldview. Nevertheless, as Wequash's words are received in England, he becomes increasingly disconnected from his tribal past and his words are interpreted within a wholly Christian framework. Puritan discourse cannot fully reconcile Wequash's motivation to its own logic, since to incorporate his motivations is, to some extent, to accept the validity of a tribal worldview.[65] The praying Indian and the New Englander are actors in the textual performance of missionary success and their repeated and reiterated performances are central to the self-fashioning of new and separate cultural categories.

MIMICRY, MERCHANDISE, AND ENGLISH RECEPTION COMMUNITIES

In most of Eliot's publications, especially the *Dialogues* and the tracts, the use of mimicry to recreate prayers, worship, and the process of religious conversion is crucial to the emergence of praying Indian identity reflecting the New England separateness and autonomy. Civil change accompanied, indeed preceded, full religious conversion and church status. With a mind to these new forms of civil organization, it is important to consider how elements of England's sophisticated mercantile economy were rhetorically styled in the mouths of native converts to boost the colony's image as a place of godly and economic success.

In Tract Six, *Strength Out of Weakness* (1652), a sequence of three letters from Eliot, Wilson, and Leverich illustrates the kind of Puritan mimicry that Indians were shown to enact as a response to missionaries' efforts. Eliot first translates Cutshamoquin's repentance for buying "strong waters" from Gorton's Plantation[66] but then goes on to relate the pearls and souls parable in which repentance is described in terms of merchandise that should be sold for a better commodity.[67] The praying Indian describes his spiritual transformation in terms of trade and recalls his spiritual revelation accordingly. In this way, the Protestant dialogue between trade and religion is encoded and posits the continuance of a specifically English Protestant, mercantile identity. In the second letter, John Wilson reiterates the pearl parable, but insists that Eliot's account is deficient on certain points, specifically as regards his account of the appearance of Natick and the gathered Indians. According to Wilson, the Englishness of the town and the people deserves more emphasis. An extensive account of the buildings and their interiors, the bridge, and the "English Apparell" of the tribal members secures the visual mimicking of Englishness.[68] Finally, Leverich, a missionary and a novice in Algonquian, recounts the emotional requirements for genuine conversion to Puritanism, and describes the emotional excess of public confessions:

> (H)aving his [Leverich's anonymous convert] countenance sad before (and as I have understood since a weeke together after our former exercise) and in speaking the teares all while trickling downe his Cheekes: After being demanded by mee what was the matter of his sadnesse, he answers mee, he did now understand that God was a just God, and for himselfe he had been very wicked, even from a childe. And another, whom I used as my Interpreter now and then in teaching them, falls suddenly and publiquely into a bitter passion, crying out, and wringing his hands, out of the like apprehension of his Condition, as he told me afterwards, and I finde no one of them (daring men) to speake of their good hearts, but some more some lesse sensible of the Contrary.[69]

The tears and wringing of hands are comparable with the public confession of convicts on the gallows and excommunicates.[70] The apparent Englishness of the confessions and the familiarity with which congregations would have understood them, and various references to colonial dissenters and a new Protestant national identity partly based on trade and commerce, are all part of the transatlantic dimension of the tracts. As the praying Indian's public confessional narrative is transferred from speech to text, it is slotted into a discourse of religion and trade. The Puritan New Englander thus emerges as spiritually renewed and justified in the mission, since civil, economic, and religious frameworks are all seen to be functioning well in the eyes of armchair missionaries in England.

In England, as these accounts were published, English audiences witnessed an increasingly successful mission growing in size and stature. From the two short paragraphs which accounted for Wequash's narrative, to the pages and pages of catechisms, public examinations, confessional speeches, and finally to the intellectual rigor of biblical exhortation from several penitents, including the Harvard educated Caleb and Joel, the image of the praying Indian was one which appeared to be on the path to what the English would call "civility." And the apparent results could appear to be spectacular: Caleb and Joel, as discussed below, famously translated a chapter of the Old Testament book Isaiah into Latin and then proceeded to interrogate its meaning according to principles of Christianity and logical reasoning.

Indeed, Eliot presents himself and the mission as the catalyst that has brought civility to a primitive race. The success of this argument rests partly on the way in which speeches are recorded and the tracts are published: in the early days, praying Indians or penitents would speak English and their words would be recoded verbatim; by the 1650s translators like Eliot would listen to Algonquian speeches and translate and transcribe them into English. In the first case, stumbling and stilted use of language was not intended as a sign of primitivism (although that is how it was perceived in England); rather, it was the genuine effects of speaking in a still unfamiliar second language. (One wonders what Eliot's Algonquian sermons sounded like to his Algonquian listeners: looks of wonder and puzzlement may have had more to do with a language barrier than the spiritual revelations he uttered.) By contrast, penitents whose words will be considered in the next chapter, including Waban, the most often cited of Eliot's converts, spoke in their own language, which was then re-written in the first language of the scribe. Despite the complexity of the translation process it is probably the main reason why these later speeches are much more fluid and fulsome than earlier accounts. There's no evidence to suggest Wequash, a warrior and a leader, was any less intelligent or rigorous in his religious understanding than Towanquick, Waban, or Caleb and Joel for that matter, but as the performances are formed in print quite a different impression emerges. The success of the mission was not necessarily a trick of translation and publication, but the Euro-centric teleology of primitive to civil to which it was affixed, certainly was.

INDIAN DIALOGUES AND THEIR ANTICIPATED RECEPTION IN ENGLAND

The voices of Native American converts continued to represent the apparent successes of Eliot's Puritan mission with the publication of *Indian Dialogues*, which appeared in the colony in 1671. Although it was not published in England and Eliot's preface suggested that it was really intended as an instruction manual for colonial and Native missionaries, Eliot sent the *Dialogues* to England, specifically to Richard Baxter. Eliot writes to Baxter in 1671: "I have drawne up a few instructive dialogues wch are also p'tly historical. One of wch my good friend will also pr(e)sent you wth."[71] Eliot's intentions in doing this must remain conjectural, but, given that most of the manuscript documents he sent to England were explicitly for publication, it is likely that *Indian Dialogues* also had an English audience in mind. It is also the case that they were intended for an audience at the Royal Society. In correspondence with John Winthrop Jr., Henry Oldenburg comments that he has received Winthrop's letter but, alas, he states: "I have not yet ye Indian dialogue and the sheet call'd ye Indian A,B,C; nor doth the Master yt brought

ye letter, remember yt any such book was left wth him at Boston."[72] Bearing
in mind Eliot's other transatlantic correspondence, *Indian Dialogues* can, and
perhaps should, be read as a promotional tract: Indian confessions were sent
to England for inclusion in Tracts; *The Christian Commonwealth* was sent to
England to be published as part of the millennial debates of the 1650s; his
"Learned Conjectures" included in *Jews in America* were intended to encourage millennial optimism; and the New Testament as well as the complete
Bible were sent to England to excite the English imagination and admiration
and, ultimately, promote the missionary cause. Eliot had a community of
English readers in mind for *Indian Dialogues* when creating the voices and
dialogues of his Indian speakers, and that community may have included
England. After all, he published the document in English when he had the
skill and means to publish it in Algonquian.

Others have taken a different view: Thomas Scanlan makes the case for a
colonial audience for the *Dialogues* because they were not published in England and were published in a literary format which was recognizable to those
classically educated scholars and ministers of New England.[73] As well, it
would be wrong to discount the putative audience, Indian missionaries, completely. In his Preface to *Indian Dialogues*, Eliot defends the use of this
specialized conversational form, the dialogue, as an appropriate tool for religious instruction:

> These dialogues are partly historical, of some things that were done and said,
> and partly instructive, to show what might or should have been said, or that
> may be (by the Lord's assistance) hereafter done and said, upon the like
> occasion. It is like to be one work incumbent upon our Indian churches and
> teachers, for some ages, to send forth instruments to call in others from pagan-
> ry to pray unto God. Instructions therefore of that nature are required, and
> what way more familiar than by way of dialogues?[74]

Eliot's assertion that the familiarity of the dialogue is reason enough for its
use as a model for religious instruction is certainly a contentious one, as
Scanlan argues, but the conversational tone and dramatic rendering of the
four separate dialogues contained in the piece are reasonably easy to interpret. Indeed, Frank Kelleter suggests three different audiences for the *Dialogues*: the commissioners of the United Colonies (colonial), the Puritan
missionary (Indian and English), and a Protestant readership in America and
England.[75]

It is difficult to decide which audience would be most influenced by
Eliot's fictional performance of native conversion, particularly the fictional-
ized representation of Metacom in Philip Keissacot. Would potential Algonquian converts be encouraged to follow their sachem; or would colonial
readers, eager to erase the perceived threat of tribal practice and cultural
difference, be comforted by imagining the religious and cultural conversion

of the powerful Native leader? Whatever the answer, the reader must find it within Eliot's complex rendering of the contesting forces of religious and political identities in the seventeenth-century Atlantic world.

CONTESTING RELIGIOUS AND POLITICAL FORCES: *INDIAN DIALOGUES* IN THE ATLANTIC WORLD

Eliot also wanted his readers in England to engage with a very specific political and religious agenda. He had already made clear his opinions of the English monarchy and the civil structures supporting it in *The Christian Commonwealth*. Although the treatise had been banned and Eliot forced to apologize, his correspondence with Baxter in the 1660s, as discussed in chapter 1 of this study, reveals that his sentiments on these matters remained unchanged. The expression of these sentiments, however, had undergone a certain degree of revision, and in *Indian Dialogues* Native American voices are used as convenient foils to mask Eliot's own political and religious proclivities.

One of the most authoritative voices in Native New England, and the one Eliot was most keen to hear uttering words of confession, was that of Metacom, King Philip, leader of the Wampanoag. Through the utterances of Philip Keitasscot, a thinly veiled representation of Metacom, and through his exchanges with various Native missionaries, including Anthony and William, Eliot's views on the political and religious contest of power in the Atlantic world become clear. In colonial literature of this period the roles assigned to Metacom by colonial writers vary between that of a barbarous heathen, a warlord, a penitent, and a cowardly, defeated sachem.[76] In each case the audience and political context determine the role which he was assigned. Philip's role in these *Dialogues* points to the political sensitivities of Eliot's intended audiences for this publication: quite apart from his role as a tribal leader and the fact that he was continually at odds with the ever-encroaching presence of colonial New Englanders, Metacom is deliberately situated in this text in a power play between the forces of Catholicism and Protestantism, as well as between English Monarchical forms of authority and the United Colonies' theocratic forms of government. It is through the kingly conversion of Metacom, through the fictional speech and speeches of Eliot's most longed for native penitent, that Eliot constructs a delicately balanced relationship with audiences on either side of the Atlantic.

Pertinent to an English audience in particular is the implicit criticism of Catholicism. Philip asks for an explanation of the "vile ministers" of Catholicism that Native missionaries describe to him, and William's account of Catholicism demonstrates that Eliot is asking his English audience to situate his New England mission within an Atlantic context where Protestantism and

Catholicism, English, French, and Spanish forces vie for control of the New World:

> I have heard that in the other part of the world there be a certain people who are called Papists, whose ministers and teachers live in all manner of wickedness and lewdness, and permit and teach the people so to do . . .
>
> Some sachems are as bad as the ministers, and of the same mind with their ministers. . . . Other sachems that are wiser and better minded, yet they cannot help it, because their ministers are so rich, and by that means have so many people depending on them, that their sachems dare not meddle with them. And their ministers take a cunning course to keep themselves and their successors rich, for they will not suffer another to marry, whereby they should have lawful children to inherit their riches. But when they die, the next minister hath all, or most of the riches that he had. And to the end, they may keep one another from marrying, they suffer one another to keep whores, so that they have bastards good store, but no lawful children. [77]

The local hierarchy of sachems (presumably priests) and ministers (bishops) is further developed to take into account the corruptions of those whom William calls the "Devil's ministers," including, cardinals, Lord Archbishops, and their "one chief," the Pope. All kinds of lustful, conceited, and depraved behavior is apparently committed by those nominated to be at the very pinnacle of the Catholic hierarchy, in stark contrast to notions of honesty and "equality"[78] embraced by Puritan Congregationalists. Indeed, Eliot reserves the greatest respect for the Protestant colonial authorities in New England, when William responds to Philip's concerns that he might lose out financially if he converts to Protestantism.

> KEIT: The first objection that I have is this, because you praying Indians do reject your sachems, and refuse to pay them tribute, in so much that if any of my people turn to pray unto God, I do reckon that I have lost him. He will no longer own me for his sachem, nor pay me any tribute. And hence it will come to pass, that if I should pray to God, and all my people with me, I must become as a common man among them, and so lose all my power and authority over them. This is such a temptation as no other I, nor any of the great sachems, can tell how to get over. [79]

The practical considerations of civil and social consequences are vividly realized in Philip's objections to religious conversion. As is the case with Puritan hierarchy, leaders expected respect, and William, a praying Indian and one of Dialogue III's missionary voices, assures Philip that his position of authority and his income need not be threatened by religious conversion: "Christ Jesus hath commanded to give unto Caesar the things that belong to Caesar, and to God the things that belong to God. And thus we have been taught. All the time that Cutshamoquin lived, our town did always honor, obey and pay tribute unto him."[80] William chooses a non-Christian leader of significant stature and importance, Caesar, to parallel Philip's experience, and then localizes the comparison by continuing his defense of civil and social hierarchy through the example of Cutshamoquin. Still, it is the broader scope that more fully substantiates William's cause and implicates Philip in a wider, transatlantic hierarchy. Through prayer and successful conversion, William contends that although Philip may lose current family ties and friendship, he will gain far more as recompense:

> Again, suppose you lose a few subjects that hate praying to God, but yet you shall gain a more intimate love of the Governor, and Magistrates, and good people of Plymouth, who were ever good friends to your father Onsamequin, and to you hitherto. But if you pray to God, you shall find deference. They will more honor, respect, and love you, than ever they did. They will embrace you as a brother in Jesus Christ. Yea, farther, the Governor and the Magistrates of Massachusetts will own you, and be fatherly and friendly to you. The commissioners of the United Colonies will own you. Yea more, the King of England, and the great peers who are heads of the Corporation there, who yearly send over means to encourage and promote our praying to God, they will take notice of you.[81]

As this new hierarchy is described, Philip's position as ruler is substantially curtailed, although (according to William's logic) the financial compensation and the implied security of a larger political and judicial body should be enough to persuade Philip of the true value of conversion. While Eliot endorses the role of the King of England and his support of the colony, he does so with little enthusiasm. It is the men of the Corporation in England who are described as "great," and it is the governors, magistrates, and commissioners of Massachusetts and Plymouth who will, it is argued, deal most favorably with a converted sachem.

Charles I and II were no favorites amongst the Puritan colonizers, and the Catholic sympathies of both monarchs are surely implicit targets in his attack on Catholicism and its abuse of hierarchical powers. In contrast and by implication, his support of the civil structures of Protestant New England as well as the missionary Corporation in England, provide a telling indication of where Eliot's sympathies lie. More than that, and more importantly, if Philip can adapt the internal consistencies of his own worldview and accept Eliot's Congregational form of Protestantism, then might not the good Christian reader in England demand that their own civil and religious leaders be equally capable of such spiritual renewal? By situating Philip's conversion in an Atlantic context which subtly challenges monarchical forms of government with the theocratic forms of government of New England, Eliot uses the Native speech of the Native leader to probe the reader's response and ask him or her to consider comparable civil and religious structures in England.

The Stuart monarchy was also the implied target of Eliot's concerns over the ways in which materialism was a barrier to spiritual renewal. Throughout the *Dialogues* and especially in Dialogue I, Kinsman, the Native everyman, assesses the colonizers who do not live by the austere standards set by Puritan teachings. He draws attention to the fact that in the past twenty years of Piumbukhou's praying to God, he has not yet become rich: "Alas, you are not like the English; and therefore I doubt upon this point. It is not as you say, that praying to God teacheth you the right way to be rich."[82] Piumbukhou responds:

> There be two sorts of riches; earthly riches, of which only you speak, and heavenly riches, which God's word calleth true riches. These earthly riches, are but temporary, and shall soon perish. But the true riches are heavenly, and eternal. They last forever. And we have spent these twenty years in seeking chiefly after heavenly riches. [83]

The earthly riches which the English are accused of acquiring include land, cattle, clothes, and "great houses," and it is difficult to determine from this list which of Eliot's audiences would define these items as riches. It is unlikely that traditional tribal culture would recognize this kind of ownership, specifically the ownership of clothes, houses and land, as a sign of wealth. One can only conclude that the target audience is an English and/or colonial one.[84] Within this verbal exchange, the Indian voices fade as the voice of the Puritan missionary becomes more apparent. However, the Indian mask which Eliot wears serves him well since he is able to critique English society and social hierarchy, without too much fear of reprisal.

What is more, it is Eliot's insistence that the problems of materialism in the colony for the past twenty years, and perhaps in England, have been an issue that really holds the Atlantic potential of these *Dialogues* in place. Approximately twenty years before the publication of the tracts, Charles I was executed. Eliot's feelings about Charles I, the civil and ecclesiastical framework supporting him, and his vast material wealth, are well documented, not least in *The Christian Commonwealth*. Many of the criticisms he places in the mouths of Piumbukhou and Kinsman about the colony's desire for wealth and fortune double as a critique of past and present English monarchs. He had made these criticisms before, but by the 1670s had a keener awareness of his audience's expectations and did not use the same tone in the 1670s in the *Indian Dialogues* as he used in the 1650s. That said, just as *The Christian Commonwealth* supported a radical break with monarchical hierarchy and offered an alternative civil and ecclesiastical order similar to the example set by the praying towns, so the *Indian Dialogues* asks his English audiences, be they monarchs or simply Christian readers, to be instructed and inspired by the same "heavenly" "riches" and "true wealth" that motivates the spiritual renewal of Eliot's Indian speakers.[85]

The *Dialogues* come to mean something different to three separate audiences: praying Indians might see it as a critique of colonial society; colonial readers may understand this as Eliot's support of a simpler, less commodified society and perhaps a critique of their past experience in England; and an English audience may well identify Eliot's critique of a colony in the grasp of materialism. Ultimately, Eliot expects his text to perform differently within the colonial and the transatlantic space.

A full interrogation of *Indian Dialogues* demands that it be placed within the bounds of the political and religious contestations of power in the Atlantic world of the seventeenth century. As tribal chiefs and the native everyman become Christian, typological interpretations of native conversions are entrenched, material wealth is denounced, Catholicism is vilified, and New England civil structures are seen to be the nearest reflection of biblical example, English readers are asked to imagine that their Protestant mission to New England is successful and through that their battle for ownership of the New World is morally secure. Further, if sachems of New England can embrace the spiritual demands of Christianity through the demands of Congregational forms of civil and social organization, English readers are encouraged to imagine New England as a site of significant spiritual renewal and are subsequently asked to question their own monarchical hierarchy and its religious practices. The force of the political and religious upheaval of the Atlantic world is not far from the surface of *Indian Dialogues,* and it takes a readership familiar with the political and religious concerns of England and the tensions this caused in New England to fully decode its implications.

Reading the mission in England was, therefore, not a simple matter of letting the "work it selfe speake," as Eliot would have it.[86] Rather, by harnessing the qualities of particular literary speech acts, specifically, letters, narratives, and fictional dialogues, Eliot and his fellow New Englanders were able to reconstruct the speech and speeches of praying Indians in order to furnish their own ambitions toward religious, civil, political, and even economic autonomy. Careful application of the implied immediacy of spoken utterances in the form of written prose meant that praying Indian performances were communicated to English readers by New English mediators who used this authoritative position superior to each of the putative interlocutors. The role of the praying Indian, however, is a complex performance of assimilation and resistance. Puritans understood Indian conversion as genuine, and it seems that Indians certainly meant what they said, but the actors and audiences in this performance interpreted the scene from very different ideological, economic, social and religious positions. Praying Indians meant to reconcile two very different cultures and belief systems to ensure their survival, yet, at the same time, English audiences were asked to witness the success of the mission and infer from this the potential of England to become a spiritually superior and financially secure nation that would rival France and Spain in the race to conquer the New World.

While the praying Indians were not conscious of English audiences in their conversations and public performances, the translator and scribe had this distant audience fully in mind, and the differences between the initial speech act and the transatlantic literary speech act were exploited to the fullest. In this way the Puritan New Englander emerges as the overseer, the one who controls the image and representations of others: specifically, Indians in the New World and English Protestantism in the Old World. By contrast, and by their own reckoning, New England Puritans were superior to each of these cultural types because they created and propagated a new religious climate in a New World environment; further, they assumed an elevated religious and cultural status through what they perceived to be a unique understanding of the spiritual prophecy wrapped up in their errand in the wilderness.

In the following chapter the complexities of the performance and speech acts of Native converts are considered more fully through an analysis of the very spaces in which the words are uttered. While this chapter has focused on Eliot's English reception community, the next chapter will consider communities of colonial and Native speakers and listeners who gathered in specific domestic, religious, and academic spaces to both deliver and receive speeches of religious conversion.

NOTES

1. John Eliot, and Thomas Mayhew Jr. *Tears of Repentance: Or, A Further Narrative Progress of the Gospel amongst the Indians in New-England* (London: Peter Cole, 1653), in *The Eliot Tracts: With Letters from John Eliot to Thomas Thorowgood and Richard Baxter, ed. Michael P. Clark* (London and Westport, CT: Paeger, 2003), 259.

2. John Eliot, trans. *Mamvsse Wunneetupanatamwe Up-Biblum God. (The Holy Bible containing the Old Testament and the New)* (Cambridge, MA: Printed for Samuel Green and Marmaduke Johnson, 1663), A3.

3. William Kellaway, *The New England Company 1649–1776: Missionary Society to the American Indians* (Westport, CT: Greenwood Press, 1975), 22.

4. Phillip H. Round uses the term "truth-telling" to focus on the implied truthfulness of letter writing, and further suggests that this is used as a strategy through which the colony might be defended from its critics. Phillip H. Round *By Nature and By Custom Cursed: Transatlantic Civil Discourse and New England Cultural Production, 1620–1660* (London and Hanover, NH: University Press of New England, 1999), 260.

5. Evidence of *Indian Dialogues'* intended English audience is confirmed by its being sent to Richard Baxter by John Eliot, and from John Winthrop Jr. to Hans Oldenburg of the Royal Society. *See* "John Eliot to Richard Baxter, 27th Jun 1671," in *Some Unpublished Correspondence of the Rev. Richard Baxter and the Rev. John Eliot, "The Apostle to the American Indians," 1656–1682*, ed. F. J. Powicke, The John Rylands Library (Manchester: Manchester University Press, 1931), 462; "Hans Oldenburg to John Winthrop Jr., March 18th 1671/72," in *Correspondence of Hartlib, Haak, Oldenberg and Others of the Founders of the Royal Society,*

with Governor Winthrop of Connecticut, 1661–1672, ed. Robert C. Winthrop (Boston: Press of John Wilson and Son, 1878), 46.

6. Edward Winslow, *Good News from New England* (London: printed by Matthew Simmons, 1648), 3, 24, 25. Another positive contemporary account of Massachusetts includes Thomas Lechford's *Plain Dealing, Or, News from New England* (London: Printed for W. E. & I. G. for Nath Butler, 1642), which describes the civil and political organization of the colony and provides a detailed account of religious rites and elections in the New England Congregationalist church.

7. Thomas Morton, "New English Canaan (1637)," in *The Literatures of Colonial America: An Anthology*, ed. Susan Castillo and Ivy Schweitzer (Oxford: Blackwell, 2001), 241.

8. John Clarke, *Ill News from New England' persecution...* (London: Printed by Henry Hills, 1652), 31.

9. .Castillo and Schweitzer, *The Literatures of Colonial America*, 267.

10. For an account of the uses of Las Casas' work, see E. Shaskan Bumas, "The Cannibal Butcher Shop: Protestant Uses of las Casas's *Brevisima Relacion* in Europe and the American Colonies," *Early American Literature* 35, no. 2 (2000): 107-36; and William S. Maltby, *The Black Legend in England: The development of anti-Spanish sentiment, 1558–1660* (Durham, NC: Duke University Press, 1971).

11. "William Steele, President of the Corporation for propagating the Gospel," in Henry Whitfield, *Strength out of Weaknesse, Or, A Glorious Manifestation of the Further Progresse of the Gospel among Indians in New England.* (London: Printed by M. Simmons for John Blague and Samuel Howes, 1652), Appendix, rpt. in Clark, *Eliot Tracts*, 246–47.

12. George Parker Winship, *The Eliot Indian Tracts* (Cambridge, MA: Harvard University Press, 1925); Kellaway, *New England Company*.

13. *"Minutes: M.H.S.* Ms., 6, 26 Feb. 19 March, 1658/9," quoted by Winship, *The Eliot Indian Tracts*, 11. Kellaway further stresses the involvement of English ministers in London and their part in the process of the publication and authorship of the dedicatory epistle of each Tract. *See* Kellaway, *New England Company*, 23–24.

14. Thomas Shepard, *The Day-Breaking if not The Sun-Rising of the Gospel, With the Indians in New England* (1647), in Clark, *Eliot Tracts*, 82.

15. Anthony Pagden, *European Encounters with the New World: From Renaissance to Romanticism* (New Haven, CT: Yale University Press, 1993), 51.

16. Pagden, *European Encounters*, 51. *See also* Michel de Certeau, *Heterologies: Discourse on the Other* (Minneapolis: University of Minnesota Press, 1986).

17. Pagden, *European Encounters*, 55–56.

18. *New England's First Fruits* (London: Printed by R. O. and G. D. for Henry Overton, 1643), in Clark, *Eliot Tracts*, 76-8.

19. Eliot, *Tears of Repentance*, 262.

20. Ibid., 267.

21. These dedicatory addresses to the Reader point to much larger debate which simmers throughout the tracts during the Interregnum. With regard to the millennial debates, which were circulating in England at this time, Mather's parting shot to English readers would not have gone unheeded. As noted in the previous chapter in relation to John Eliot's *The Christian Commonwealth*, fifth-monarchists had claimed that England would be the site of Christ's second coming, most notably in William Aspinwall's *A Brief Description of the Fifth Monarchy, Or, Kingdom* (London: Printed by M. Simmons and are to be sold by Livewell Chapman, 1653), but Mather's dedication hints that without sustained and comprehensive spiritual and civil change England may not be able to live up to the millennial potential which Aspinwall and other Fifth Monarchists predicted. *See* fuller discussion of these themes in chapter 1.

22. "With the execution of Charles II (sic I) in 1649 and the establishment of the Protectorate under Oliver Cromwell in 1653, the metropolis ceased to be, for many New Englanders, the unregenerate, 'custome-sick' cultural space they had fled in the 1620s and 1630s and became instead the focus of their most inspired millennial expectations. Future New England leaders like Increase Mather, John Leverett, Edward Winslow, and others, re-emigrated to the mother country. . . . During the years 1642–1656 a full one third of Harvard students graduates returned to England." Round, *By Nature and By Custom Cursed*, 255.

23. "Tis incredible what an advantage to preferment it is to have been a New English man." "Mather to John Rogers, 1651," in *Collections of the Massachusetts Historical Society* (hereafter cited as *MHSC*), 4th ser., vol. 8, 1868. Quoted by Round, *By Nature and By Custom Cursed*, 255.

24. *New England's First Fruits*, 67, 74.

25. Eliot's letter is dated, October, 29 1649 and is included in: Henry Whitfield, *The Light Appearing More and More Towards the Perfect Day* (London: J. Bartlet, 1651), in Clark, *Eliot Tracts*, 194–97: 195.

26. Thomas Shepard, *The Clear Sun-shine of the Gospel* (London: J. Bellamy, 1648), in Clark, *Eliot Tracts*, 108.

27. Whitfield, *The Light Appearing*, 208.

28. Edward Winslow, *The Glorious Progress of the Gospel* (London: Printed for Hannah Allen, 1649) in Clark, *Eliot Tracts*, 166–67.

29. Thomas Shepard, *The Clear Sun-shine of the Gospel*, 105.

30. Thomas Scanlan goes so far as to argue: "The Indian tracts, therefore, were nothing short of allegories of an idealized Protestant national identity that was characterized, not by division and strife, but by holiness and harmony. The Indian tracts gave the English a chance to imagine their nation, not as it was, but as they would like it to be." Thomas Scanlan, *Colonial Writing and the New World 1583–1671: Allegories of Desire*. (Cambridge: Cambridge University Press, 1999), 158.

31. William Kellaway discusses the problems with land procurement in the Home Counties and in London in chap. 1 of *New England Company*, 38–40. He also provides a detailed account and defense of Peter and Weld in "The Collection for the Indians of New England, 1649–1660." He also provides a detailed account and defense of Peter and Weld in "The Collection for the Indians of New England, 1649-1660," *Bulletin, John Rylands Library* 39, no. 2 (March 1957): 451–54. *See also* Raymond P Stearns, "The Weld-Peter Mission to England," *Publications of the Colonial Society of Massachusetts* 32 (1934), in *Transactions of the Colonial Society of Massachusetts, 1933–1937* (Boston: Colonial Society of Massachusetts, 1937), 188–246.

32. Whitfield, *The Light Appearing* 2003, 175.

33. Whitfield, *Strength out of Weaknesse*, 247.

34. John Eliot, *A Late and Further Manifestation of the Progress of the Gospel Amongst the Indians in New-England* (London: Printed by M. S., 1655), in Clark, *Eliot Tracts*, 320.

35. Eliot, *Mamvsse Wunneetupanatamwe Up-Biblum God* (1663), n.p.

36. In fact, Eliot's motivations might be paralleled with those of John Foxe and Thomas Beard. Hill contends: "John Foxe attributed 'this gift of printing' to direct divine intervention. . . . Thomas Beard, Oliver Cromwell's mentor and friend, followed Foxe in seeing divine Providence behind the coincidence in time of the invention and development of the printing press and the translation of the Bible into English." Christopher Hill, *The English Bible and The Seventeenth-Century Revolution* (London: Penguin Press, 1993), 9–10. Similar imperatives may well have occurred to Eliot since his painstaking efforts to translate the Bible into Massachusett were finally realized in 1661 with the publication of the New Testament, some twenty or so years after the arrival of the printing press in the New England colony.

37. Eliot, *Mamvsse Wunneetupanatamwe Up-Biblum God* (1663), n.p.

38. Ibid., n.p.

39. Mary Armyne [Huntington copy] was a donator to the Corporation for Propagating the Gospel and friend of Baxter; Richard Baxter, Eliot's friend and correspondent, Robert Boyle, president of the New England Company. Ralph Frecke, was sent a copy of the Massachusetts Bible for his donation of Bryan Walton's Polyglot to Harvard Library (James Constantine Pillings, *Bibliography of the Algonquian Languages* [Washington, DC: Government Printing Office, 1891], 285). Even into the eighteenth and nineteenth centuries, in New England, copies of the Bible were passed down as heirlooms; for example, one owner writes: "The property of Anna Pecke presented to hir by her grandfather" and a later signature, presumably of a descendant, reads: "Angelina Peck—Pawtucket, 1831" (150). Wilberforce Eames has recorded a list of owners in his contribution to Pillings' (126–85).

40. Hill, *English Bible*, 56.

41. According to Eames, five hundred New Testaments and 1,040 complete Bibles were printed in New England between 1661 and 1663. Robert Boyle recorded his experience of the Charles II's response to the Bible in a letter dated April 21, 1664. Boyle confirms Charles' vague interest, but after glancing through it is easily distracted by another visitor, an unexpected "Enuoye" from the "Emporour." (Pillings, *Bibliography of the Algonquian Languages*, 136, 140–41).

42. Eliot and Mayhew Jr., *Tears of Repentance*, 263.

43. Linda Gregerson, "The Commonwealth of the Word: New England, Old England, and the Praying Indians," in *British Identities and English Renaissance Literature*, ed. David J. Baker and Willy Maley (Cambridge: Cambridge University Press, 2002), 179.

44. Henry Newcome, minister of Gawsworth, Cheshire, 1652/3. *The Autobiography of Henry Newcome*. 1st ser., vol. 26 (N.p.: Chetham Society, 1852), 43. Quoted by Kellaway, *New England Company*, 29.

45. "Richard Bigge's letter to William Cooke, treasurer for the County of Wiltshire, 21 May 1653," Bodleian, Ms.Rawlinson C934, f72. Quoted by Kellaway, *New England Company*, 29.

46. Bigge quoted by Kellaway, *New England Company*, 29.

47. Kellaway, *New England Company*, 29.

48. Details of contributions from various parishes are held in the *New England Company Archives*, Bodleian Library, Oxford, Rawlinson Collection, C943, 54–73.

49. Edward Winslow, *Glorious Progress of the Gospel*, 167.

50. I am using the term eloquence as Sandra M. Gustafson uses it in, *Eloquence is Power: Oratory and Performance in Early America* (London and Chapel Hill: Published for the Omohundro Institute of Early American History and Culture, Williamsburg, Virginia, by the University of North Carolina Press, 2000).

51. Gustafson, *Eloquence is Power*, xvi.

52. Whitfield, *Strength out of Weaknesse*, 236.

53. Thomas Shepard, *Clear Sun-shine of the Gospel*, 138.

54. Ibid., 137.

55. Round, *By Nature and By Custom Cursed*, 260.

56. John Eliot, *A Further Accompt of the Progresse of the Gospel Amongst the Indians of New England* (London: M. Simmons, 1659), in *The Eliot Tracts: With Letters from John Eliot to Thomas Thorowgood and Richard Baxter, ed. Michael P. Clark* (London and Westport, CT: Paeger, 2003), 332.

57. *New England's First Fruits*, 62.

58. Edward G. Gray, *New World Babel: Languages and Nations in Early America* (Princeton, NJ: Princeton University Press, 1999), 94, 98.

59. Holstun argues: "For Eliot the Indians represent not some race of natural men radically other to Western men but a missing link in scriptural history and anthropology. The discovery and the conversion of the Indians signify an ultimate (or penultimate) unity of peoples and of history, not a static logical binary between nature and civility. Puritan anthropology, sketchy as it might be, is thoroughly historical. . . . The Indians are not anti-Christian and anticivil like popish Europe and prelatical England; they are pre-Christian and precivil." (James Holstun, *A Rational Millenium: Puritan Utopias of Seventeenth Century England and America* [New York: Oxford University Press, 1987], 113, 115).

60. Following the Pequot wars, Round argues that codes of honor and courage were emphasized to boost the reputation of the colony, and the morale of a nation: "Representations of the Pequot War thus created an arena for the performance of honor and courage at a time when civility was becoming increasingly difficult to recognize and older, aristocratic models of honor and nobility no longer seemed relevant. By performing their courageous ideals in a transatlantic context, Underhill's and Vincent's texts provided metropolitans with a new register for achieving social stability." (Round, *By Nature and By Custon Cursed*, 243–44) After the war, with fewer opportunities to incorporate notions of nobility and honor, missionary success through the creation of the praying Indian allowed similar pride and morale to develop in both New and Old England. (Round, 233–34) *See also* John Underhill, *Newes From America* (London: Printed by I D. for Peter Cole, 1638); Philip Vincent, *True Relation of the Late Battell Fought*

in New-England, between the English and the Pequet Salvages. London: Printed by Thomas Harper, for Nathanael Butter and Iohn Bellamie, 1638).

61.   *New England's First Fruits*, 61.

62.   Ibid., 62.

63.   Phillip Round interrogates Wequash's speech further and suggests: "At first Wequash speaks a vivid vernacular, saying that he 'had low apprehensions of [the English] God, having conceived him to be (as he said) but a *Musketto* God, or a God like unto a flye. As the story progresses and Wequash becomes more susceptible to the ministration of the reformers, however, his speech becomes more and more stylized. When Wequash finally reveals his longing for Christian knowledge, he does so in language that would come to characterize white representations of native speech for several hundred years: '*Wequash, no God, Wequash know no Christ.*' Indian speech like that of Wequash serves as a dialogic counterpoint to the 'excellent conversation' of the Bay Colony inhabitant. His halting and humble utterance provides evidence of the efficacy of the Massachusetts reformers' efforts to convert the Indians through paternal instruction and honor culture emulation" (Round, *By Nature and By Custon Cursed*, 247).

64.   Judith Butler, *Excitable Speech: A Politics of the Performative* (New York: Routledge, 1997), 5.

65.   For further analysis on the performance of praying Indians and Native American identities more generally, see Joshua Bellin, "John Eliot's Playing Indian," *Early American Literature* 42, no. 1 (2007): 1–30; Susan Castillo, *Colonial Encounters in New World Writing 1500-1776: Performing America:* (London: Routledge, 2006); Kenneth M. Morrison, "'That Art of Coyning Christians': John Eliot and the Praying Indians of Massachusetts." *Ethnohistory* 21, no. 1 (Winter 1974): 77–92.

66.   This is an obvious attack on the colonial dissenter and for further discussion of Gorton's opposition to Puritan orthodoxy in New England, see Philip F. Gura, *A Glimpse of Sion's Glory: Puritan Radicalism in New England, 1620–1660* (Middleton, CT: Wesleyan University Press, 1984).

67.   Henry Whitfield, *Strength Out of Weaknesse*, 228.

68.   Ibid., 232.

69.   Ibid., 235.

70.   This is comparable with the "mimicked" colonial discourse of the Salem witch trials which Gustafson describes: "Mimicking the verbal skills of the ministry, the demoniacs (the possessed women) provided a mirror for the colony's spiritual leaders, who heard in their speech the voices of God and Satan battling over the colony's future" (Gustafson, *Eloquence is Power*, 41). Also, Phillip H. Round notes the trials and punishments of excommunicates in, *By Nature and by Custom Cursed*. For an excellent account of the rituals of trials, punishments and executions in New England generally, *see* David D. Hall, *Worlds of Wonder, Days of Judgement: Popular Religious Belief in Early New England* (Cambridge, MA: Harvard University Press, 1990).

71.   "John Eliot to Richard Baxter, 27th Jun 1671," in Powicke, *Some Unpublished Correspondence*, 462–63.

72.   "Hans Oldenburg to John Winthrop Jr, 18 March 1671/72," in Winthrop, *Correspondence of Hartlib, Haak, Oldenberg*, 46.

73.   Scanlan, *Colonial Writing and the New World*, 173–74.

74.   John Eliot, *Indian Dialogues: A Study in Cultural Interaction* (Cambridge, MA: Printed by M. Johnson, 1671), rpt. Contributions to American History Series, ed. Henry W. Bowden and James P Ronda, vol. 88 (Westport, CT: Greenwood Press, 1980), preface, n.p.

75.   Frank Kelleter, "Puritan Missionaries and the Colonization of the New World: A Reading of John Eliot's *Indian Dialogues* (1671)," in *Early America Re-Explored: New Readings in Colonial, Early National and Antebellum Culture*, ed. Klaus H. Schmidt and Fritz Fleischmann (New York: Peter Lang, 2000), 82–83.

76.   During King Philip's War many letters were written from New England to London including those written by Edward Wharton, under the title: *New England's Present Sufferings, Under their Cruel Neighbouring Indians* (London 1675). Other letters, including those from James Cudworth, John Easton, Nathaniel Thomas, John Levertt, Edward Palmer, John Free-

man, and Samuel Gorton (Jr.) at the request of Sachem Philip, are included in the *MHSC* , 1st ser., vol. 4 (Boston, 1799), 80–94. Further publications in relation to the conflict and represent Metacom as violent warrior, include: Mary Rowlandson, *The Sovereignty and Goodness of God*, (Cambridge MA: Samuel Green, 1682) in, *Early English Books Online* at http:// eebo.chadwyck.com/home (accessed April 3, 2013); Benjamin Church, *Entertaining Passages Relating to King Philip's War*, 1716, in *The Literatures of Colonial America: An Anthology*, ed. Susan Castillo and Ivy Schweitzer (Oxford and Malden, MA: Blackwell Publisher, 2001); and William Hubbard, *A Narrative of the Indian Wars in New England* (Brattleborough, VT: William Fessenden, 1814) Early American Imprints, 2nd ser., microform, 31766.

77. Eliot, *Indian Dialogues*, 136–37.

78. Ibid., 127.

79. Ibid., 121.

80. Ibid., 122.

81. Ibid., 126.

82. Ibid., 66.

83. Ibid.

84.   Thomas Scanlan claims: "Rather than constructing the *Dialogues* for English readers, who desired to reimagine themselves and their nation through the representations of native people, Eliot attempts to demonstrate to his fellow colonists that the work of converting the native people can produce "merchandize" for domestic consumption." (Scanlan, *Colonial Writing and the New World*, 165) Certainly, I agree that this is a fair account of the colonial response but there is scope to claim that both English and colonial audiences need to be considered in any attempt to understand the use and purpose of the *Dialogues*.

85. Eliot, *Indian Dialogues*, 66.

86. Eliot, *A Further Accompt of the Progresse of the Gospel*, 332.

Chapter Three

Speech, Space, and Religious (Re-)Affirmation

Before Eliot and his fellow ministers could shape and direct the written text of Native conversion narratives to audiences of English readers, Native penitents gathered together to express their religious experiences to each other and to audiences of the colonial elite in New England. In the homes and meeting houses of seventeenth-century New England, native and colonial interlocutors uttered words of prayer and religious conversion. It is fair to say that colonial ministers, missionaries, and magistrates continued to control many of the rules concerning religious speech, through the organization of prayer, as well as the forms and functions of sermons, examinations, and confessions. The extent to which colonial missionaries also controlled and shaped the *spaces* in which these religious utterances took place, and the impact which these spaces had on the reception of religious utterances, is the focus of this chapter.

With the aim of exploring perceptions of space in colonial New England, this chapter considers the ways in which private and public spaces were defined and interpreted by Puritan settlers. Importantly, it also considers the extent to which Christian Indians slotted into that environment, especially in relation to the spaces in which they performed their religious conversion. The spoken confessions of praying Indians have attracted significant critical attention in recent years with many commentators stressing the performative nature of these religious utterances. Phillip H. Round argues that the effect of the written traces of these religious utterances as they were sent to England caused the praying Indian identity to emerge performatively within an epistolary tradition which harnessed the truth-telling rhetoric of the private letter. [1] In slightly more recent studies, Sandra Gustafson, Kristina Bross, and Joshua Bellin have each relied on theories of speech and/or performance to generate

new and influential readings of the prayers and confessions of praying Indians.[2] While these readings have allowed for a more nuanced account of
Algonquian conversion, revealing the pressures brought to bear on indigenous people in a colonial environment, they have not considered the more
local aspects of how space was conceptualized and physically delineated as
part of this religious process.

In each tradition, western and native, certain spaces are shaped and remembered through the activities and memories of particular communities.[3]

Following Michel de Certeau's analysis of place, which he describes as a
"configuration of positions" and an "indication of stability,"[4] I want to consider the impact which specific delineations of space has on the religious
speech and speeches of praying Indian penitents. By considering the kinds of
spaces in which Puritan and praying Indian interlocutors exchanged views,
interrogated each other's beliefs, and prepared the way for spiritual conversion, it is possible to further understand the subtle nuances of spiritual adaptation which took place in and around Massachusetts Bay in the early years
of colonization.

OPENED AND CLOSED DOORS: DEFINING SPACE AND
THE ETIQUETTE OF SPEECH

John Eliot's concern with defining and codifying space was not limited to his
interactions with indigenous people of the Massachusetts Bay area; indeed,
he was keenly aware of the usefulness of a spatial metaphor to distinguish
New England Puritans from Old English Protestantism. In the early 1650s, as
part of his millennial-inspired exchanges with readers in England, John Eliot
invested a significant amount of rhetorical capital in describing both the
Puritan migration and his subsequent missionary endeavor through the metaphor of space:

> [W]hen God opened a door of quiet departure, and liberty to enjoy the holy
> worship of God, not according to the fantasies of man, but according to the
> word of God, without such humane additions and novelties, we thought it
> better for us to give way by departing quietly and leaving the field to them that
> were masters of it, than to stand up longer in opposition; and I cannot see why
> any should cast upon this our quiet departure the imputation of rending. We
> have reason to think, that many who sate at the helm, did like well of that our
> departure, and said let them go in peace, expecting to have stood their ground
> the more firme by our removal.[5]

This "door" of departure is the space through which they might take their
orderly and quite retreat from the open "field" of religious conflict. It is
perhaps no coincidence that the "door," a spatial marker which allows access

to private and social spaces, is the marker for the Puritan colonizers' departure into their own civil space in New England. Eliot was not the first to identify these spatial allusions in connection with the Puritan migrations: John Cotton spoke of a "peaceable roome" ready and waiting in New England and John Winthrop spoke of a "shelter" as well as his more durable image of a "citie upon a hill."[6] Deliberate demarcations of controlled and enclosed spaces provided Puritan New Englanders with an effective image through which to separate themselves from their English brethren, but with the construction of new homes, meetinghouses and towns, these demarcations also helped regulate the spaces of Christian living in what was perceived to be a vast open wilderness.

Indeed, as Sacvan Bercovitch has most persuasively argued, the wilderness provided a further and more enduring conception of space which harbored both the purpose and rewards for New England saints.[7] In "Learned Conjectures," Eliot challenged his detractors in England by stressing that the colony was indeed a "wildernesse" with "difficulties, uncertainties, temptations, & raw beginnings," and that "by coming hither, (the New Englander has) changed a comfortable being for the outward man into a condition full of labour, toile, sorrow, wants, and temptations of a wildernesse, which dwellers in *England* cannot so well see, weigh, or pitty, but the Lord can."[8] With the repeated image of the wilderness, the reader is made aware that it is the very threat of the vast, seemingly uncontrolled and open space of the landscape that holds its promises: the harsher the better for the penitent or godly man or woman who might find the omniscient presence of the Christian God in this providential space of religious fulfillment.

From the "peaceable rooms" of contemplation in towns and praying towns of New England, to the vast, seemingly limitless space of the wilderness of the New World, the language of space in seventeenth-century New England provided a framework for spiritual survival and renewal. It should also be noted that Native penitents were also sensitive to the limits of space and place. Indeed, very early on in the mission, Algonquian penitents asserted this interest when they propound a series of questions about the geographical location of Christ.[9] The questions asked of Eliot are all about the *where* of the Christian tradition and Christian memory rather than *what* of Christ's teachings. This tells us that Native participants in Eliot's religious meetings had a keen, collective interest in discovering the place or site of Christian teachings and that they were equally well-practiced in using the language of space and place to make sense of spiritual experiences. In tribal traditions a significant religious event could give meaning to a particular place, and a particular place might help give meaning to a significant religious speech or performance.[10] However, Native penitents would find that as part of their religious instruction they would have to adapt the ways in which they understood the practice of delineating space.

A fine illustration of Native adaptation to colonial forms of spatial etiquette is the image of a closed door to which penitent Indians were introduced in their journey toward religious conversion and church membership,
an ironic contrast to the *open* door through which Eliot imagines the Puritan
migrants passed as they sailed for the New World. As part of the civil and
social refashioning of penitent Indians into communities of Christian believers, new covenants and rules of behavior were set down as precursors to full
acceptance into the Christian community. On one occasion in 1646 this led
"Sachims and other principall men"[11] from the Concord area to agree to
twenty-nine points of order which were intended to demonstrate their adoption of certain elements of etiquette and social organization in accordance
with English tastes. Among some fairly serious social and civil rules of
behavior is the demand to knock on a door before entering.[12] The closed door
perhaps signals that the rules which delineated space were being firmly im-
posed on Native culture before the first praying town was even built. Native
penitents had to reconcile themselves to the fact that access to certain spaces
which housed religious, educational, civil, and judicial activity was often at
someone else's discretion. If Native communities were to have access to
these places of religious, civil, educational, and judicial authority, their engagement with the politics of space of the colonizer had to be carefully
negotiated.

This negotiation of space existed hand-in-hand with an understanding of
the etiquette of speech. The debates, prayers, sermons, and confessions, all of
which were uttered and heard in the colonial towns, praying towns, meeting
houses, colleges, and wigwams in and around Massachusetts Bay, were each
defined by an etiquette of speech. The rules guiding these kinds of public
verbal performances can be usefully understood through Mary Louise Pratt's
account of "turn-taking." Central to Pratt's thesis is her focus on what replaces "turn-taking relations" of natural conversations when more formal
modes of speech, like sermons or examinations, are enacted.[13] Pratt recognizes that at the heart of any communicative act, written or spoken, is the
negotiation of meaning between the speaker and the audience. Part of Pratt's
analysis rests on the assumption of equality; that is, the taking of turns will
be determined by a group of peers who will naturally give and take their
place on the floor. For example, during a sermon the congregation would
expect to be silent but during catechism they would be expected to partici-
pate. In the context of Algonquian religious utterance in seventeenth-century
Massachusetts, the content and environment of these specific speech acts
identify the "rights, obligations, and expectations"[14] of both speaker and
audience.

Through close consideration of different locations, including Harvard
College, the Indian College at Harvard, Natick, Waban's wigwam, meetinghouses, and a child's grave, the remainder of this chapter will examine the

ways in which certain spaces are appropriated in such a way as to inform the
interpretation of praying Indian religious utterances. To begin with, I'll consider the Cambridge Synod, the intellectual and religious hub of colonial life
in the seventeenth century.

INTELLECTUAL AND EDUCATIONAL ESTABLISHMENTS

In 1648, Thomas Shepard describes that participation of Algonquian penitents in the Cambridge Synod:

> The first day of the Synods meeting at *Cambridge*, where the forenoon was
> spent in hearing a Sermon preached by one of the *Elders* as a preparative to the
> worke of the Synod, the afternoon was spent in hearing an *Indian* Lecture
> where there was a great confluence of *Indians* all parts to heare Mr *Eliot*,
> which we conceived not unseasonable at such a time, partly that the reports of
> Gods worke begun among them, might be seen and beleeved of the chief who
> were then sent and met from all the Churches of Christ in the Countrey, who
> could hardly beleeve the reports they had received concerning these new stirs
> among the *Indians*, and partly hereby to raise up a greater spirit of prayer for
> the carrying on of the work begun upon the *Indians*, among all the Churches
> and servants of the Lord Jesus: The Sermon was spent in shewing them their
> miserable conditions without Christ, out of *Ephes*. 2.1. that they were dead in
> trespasses and sinnes, and in pointing unto them the Lord Jesus, who onely
> could quicken them.
>   When the Sermon was done, there was a convenient space of time spent in
> hearing those questions which the *Indians* publickely propounded. [15]

Although the exact location of this particular synod meeting is not specified,
it seems likely that it took place in Thomas Shepard's church: Shepard is in
attendance, it was the First Church and meetinghouse in Cambridge, and it
was used by Harvard students and faculty in the early days of the college. [16]
The fact that Algonquians were invited to the Cambridge Synod is surprising; let us not forget that this was a closed space of serious debate where
decisions affecting church membership and church policy were thrashed out.
Indeed, this synod meeting led to the publication of "The Cambridge Platform (1648)"; prompted by the seemingly freewheeling spiritual revelations
of Anne Hutchinson and Roger Williams, ministers and intellectuals in the
colony saw the dangers of absolute independence for each congregation and
the 1646-1648 synod intended to address this crisis. In these circumstances
the 1646-1648 synod was called to establish a "platform of discipline" which
would unite congregational churches in common codes of practice. [17] The
result, it was imagined, would allow churches to maintain their independence
to some degree but it would also provide some much needed uniformity,
necessary to fend off attacks from local disputants as well as the long arm of

the English monarch or parliament. Among other things, this document codified certain common practices, for example, it defined the New England way
of electing Church Officers.[18]

The Cambridge Synod was a powerful and controversial feature of religious and civil governance in New England. In theory at least, at these meetings ministers would persuade and convince wrongdoers to repent and
change their ways. As such the synod would not have any "compulsive
power"[19] for fear it might follow too closely the Presbyterian model by
denying the independence of individual churches; in reality, however, the
magistrates were on hand to enforce any point of civil order, and they af-
fected the lives of Puritans and non-Puritans alike. Entry into the spaces in
which these synods were held, therefore, together with an invitation to speak
to the gathered listeners, was no small achievement. When Eliot attended the
1648 synod with Algonquian penitents who not only listened to his sermon
but were invited to take the floor and question the missionary on religious
matters, he was introducing penitents to New England's theological and intellectual elite. The fact that their debates focused on the colonists' internal
crisis and outward reputation perhaps gives a clue as to why this Indian
lecture took place at all.

Crucially for the missionary-colonizer, the event responds to the persistent claims from outsiders that New England was not living up to the demands of its original charter to convert Native Americans to Christianity.
However, there is more going on at this meeting than simple political ap-
peasement: penitents are called to listen to Eliot's sermon on Christian beliefs but they are also called to interrogate those teachings. On the one hand,
this performance at the Synod might be seen as a stunt to give the New
England saints hope that despite their internal and political difficulties, God's
word continues to travel through them to the so-called unconverted heathen.
On the other hand, by becoming attuned to the rules and obligations of this
particular speech situation, where speakers and audience give and take control of the floor, an interesting dynamic in the power relationships between
colonial and native interlocutors can be identified.

As Eliot takes the floor to recite his lecture, his audience of invited guests
grants him control of that floor in mutually accepted "rights and obligations."[20] The roles are then reversed as the previously silent audience is
granted access to the floor and become verbal participants in the day's proceedings. The space of this verbal performance, the Cambridge Synod,
makes this an unusual, perhaps unique, event. Further, the authority and
power which this civic and religious space holds have an impact on the status
and agency given over to Algonquian participants as they are granted the
right to challenge and question their colonial interlocutor. Rarely were Puritan leaders put on the spot to defend or explain their faith. Anne Hutchinson
was vilified for such a move some ten years earlier and, yet, at the heart of

New England's religious and civil authority, Algonquian speakers are given the opportunity to control the floor and question the faith of the saints.

The kinds of questions which were posed concern the original site and current location of Christ:

> [O]ne question was, *What Countrey man Christ was, and where he was borne?*
> Another was, *How Farre off that place was from us here?*
> Another was, *Where Christ now was?*
> And another, *How they might Lay hold on him, and where, being now absent from them?* with some other to this purpose; which received full answers from severall hands.[21]

As noted above, their desire to pinpoint the original site of Christianity reflects the practice of attributing spiritual significance to particular parts of a knowable landscape. The way that the questions are phrased, suggests that they are attempting to understand Christianity through the same rubrics of spirituality that they have always held; that is, through the existing relationship they held between their spiritual history and specific geographical locations.

Both in terms of the space of this religious utterance, as well as the spatial concerns which constitute their utterance, Native voices are able to actively share the floor at the heart of New England's church-governance. By doing so, Native penitents fashion an understanding of Christian beliefs by interpreting elements of this new faith into a pre-existing, tribal model which connects place and spirituality. From their participation in this event, they demonstrate that theirs was not a path of passive acceptance but of active participation. Native speakers may have been guests of the synod, ostensibly invited to demonstrate to those doubters in the colony and beyond that, despite views to the contrary, the mission was developing successfully. In this verbal performance, and in the negotiation of, and preoccupation with, matters of space, the Puritan audience saw the grassroots of religious conversion, but Native voices were more likely speaking a language of religious adaptation.

Spaces of education provided another important context for religious performances and negotiations of faith. Native participation in New England's intellectual circles became a feature of life for some individuals in the 1650s and 1660s, when Harvard proposed an Indian College which would be an annex to the original college. The proposition was not without controversy, and the initial idea may well have been a bit of a ploy to exact funds from the missionary budget to help with the costs of developing the expanding Harvard. Certainly, after the brick building of the Indian college was completed and there was accommodation for twenty or more students, non-Native students who could not be housed in the original building were housed in the Indian College while the college waited for Native scholars to qualify for entry.[22] Native scholars were finally enrolled in 1658, when two students in particular, Caleb Cheeshahteaumauk and Joel Iacoomis, distinguished them-selves before the president of Harvard, Charles Chauncy, during an examina-tion of their linguistic, rhetorical and reasoning skills. The examination pro-cess mirrored that experienced by their fellow New English students. Unfor-tunately, there is no transcription of the event, but there is a record of the examination in a note from Chauncy[23] and it is also referred to by John Winthrop Jr. in a letter to Robert Boyle of the Royal Society in London.[24]

Although the space of this public commencement exercise is unspecified, it is likely that it took place in the hall of the original Harvard College. In 1643, the edifice of the College is described as "fair and comely within and without, having in it a spacious Hall; (where they daily meet at Common Lectures) Exercises, and a large Library with some Bookes to it."[25] Samuel Eliot Morison describes what the interior of this hall may have looked like:

> It was probably plastered on three sides, certainly glazed with 112 square feet of glass, and provided with long refectory tables and backless forms and, in all probability, a dais at the east or further end for a "high table" where the fellows and fellow-commoners dined. At the about the center of the north side was the fireplace. The dimensions of the hall, about 20 feet by 50 feet were sufficient to seat the entire college at its highest point of enrolment (about fifty) in the seventeenth century, and were about the same as those of the smaller college halls in England.[26]

In what must have been an impressive, enclosed, and, perhaps, intimidating space, Caleb and Joel were examined before magistrates, elders, and Har-vard's president, demonstrating the conflation of the mission with the civil and educational matters. The nature of the examination, which acknowledges significant intellectual ability and linguistic dexterity on the part of both Algonquian speakers, confirms their access to a powerful and influential audience. The fact that they are being judged on their performance means that the center of power in this exchange rests with the colonial audience, in this case President Chauncy, and in this they are no different from their fellow New England students.

Despite shared educational systems and common public examinations, the attendance of Indian scholars at the Indian college is not an uncomplicat-ed acceptance of Christianity and colonial authority; if it was the college would most likely have been far more successful. Although their greatest hopes, Caleb and Joel, did not survive—one drowned and the other died of consumption[27] —John Wampus (Wompas), their contemporary, was able to learn enough about colonial judicial systems and real estate, presumably through the very collegiate lifestyle meant to secure religious piety and intel-lectual depth, to secure a healthy living as a mariner and realtor.[28] His ven-tures did not always turn out well, but when he was jailed for his debts he

was lucky to have learned enough about the English legal system and bureaucracy to successfully petition the King in England to ask for pardon.

In fact, the Indian college did not produce any native missionaries: few
students lived long enough to realize the founders' dream, and those who did
were not inclined to the religious life.[29] Certainly, the college came to encap-
sulate the precarious nature of colonial life for Christian Indians of Massachusetts Bay, but it also provided an intellectual space for Christian Indians
to explore and examine the religion and politics of their colonial neighbors,
and as the case of John Wampus highlights, it allowed them to consider their
own path in the new circumstances of the world they now shared.

In both of these colonial spaces, the Cambridge Synod and Harvard College, Algonquian individuals either studied or questioned the religion of the
colonizer. Each intellectual exchange and endeavor signals a level of interaction between Algonquian and colonial interlocutors, which resists an assumption of automatic and complete dominance of one group over another.
Rather, the speeches, examinations, and verbal exchanges in colonial spaces
show a tendency for Algonquian participants to negotiate their own beliefs in
a new religious, political, and physical environment. This is not to suggest
that absolute equality existed between the two parties; the devastating effects
of new diseases and the encroachment of colonial authorities on Native
American land were significant realities with which Algonquians had to
contend. My point is not to dispute this reality but to consider that changes in
religious and civil practices were the result of intellectual engagement, not
blind acceptance or simple survival politics. Decisions were made on the
basis of a broad and deep understanding of religious and civil structures,
gleaned from lecture days or formal schooling, and religious affiliation was
either accepted or rejected only after this process was complete. The very
fact that Algonquian leaders and students could test the limits of the new
religion at the center of New England's religious, civil, and educational
establishments demands substantial recognition of their own involvement in
negotiating changes to their faith.

FROM WABAN'S WIGWAM TO THE PRAYING TOWN

At around the same time that Eliot was inviting penitents to the Cambridge
Synod, he was also visiting native penitents in their own homes. These smaller, more intimate meetings, often held in Waban's wigwam, provide an entirely different spatial dynamic to the official meetings and examinations
held by colonial elites. In the second of Eliot's tracts, *The Day-Breaking*,
Puritan and Native responses to social and civil spaces become intertwined
as the move from wigwam to praying town began. Implicit in this account of
space is a deep-seated understanding by New England authorities that certain

kinds of space, domestic and social, can and do pave the way for religious conversion. As the mission develops, therefore, the spaces in which Native penitents conduct their religious practice changes from the wigwam to the meetinghouse to the praying town. An account of these spaces, and the significance that New England Puritans attached to them, has an impact on the ways in which religious performances might be interpreted.

In *The Day-Breaking*, the four visits which were made to Waban's wigwam are individually described. In general, sermons were heard, prayers were offered up, and native voices were recorded interrogating Christian faith through extensive question and answer sessions.[30] In addition, readers in England were also provided with what they would have perceived as welcoming details of Native penitence: the image of a native man weeping uncontrollably at the revelation of his sinful state,[31] and children performing their catechism by rote, receiving small gifts of food and clothing for their troubles.[32] Like other missionary pamphlets, the tract succeeds in its attempt to convince its English readership that the mission is taking hold in a small but effective way.

This particular tract distinguishes itself from the other Eliot tracts through its attention to small things and small places. Indeed, the epigraphs for *The Day-Breaking* include two biblical quotes emphasizing small successes: "Who hath despised the day of small things?" (Zach. 4:10) and "The Kingdome of heaven is like to a graine or mustard seed." (Matth. 13:13).[33] By contrast, the first of the missionary tracts, *New England's First Fruits,* split its narrative between several different sites of religious conversion and education, from the conversion of individuals like Wequash, to a summary of the curriculum at Harvard College. *The Day-Breaking* strikes a more intimate tone by encompassing all the missionary success of this tract within the tribal space of Waban's wigwam. For the readers back home in England, what could be more effective? Tribal voices are heard speaking and performing their religious conversion in their own home and are seen to be actively pursuing an intellectual understanding of Christianity as they relentlessly question the missionary and his religious practice. Indeed, after three hours of this questioning at their first meeting on October 28, 1646, the ministers and missionaries were "resolved to leave them with an appetite,"[34] allowing reflection and follow up at later meetings that year. During November and December those follow-up meetings took place, and on one occasion at least the "conference" between native and colonial interlocutors lasted through the afternoon and into the night.[35]

In this early tract Algonquian is also confirmed as a language of Christianity when at the second meeting, November 11, there are fifteen minutes of prayer in Algonquian,[36] and Eliot's missionary ideal of native converting native (as is later dramatized in his *Indian Dialogues*) appears tangible when Waban is overheard repeating and explaining the preacher's words to his gathered company, following this with prayers throughout the night.[37] Waban's wigwam, a home and a social space for increasing numbers of potential penitents (if this tract is to be believed), held within it the whole journey of religious transformation and conversion: Waban listened to the Christian teaching, he interrogated, learned, prayed, converted, proselytized, and actively encouraged his fellow tribesmen to do the same.

The depiction of this specific space, a relatively small enclosed space in a vast and notoriously harsh landscape, is no accident. The New England missionaries wanted to make religious conversion appear local, personal, and familiar to both Native and English audiences. Penitents who frequented Waban's wigwam interrogated Christianity in a familiar space, surrounded by familiar people, and they prayed and conversed largely in their own language. Meanwhile, English audiences understood that the space of a native home, albeit the unfamiliar shape of a wigwam, offered certain assumptions about the acceptance of domestic space and its incumbent features of "civility," which Puritan religious missionaries required before full church membership could be considered. Over the course of just a few months, three elements of the mission's success are accounted for: firstly, at each meeting larger crowds gather in Waban's wigwam to hear Eliot preach; secondly, the native language, Algonquian, is gradually incorporated into the lectures, sermons and prayers; and, thirdly, an Algonquian penitent is depicted explaining the religious teachings of Christianity to fellow Algonquians and embracing the role of teacher and missionary.

The intimacy of domestic space and the power of that space to establish effective religious conversion are also a feature of later letters and confessions: in 1652, Thomas Mayhew wrote about the conversion of a man, thirty years old, and son of a prominent Native tribesman, whose initial understanding of Christianity came from a long late-night conversation which he had with Mayhew in the privacy of his own home.[38] On another occasion, William of Sudbury, Nataous, notes that in his difficult journey toward religious conversion, it was through his visits to the homes of ministers and other English settlers that he began to hear about God and, after many false starts, began to pray. Nataous comments that when he resisted God his home was a place where he was "angry," full of lust and the worship of many gods. Significantly, this behavior is aligned with the wilderness, where he confesses he "lyes" and is angry.[39] In a very deliberate move by the colonial-missionary, spatial distinctions are used to confirm both the veracity of native conversion to Christianity as well as the growth of English-style civility. Ultimately, it is through a so-called civilized domestic space that the seeds of religious conversion are planted and seen to grow.

The potentially *civilizing* nature of space is further developed when the domestic spaces of religious conversion are replaced by the public spaces of the meetinghouse and the praying town. Recently, commentators have focused on the meetinghouse as a central feature of this new theocratic society, and this is not surprising. After all, the meetinghouse was the only space left to Puritans which might be deemed something close to a sacred space. As David D. Hall, Jane Kamensky, Ann Kibbey, and Patricia Caldwell have all illustrated in different contexts, Puritans of England and New England dispensed with physical manifestations of God's symbolic presence on earth by ripping out altars and all Christian iconography, making man's material imaginings of God secondary to the grace which god revealed to them. As a result, meetinghouses had a pivotal role to play in providing a symbolic space for the communities of saints all over New England to meet, worship, and sustain the bonds of community. Despite their desire to dispense with material manifestations of worship, the meetinghouse was a strong sign that God was present in the hearts of individuals but also in the collective heart of the community. So much so, that when Richard Mather marvels at the craftsmanship of the meetinghouse at Natick, the foremost praying town, the enclosed space of the meetinghouse becomes a powerful sign of the redemption of the town's inhabitants.[40]

In Eliot's own account the links between the enclosed space of the meetinghouse and religious redemption are more forcefully forged. Before relaying the fulsome confessions of the praying Indians in *Tears of Repentance*, Eliot draws particular attention to the effects of the spaces and buildings which Natick now affords its inhabitants:

> [N]ow being come under Civil Order, and fixing themselves in Habitations, and bending themselves to labor, as doth appear by their works of Fencings, Buildings &c. and especially in building, without any English Workmans help, or direction, a very sufficient Meeting-House, of fifty foot long, twenty five foot broad, neer twelve foot high betwixt the joynts, wel sawen, and framed (which is a specimen, not only of their singular ingenuity, and dexterity, but also of some industry) I say this being so, now my argument of delaying them from entering into Church-Estate, was taken away.[41]

In this newly ordered and spatially acceptable habitation, at least from Eliot's point of view, the meetinghouse became a symbol of their civility and their religious redemption: this space was created to house their religious education and conversion, and its material existence should usher in their status as church members. Indeed, the misfortune of one penitent, Antony, who suffered a cracked skull in an accident during the construction of the meetinghouse, impresses further significance on the creation of space. Rather than let Antony tell his own story, Eliot prefaces his confession with an account of the event: "*I did fear that such a blow in their Labor might discourage them from Labor, I have found it by Gods blessing otherwise; yea, this man hath performed a great part of the sawing of our Meeting-House, and is now sawing upon the School-House, and his recovery is an establishment of them to go on; yea, and God blessed this blow, to help on the Work of Grace in his soul.*"[42] Not only does the finished building provide the promise of religious redemption but accidents during its very construction are demonstrably welcome signs, to Eliot at least, of God's providence. The New England missionary commentators chose, quite deliberately, to use the enclosed space of the meetinghouse to demonstrate Native willingness to convert to English forms of religious, legal, and civil society, and confirm the providential nature of their mission.

To draw these strands together, it is worth clarifying that the building blocks of the growing mission were figured in the gradual expansion of spaces in which Indians rehearsed and interrogated their religious faith. From the relatively small space of Waban's wigwam, to the more English-style public space of the meetinghouse, the spaces in which praying Indians performed their religious faith were significant markers on their road to conversion and church membership. The first of the praying towns, and the final marker on the road to religious conversion, was established in 1651, when Natick formally adopted the civil and ecclesiastical measures that the court in Boston had initially set out in 1647.[43]

Commentators on the mission were not slow to recognize the significance of the spatial layout of Natick in particular. Before Eliot characterized Natick as harboring the millennial potential for all New England,[44] various commentators, including John Wilson, Richard Mather, and Eliot himself, satisfied themselves that the building of English-style towns for Native communities would be the precursor to full church membership. While Eliot sold the creation of praying towns to English audiences as a feature of his millennial optimism in *The Christian Commonwealth*, in New England their existence was more finely nuanced.

John Wilson describes the built environment of Natick and makes much of the roads and bridges built by Natick laborers. In the same letter he also makes much of the journey which he and his fellow preachers and ministers take to attend the day's proceedings at Natick: Wilson notes that Natick lies about eight miles from Dedham, from where Governor Endicott travels, and eight miles from Watertowne Mill, from where Wilson and his party travel.[45] On the journey home, Wilson suggests that he is travelling with Eliot's brother (but it is quite certainly his son) and they discuss the piety of the penitents and their willingness to convert: Eliot's brother/son confesses that he eavesdrops on the families at Natick, and his surveillance, under the cover of darkness, confirms their true, holy intentions. Wilson's anecdote of surveillance harbors a fundamental cultural conflict which is defined through the spatial configuration of the colonial landscape. While penitent Indians practice their Christian faith, apparently unobserved, establishing irrefutable evidence of their *true* conversion, they are situated at a distance from established colonial towns, Dedham and Watertowne Mill. This physical distance also marks the distance that exists in the cultural geography of the colonial landscape. No matter how English a Native individual appeared in dress, behavior, prayers and built environments, the spatial distance between colonial towns and praying towns was a permanent marker of separation between white and Native communities. By contrast, but by the same token, the fences built around property and houses in Natick also served as a material sign of separation from the traditions of tribal societies.

Colonial missionaries and commentators were keen to note the active involvement of penitent Indians in this negotiation of space and settlement in the colonial landscape: in the same year that Waban made his land petitions (1646) which eventually led to the building of Natick, similar petitions were being made by Indians near Concord, a group who had already established twenty points of order in an attempt to encompass English-style law and etiquette into their social behavior.[46] In both cases, colonizers chose to emphasize the "civilizing" potential of the enclosed spaces, be they villages or small towns, rather than the pragmatic politics of native people, adapting to survive in this new cultural geography. From the small space of Waban's wigwam, which had been re-fashioned into a site of Christian teaching and English-style civility, to the building of meetinghouses and the legally fenced praying towns, spaces of native religious utterance had expanded into larger, codified social spaces. In this middle-ground, praying Indian communities emerged and their performances of religious speech were as complex and compromised as the ground on which their words were uttered.

SITUATING SPEECH: RELIGIOUS UTTERANCES IN NATICK AND ROXBURY

Over the course of the eleven tracts a general narrative of space emerges and the roles of speakers and audiences are established in the enclosed spaces of the meetinghouses in Natick and Roxbury. While the intimate space of Waban's wigwam was often the site of a penitent's initial introduction to Christianity, it was in the public space of the meetinghouse, either in the praying town of Natick or colonial settlement at Roxbury, that the confessions, examinations, biblical exhortations, and the final confirmation of church membership, were finally enacted.

The first of these acts of religious conversion was held in Natick. In these initial confessional speeches, the slow revelation of God's grace is envisioned through the penitent's overcoming ignorance and sin. The next step toward church membership occurred in Roxbury, 1654, where a group of elders examined penitent Indians. This second trial differed from the first because it focused on principles of faith and doctrine rather than the working of grace in their heart; the missionary was keen to demonstrate that intellectual engagement with Christianity was just as important as an emotional one. The third meeting bore witness to another intellectual exercise, the exhortation of biblical text, where short passages were examined and expounded to demonstrate a coherent understanding of the text, comprehension of faith, and some connection to the penitent's present circumstances. These acts of biblical exegesis took place in Natick, 1658, and many of the penitents linked the poor harvests and floods which they had experienced that year to the book of Genesis and Noah's story in particular. Finally, the last of the confessional narratives on which church membership rested took place in Roxbury, 1659: a private preparatory confession was delivered by each of the eight penitents before a select few elders and ministers, followed by a public confession before a council of church members, elders and ministers who had been invited from all neighboring churches. On the road to religious conversion, the purpose of Natick was to *prepare* the penitent for church membership, whereas the purpose of Roxbury was to *accept* the penitent into the church. Native space and colonial space were held in very different regard and each provided a distinct level of religious authority and control.

With this delineation and codification of space in mind, it is worth considering the confessional speeches of two prominent praying Indians in particular, Waban and Nishokhou, to demonstrate the impact which certain spaces had on extemporaneous religious utterance. The earliest of these confessions included in *Tears of Repentance* (1653), which took place in Natick, seem raw and rudimentary in comparison to the later confessions that take place in Roxbury. These later confessions are included in *A Further Accompt of the Gospel* (1659) and demonstrate skilled exhortation of biblical text. The initial utterances, however, in their raw state, demonstrate the negotiation of power relationships and the processes of cultural production between colonial and praying Indian communities.[47] By focusing on the performance of public confessional narratives in the spaces in which they were performed, a great deal is revealed about the dynamics of turn-taking relations, ownership of the floor, and the negotiation of faith in the complex cultural spaces of the praying and colonial towns.

Eliot provides the parameters of what I call the immediate speech situation of the first recorded Indian confessions in *Tears of Repentance* when he outlines the process through which native voices are granted permission to speak:

> When the Assembly was met, the first part of the day was spent in Prayer unto God, and exercise in the Word of God; in which my self first; and after that, two of the Indians did Exercise; and so the time was spent till after ten, or near eleven of the clock. Then addressing our selves unto the further work of the day, I first requested the reverend Elders (many being present) that they would ask them Questions touching the fundamental Points of Religion. . . . After a

little conference hereabout, it was concluded, That they should first make
confession of their experience in the Lords Work upon their hearts. [48]

The day is deliberately structured around specific speech acts, beginning
with prayers, exercise (biblical exegesis), and a question and answer session.
Each religious utterance demonstrates the formulaic and iterative qualities of
the performance, which must satisfy the expectations of the gathered audiences if the praying Indians are to be granted permission to speak their own
words in the form of the confession.

Waban, who eventually became the chief justice and law enforcer in the
first praying town, makes four confessions between 1653 and 1660, and each
one demonstrates his initial reluctance toward Christianity followed by his
final acceptance and repentance. David Thomson suggests that Eliot's insistence on multiple confessions over a period of time was part of his "prepara-
tionist" style of entry to church membership; in this process of conversion,
penitents would gradually declare their sins and express their true faith only
through a long period of scriptural analysis and personal reflection. [49] Waban
begins his first public confession at Natick by recounting his ignorance and
aversion to the English God:

> Before I heard of God, and before the English came into this Country, many
> evil things my heart did work, many thoughts I had in my heart; I wished for
> riches, I wished to be a witch, I wished to be a Sachem; and many such other
> evils were in my heart: Then when the English came, still my heart did the
> same things; when the English taught me of God (I coming to their Houses) I
> would go out of their doors, and many years I knew nothing; when the English
> taught me I was angry with them: But a little while agoe after the great sikness,
> I considered what the English do, and I had some desire to do as they do; and
> after that I began to work as they work; and then wondered how the English
> come to be so strong to labor; then I thought I shall quickly die, and I feared
> lest I should die before I prayed to God. [50]

His confession is a familiar account of good overcoming the temptations of
material wealth and social status. As an early convert who soon became a key
figure in the social cohesion of the praying town at Natick, and also preached
Christianity to other Indians, it is worth exploring the complexities of Waban's initial confession as it identifies debates and negotiations between
Christian and tribal concerns.

Most notably, it is only after the "great sikness"[51] and the fact that the
English were prospering that Waban considered adopting their religion and
their social structures. Waban saw that illness and disease were decimating
Algonquian communities in the New England area. Fear of these seemingly
incurable new illnesses became a familiar trope throughout his confessions as
he places significant importance on the link between physical and spiritual

welfare. In a later extemporaneous speech where Waban exhorted a passage of the Bible (this event also took place at Natick), the relationship between the spiritual body and the physical body is confirmed when Waban interprets Matthew 9:12–13, and describes Christ as the physician to the body and soul: "[W]e have many at this time sick in body, for which cause we do fast and pray this day, and cry to God; but more are sick in their souls. . . . Therefore what should we doe this day? goe to Christ the Phisitian; for Christ is a Physitian of souls."[52] This sentiment is repeated at Roxbury in the following year and recorded in *A Further Account of the Gospel*: "for Christ healeth the outward diseases of the body, but especially the inward filth of the soul."[53]

It is important to note that Waban has a pre-existing tribal belief in the connections between spiritual welfare and physical welfare. He recalls with apparent shame that he would have liked to have been a sachem, and that he was encouraged to be a pauwau, both important roles in the health and welfare of the individual and social body of Native tradition. Following this, Eliot asserts that "his gift lay in Ruling, Judging of Cases, wherein he is patient, constant and prudent."[54] Waban is a man who appears to enjoy order and hierarchy, and equates the health and continuation of the individual and the social body with faith in an adequate spiritual order. This social and religious framework chimes with Eliot's worldview, where civil and spiritual frameworks are inseparable. Thus, although Waban's conversion is viewed by his Puritan onlookers as enacting a complete disavowal of tribal practices, it is equally feasible that Waban's personal aspirations and his belief in a consistent civil and spiritual framework remain unchanged.

When Waban began his own practice of preaching, witnessed through his part in the conversion of William of Sudbury, or Nataous, the Puritan audience in the colony and England viewed it as the fruits of Eliot's labors. But it is also possible to interpret Waban's performance as a strategy of colonial mimicry; by using the shape and language of the New English Puritan confessional narrative and sermon, he reinterprets and adapts his original worldview. Natick, a place of transition and cultural change provides the necessary space for Waban and others to negotiate the pace and shape of their spiritual adaptation.

Complex deliberations of faith and spiritual identification continue in Nishokhou's narratives, specifically during the third of the trials, where biblical exegesis and logical reasoning find their way into the conversion process. Again, this expression of faith took place in Natick, 1658, and demands a more nuanced account of praying Indian faith and spirituality than a simple explanation of survival politics. In a similar way to Caleb and Joel's examination at the Indian college at Harvard, penitents were expected to incorporate knowledge and interpretation of the Bible into their own experience of spiritual revelation. Until 1663, when Eliot first published the Bible in Algonquian, praying Indians were reliant on Eliot's and Thomas Mayhew's verbal translations, as well as Eliot's smaller publications of the *Psalms* (1658), *Genesis* (1655), and *Matthew* (1655).[55] These biblical texts became manifest in the verbal utterances of the penitents: for example, when John Speene refers to Matthew, "Mat. 3. 2. *Repent for the Kingdome of heaven is at hand*,"[56] he reinforces the concept of repentance and baptism in preparation for a new spiritual beginning.

The pattern of each of these later confessions which rely on biblical exegesis is identical: after quoting two or three verses from the Bible (in these examples *Matthew* and *Genesis* are most common) each penitent develops an argument or discourse on how his chosen verse can be expounded or "improved" to provide an understanding of his own physical and spiritual situation.[57] Waban, Nishokhou, and the other penitents may not be in the same league as Caleb and Joel, whose Latin translations and interrogations of Isaiah are accounted for by Chauncy in this same tract, but the confessions demonstrate competent use of analogy and metaphor within a recognizable logical formation which "improves" scriptural meaning.[58]

Nishokhou's confession is probably the most obviously structured by logical imperatives. He chooses to expound *Genesis* 8.20, 21 and uses the story of Noah and the great flood to understand his own experience, to demonstrate his repentance, and to explore the possibility of God's forgiveness through sacrifice. In *The Logic Primer* (1672), Eliot argued that logic should serve to open scripture so that it might teach the rules for Christian living, and Nishokhou is able to quickly expound Old Testament paradigms to provide coherence for his own situation in seventeenth-century Natick. He continues to refer to biblical sources in order to emphasize the importance of sacrifice, specifically with recourse to Abraham's near sacrifice of Isaac. As this is a typical, Puritan confessional narrative, it initially demonstrates an understanding of scripture, which then leads to self-analysis. Therefore, when Nishokhou begins to draw conclusions about his sins and the process of repentance, the physical nature of biblical sacrifices become more clearly and elaborately described.

Beginning with sensory description, Nishokhou refers to the "sweet savour" of Noah's sacrifices, and later he refers to the brutal possibility of the physical sacrifice of Abraham's only son. The physical nature of these descriptions becomes an integral part of the image created: "God doth not require us to sacrifice our sons, but our beloved sins, our dearest sins. . . . (N)ow if we offer a spirituall sacrifice, clean and pure as *Noah* did, then God will smell a savour of rest in us, as he did in *Noah*, and then he will withhold the Rain, and give us fruitfull seasons."[59]

As Nishokhou draws parallels between Noah, Abraham and his own experience, the physical nature of sin is enriched by the sensory description of sight and smell. The idea that sin can be expunged, that it is produced by man but can be cut off and sacrificed to God as an offering is an unusual twist in

the tradition of sacrifice. Nishokhou inverts the tradition of sacrifice by posit-
ing that it is the *unwanted* object which should be offered up as a sign of
repentance, a complete inversion of Abraham sacrificing his most precious
and most wanted possession, his only son. This manipulation of metaphor is
particularly interesting: Nishokhou demonstrates patterns of logical reasoning and exegetical method which Eliot has taught him and which later became codified in *The Logic Primer*; however, Nishokhou modifies this method of logical construction by developing his own metaphorical associations
in order to link his spiritual and physical selves.

While the formulation of biblical exegesis through logical analysis is a
common feature to Puritan accounts of conversion,[60] Nishokhou's narrative
also demonstrates a sophisticated ability to control the discourse through his
own metaphorical connections. This is a key strategy in Nishokhou's attempts to carve a mark of Native identity onto pre-existing Puritan religious
practice. When taking his turn to speak, Nishohkou's intellectual rigor, together with his creative verbal eloquence, powerfully re-creates Puritan religious practice. Nishokhou confirms his own cultural agency by actively par-
ticipating in the shape and hue of his own Christian Indian faith.[61]

While *The Logic Primer* sought to plant European logical structures in
Native minds, in reality, the process of articulating these logical structures in
rich and imaginative language allows praying Indians the opportunity to
resist full cultural assimilation. Natick and other praying towns offered Native penitents the space to negotiate their own spiritual identities through this
process of adaptation and re-interpretation.

In addition to this intellectual interrogation of individual faith and biblical
exegesis, there is also a personal story behind this narrative: Nishokhou lost
both his children and his wife in one of the many waves of disease that swept
New England. The story of Abraham and Isaac presumably played heavily
on his mind and may well have been behind Nishokhou's initial selection of
text. Throughout the rest of his life he appeared to struggle with alcoholism
and several of his confessions include reference to this. Nishohkou's biblical
exhortation maps the personal story of a man dealing with the impact of loss
and sees him wrestle with his conscience. His speeches, interrogations, and
analogies are personal creations; they are not mere repetition of stock phrases
or religious sentiments. In all, it is a delicate patchwork of intentions and
motivations which demonstrate praying Indians' desire to re-create Puritan
religious practice and control the expression of their Christian faith.

The delicacy of this patchwork of intentions continues at Roxbury, but the
nature of the relationship between the speakers and the listeners changes a
little with the change of venue. When in Natick, the penitents, to some extent
at least, own the floor on which they utter their confessions and their biblical
interpretations. Ministers, and elders have come to visit them and appear at
least to allow penitents to speak without too much hindrance or interference.

There appears to be very little interaction between interlocutors, through questioning or examining, for example, until the penitents arrive in Roxbury, where slightly different strategies of speech and performance are employed.

The negotiation of faith at Roxbury incorporates both the "Examination of the Indians" in 1654 as well as their final confessions which were heard and accepted in 1659. The "Examination" took the form of catechism, where penitents were asked to respond to a series of questions propounded by a number of elders from the Roxbury assembly. The final confession was also spoken before a number of elders, ministers and church members from Roxbury and the surrounding parishes. This was a composite piece of oratory which combined all elements of previous confessional speeches, including recognition of their past ignorance of God and sin, signs of the revelation of God's grace in their hearts, as well as interrogation of biblical text as it related to their own circumstances. Each of these religious performances was intended to persuade the attending audience that the penitents were indeed fit for church governance, but in each case the dynamic of exchange between interlocutors is different. During the examination, penitents and elders give and take their place on the floor as questions are propounded and then answered. In contrast, during the confession, penitents are given permission by their audience to hold the floor and describe their spiritual experiences in their native language for a significant period of time with no interruption.

In their first act of public speech at Roxbury, Indian penitents take part in the performance of catechism, a speech act that measures the turn-taking relations of the speaker and the listener in very precise terms. The call and response dynamic of this public performance relies on very obvious relationships of power and cultural dominance. Among other things, penitents are tested on their understanding of sin and repentance, on the differences between their gods and the Christian God, on the Ten Commandments, and on the aspects of the holy trinity, God, Christ, and the Holy Spirit. Penitents fulfill their obligation in this verbal exchange by reciting certain words, phrases, and responses, thus maintaining the constituative elements of the catechism's established turn-taking relations. As praying Indians perform this practiced form of verbal communication, the missionary perceives that he still dominates the floor and continues to manage the parameters of all the utterances. However, if this speech act is emptied of its spiritual intentions and the speaker is interested only in his or her ability to persuade an audience that they have learned the correct responses, then the power balance which constitutes the catechism has been substantially altered. In effect, the repetitive nature of the catechism provides an easy way for missionaries to establish religious dialogue with Algonquian participants, and for Algonquian participants it is the process of repetition and mimicry through which they might fulfill the expectations of Puritan audiences. But who could say what was really in their hearts?

In the final confessions at Roxbury, the negotiation of praying Indian faith and spirituality reaches its most eloquent expression. Expressions of faith in these speeches allow the gathered audiences to witness personal struggles, personal loss and fear, as well as revelation and hope. Common to all the confessions is the desire to negotiate the terms of their faith through their own experience in order to fashion that faith in relation to pre-existing cultural expectations and values. The confessions of Waban and Nishokhou in particular demonstrate the close relationship between pre-existing values, recent personal experience and the shape of the religious faith which was formed. In Natick, Nishokhou had already expounded eloquently on the Old Testament stories of Noah and Abraham and in Roxbury he utters a similar narrative of his life. He begins by acknowledging the sins of his parents and their worship of false gods; he acknowledges the lust he felt as a young man as well as the alcoholism he experiences in later life; he then speaks of the death of his wife and child and begins to incorporate their deaths into his account of God's grace beginning to work in his heart. Nishokhou refers to both the Old and New Testaments to help illustrate his initially rocky relationship with God and, at last, his final acceptance of God's grace in his heart. In this final confession, Nishokhou provides both a personal and intellectual understanding of Christianity through his personal experiences and his biblical exegesis.

In these final extemporaneous speeches, Waban, Nishokhou, and the other six penitents undertake a complex process of what Jane Kamensky has described as saying and unsaying.[62] In the context of criminal trials and legal proceedings, Kamensky makes the case that "legal culture shared with Puritan religious culture is an intense focus on securing a wrongdoer's admission of guilt."[63] That is, the confession of wrongdoing, by re-stating past sins in front of an audience of appropriate judges, was crucial if the sin was to be unsaid or, put another way, confessed and absolved. The confessions of Waban, Nishohkou, and others, detail the process of the newly formalized ritual: they made visible their sinful hearts through words and tears, connecting their physical and spiritual selves in a ceremonial performance. To their Puritan audience, the process of saying in order to *un*say, that is uttering words of Christianity as a way to unsay the practices of tribal spirituality, was an important part of the confession and was only finalized in the meetinghouse at Roxbury. Only at Roxbury does the full impact of unsaying take effect. In this final site of confession the penitent holds the floor of the assembly and utters a public extemporaneous confession, an act of unsaying previous sins and tribal beliefs, and is regenerated into the community of speakers and believers. But that is not the final analysis.

There is a twist to this process of unsaying. The use of personal experiences, the assertion of leadership, the connections drawn between physical and spiritual health, as well as the use of metaphor and analogy to establish a richness of language, all together signal praying Indian desire to mold new religious rites and logical constructions in relation to their past and present experiences. Joseph Roach, a performance theorist whose work has shed new light on the cultural recreations which take place in a colonial landscape, has argued that "no action or sequence of actions may be performed exactly the same way twice; they must be reinvented or recreated at each appearance."[64] In Eliot's meetinghouse at Roxbury, perhaps the very heart of the mission itself, praying Indians negotiate the constraints of Puritan discourse when they reinvent the spiritual confessional narrative and, by doing so, they renew their own practices of ritual performance to meet the demands of a new Christian and colonial environment. They say the correct words in the correct way, but they unravel the limits of Puritan discourse by re-saying and reinventing their own pre-existing tribal beliefs. Penitent Indians are not necessarily unsaying their tribal past; rather, they *re*say their tribal future through a process of adaptation, not assimilation.

Over the course of Eliot's eleven tracts intimate spaces were replaced by public spaces of the meetinghouses in both Natick and Roxbury. In the final tract, *A Brief Narrative*, published in 1670, readers are offered an account of nine successful praying towns in the Massachusetts Bay area and the church membership which praying communities enjoyed. Eliot's description of the sites of the praying towns offers a brief cultural geography of the mission which has come full circle since the publication of *First Fruits* in 1643. The loose geographical spread of the penitents in *First Fruits* was replaced in later tracts with the very specific spaces of religious utterances in Waban's wigwam, or meeting houses in Natick or Roxbury, and, in Eliot's final tract, the spread of the mission is again stressed in the more detailed description of the settled praying towns.

Around the same time as this final tract, 1670, the "symbolic space" of the praying town, which David Thomson argues was a site of "religious transformation and communal scrutiny,"[65] would be re-created again by Eliot in his *Indian Dialogues*. In this semifictional account, the same concerns with domestic space, Waban's wigwam, and the missionary's journey through the woods or the wilderness situate the dialogues in a similarly symbolic space. In dialogue 1, Kinswoman's home is the sight of initial resistance, but this is soon replaced by prayer and repentance; Waban is situated at Natick and Nishokhou at Nipmuk, highlighting the spread and success of Eliot's mission. In dialogue 2, Waban travels to Nipmuk as a native missionary, spreading the word as he goes and converting the fictional Penevot on the way. It is in the woods, however, that Eliot's most ambitious prize awaits: In dialogue 3, Philip Keitassoot, a thinly veiled Metacom, examines the principles of Christianity through his conversations with Antony and William, as they bring Philip to understand what is meant by Scriptures and the Word of God. More potently, perhaps, in relation to issues of space and performance, Philip is initially wary of the public enactment of Christianity in his town:

> You go too fast. Your answer goes beyond my proposal or their request. We spake onely of private conversation. I said nothing of the Sabbath, nor of their public teaching. This is a greater matter. But go to, seeing you have made the motion. I will not refuse it. What say you my friends? You hear what these people desire. Will you tarry the sabbath among us, and teach publicly among my people? For if you accept the motion, we shall take a course to give notice thereof to all parts of the town. [66]

The religious performance takes place and eventually, after much debate and soul-searching, Philip utters his famous and fictional extemporaneous plea to convert to Christianity:

> I am more then satisfied. I am ashamed of my ignorance, and I abhor myself that ever I doubted of this point. And I desire wholly to give my-self to the knowledge of, and obedience to the Word of God, and to abandon and forsake these sins which the word of God reproveth and condemneth. [67]

In these symbolic spaces, the domestic space of the wigwam or in the open space of the woods, each of which is codified and refined in the tracts of the semifictional *Indian Dialogues*, Eliot continues to consider the delineation of space as an integral part of the description and success of his mission. In the wake of King Philip's war, 1675, few of the praying towns survived and the spatial symbols of Eliot's success were seriously diminished, reflecting the poor state of the momentum behind the mission in these turbulent years. The relatively safe space of the praying towns was in significant doubt, but Natick, the strongest of the towns, did survive and it was there that several praying Indians would utter their final, dying words of religious faith and hopes for continuity.

FINAL WORDS: DEATH, DYING, AND NATICK

Eliot's final publication, *Dying Speeches of Several Indians*, contained the last words of eight converted praying Indians as they perform a dying speech act to a gathered audience of family and friends. In each episode, the dying speech is framed with a short introductory biography of the individual. In his introduction of Waban, Eliot swamps his personalized, local experience of conversion with an account of his role in the civil and ecclesiastical framework of the praying towns, specifically, Waban's role at Natick: "(H)e was chosen Ruler of fifty, he hath approved himselfe to be a good Christian in Church Order, and in Civil Order, he hath approved himselfe to be a Zealous, faithfull and stedfast Ruler to his death."[68]

Foremost, the speeches are unbroken and uninterrupted accounts of the individual Christian Indian's life. Antony's speech serves as a good example to demonstrate how repentance and instruction play a part in the performative effects of the spiritual monologue. Antony, who had been a teacher, confesses that he was a "backsliding Hypocrite" who sinned, repented, was forgiven by both Eliot and Gookin, and yet sinned again. Unusually, he is specific about his vice, and confesses that: "Love of strong drink is a lust I could not over come."[69] He even goes so far as to advise Daniel: "beware, that you, love not strong drinks as I did, and was thereby undone."[70] Finally, in common with the other deathbed speeches, he encourages his children to "forsake not praying to God, goe not to strange places where they pray not to God, but strongly pray to God as long as you live."[71] When Antony repents, he seeks God's forgiveness, therefore the speech act, his final confession, has very specific desired effects: "I desire to dy well. . . . Oh Lord save me and deliver me by Jesus Christ, in whom I believe: send thy Angels when I dy, to bring my poor soul to thee, and save my poor sinfull soul in thy heavenly Kingdom."[72] Antony's speech, and those of the other dying speakers, differ from the confessional narratives of earlier tracts because the speakers assume complete authority as they address their listening audiences (in Antony's case, his children and Daniel) and instruct them to follow their example of repentance. Specifically, in his speech to Daniel, Antony instructs him to resist the temptation of "strong drink" and avoid defiling his teaching by drunkenness.[73]

Some commentators suggest that the delivery of such speeches has a tradition in Native culture and a dying speech would signal a good death and often have the function of passing wisdom to a new generation.[74] The *Dying Speeches*, then, can be understood as a hybrid verbal utterance uniting two cultural traditions and addressing two communities of reception: to a colonial audience, the spiritual monologues of dying Native penitents serve to demonstrate their Christian credentials and, to a Native audience, the speeches also demonstrate the continuance of cultural tradition through the transmission of wisdom and experience from one generation to the next.

Similar performances of adaptation occur in other death rituals. Thomas Shepard, a New England minister, retells the story of the events at the burial of a child from Noonantetum and the graveside speech which was witnessed by Edward Jackson. Gravesides are unusual spaces because they are not always controlled by the same power structures that shape the spaces of meetinghouses, wigwams, or churches and in this case the grave is sited on undisputed ground. On this occasion the Indians from Noonantetum ask how the child might be buried in the English fashion, the implicit Puritan logic of the text suggesting their ready acceptance of English rituals.

Tutaswampe, described as a very "hopefull"[75] Indian is asked to lead prayers, which he does under the shelter of a tree close to the graveside. Shepard notes: "[A]lthough the *English* do not usually meet in companies to pray together after such sad occasions, yet it seems God stird up their hearts thus to doe; what the substance of their prayer was I cannot certainly learn. . . . Tutaswampe did expresse such zeale in prayer with such variety of gracious expressions, and abundance of teares, both of himself and most of his company, that the woods rang againe with their sighes and prayers."[76] All of this happens while Jackson looks on, uninvolved, from a distance. The outpouring of grief is considered to be somewhat un-English, but this is not the only thing that distinguishes the group from their English counterparts. Shepard suggests that by burying the child in the Christian manner they demonstrate their acceptance of the English practice.

Shepard assumes that by gathering together in this way to perform vocal and emotional acts of prayer and grief, Tutaswampe and his company are adapting the English ritual of burial to suit their own response to this untimely death. What Shepard and Jackson witness, however, is not necessarily wholesale conformity to prevailing English traditions but, rather, a negotiation of faith which highlights Algonquian participation and control in establishing new forms of funeral rites. This conclusion resonates with what Douglas L. Winiarski has described as the hybrid nature of Native Christian mortuary rituals in the New England colony.[77] This argument is further enhanced by Craig White when he suggests that the very fact that Toteswampe and his group of mourners stood under a tree has significant implications for the integration of spiritual ritual. White details pre- and post-contact understanding of trees as a metaphor of spiritual significance[78] and also details the metaphorical use of trees in the confessions of Anthony, Nishohkou, and others, which are used to illustrate his point about the integration of native and Puritan beliefs. White stresses that "trees grew on likely spots for encounters with the powerful other-than-human beings who dwelt there."[79] Therefore, the site of the child's burial, as well as the hybrid nature of the performance itself, indicates that this space of religious utterance held tremendous tribal, spiritual significance for the participants in this event and, yet, this significance goes completely unnoticed by the Puritan observers of this funeral ceremony. The onlooker and the recorder of the event, Jackson and Shepard, are both excluded from the true intricacies of spiritual adaptation and continuance of the Native community.

By listening to individual voices in their place of first utterance, the implications for Native agency in the creation of a new spiritual identity are revealed in a more nuanced context. On each occasion Native voices can be heard uttering the concerns of Christianity, often through a framework of pre-existing ritual acts and spiritual beliefs. In each cultural space and by the end of the conversion process, praying Indians had actively sought to establish a role for themselves in the new colonial circumstances of seventeenth-century Massachusetts Bay. In a total speech situation which recognizes the power relationships of colonial dominance, as well as Indian determination to negotiate new forms of spiritual practices and social structures, the speech acts of Caleb, Joel, Waban, Nishokhou, Tutaswampe, and others, demonstrate an ability to re-create a Puritan performance in terms which show their determination to stay actively involved in the negotiation of their religious beliefs and social organization.

The carefully nuanced identity of Algonquian Christian Indians would partially unravel in the wake of the conflict in 1675. During this war, most Algonquians, praying or not, were taken captive by colonial authorities and sent to Deer Island, where many died or were sold into slavery.[80] This prompted Eliot to send a petition to the General Court at Boston in an attempt to secure the safety of Christian Algonquians and guarantee that they would not be sold or transported.[81] Given the bloodshed which ensued, it is perhaps not surprising that after the war had ended the mission drifted due to a general lack of colonial support. Bross suggests in light of Eliot's *Dying Speeches*, where he states—

> Here be but a few of the Dying Speeches and Counsels of such *Indians* as dyed in the Lord.
>   It is an humbling to me that there be no more, it was not in my heart to gather them[82]

—the sustaining image of John Eliot is that of a jaded missionary.[83] Certainly, there is some truth in this: by comparing the last of Eliot's original publications, *Indian Dialogues* (1671) and *The Dying Speeches of Several Indians* (1685), we are left with either the devastating irony of Philip's fictional conversion in the woods, or the haunting deathbed speeches of Christian Indians like Piambohou who, Eliot tells us,

> was the Second man next to Waban that received the Gospel, he brought with him to the second meeting at Wabans house many, when he formed them into a Government, he was chosen Ruler of ten, when the Church at Hassenamessit was gathered, he was called to be a Ruler then in that Church, when that was scattered by the ware, they came back to Natick Church, so many as survived, and at Natick he dyed.[84]

Quite fittingly, Piumbohou embraced his Christian identity in key spaces of religious utterances, Waban's house, a praying town and, finally, Natick, a space spiritually defined by its Christian Indian inhabitants. From the very first utterances of religious conversion to the dying speeches at Natick, Christian Indians undertook a process of spiritual adaption, conscious of the need to negotiate the spaces in which their voices were heard.

NOTES

1. See Phillip H. Round, *By Nature and By Custom Cursed: Transatlantic Civil Discourse and New England Cultural Production, 1620–1660* (London and Hanover, NH: University Press of New England, 1999).

2. Sandra M. Gustafson, *Eloquence is Power: Oratory and Performance in Early America* (London and Chapel Hill: Published for the Omohundro Institute of Early American History and Culture, Williamsburg, Virginia, by the University of North Carolina Press, 2000); Kristina Bross, *Dry Bones and Indian Sermons: Praying Indians in Colonial America* (London and Ithaca, NY: Cornell University Press, 2004); Joshua David Bellin, "John Eliot's Playing Indian," *Early American Literature* 42, no. 1 (2007): 1–30.

3. For a fuller discussion of space, see Gaston Bachelard, *The Poetics of Space*, trans. Maria Jolas (Boston: Beacon Press, 1994); Michele de Certeau, *The Practice of Everyday Life*, trans. Steven F. Rendall (Berkeley: University of California Press, 1984); Henri Lefebvre in *The Production of Space* (Oxford and Cambridge, MA: Blackwell, 1991). For an account of the changing nature of settlement in Native societies in New England at this time, see Anne Keary "Retelling the History of the Settlement of Providence: Speech, Writing, and Cultural Interaction on Narragansett Bay," *New England Quarterly* 69, no. 2 (June 1996): 250–86. More generally, see Keith H. Basso, *Wisdom Sits in Places: Landscape and Language among the Western Apache* (Albuquerque: University of New Mexico Press, 1996); Lisa Brooks, *The Common Pot: The Recovery of Native Space in the Northeast* (Minneapolis: University of Minnesota Press, 2008); William Cronon, *Changes in the Land: Indians, Colonists, and the Ecology of New England* (New York: Hill and Wang, 1983); Tracy Neale Leavelle, "Geographies of Encounter: Religion and Contested Spaces in Colonial North America," *American Quarterly* 56, no. 4 (2004): 913–43.

4. de Certeau, *Practice of Everyday Life*, 117.

5. John Eliot, "Learned Conjectures," in *Jews in America*, ed. Thomas Thorowgood, 2nd ed. (London: Printed for Henry Brome, 1660), 22.

6. Jane Kamensky, *Governing the Tongue: The Politics of Speech in Early New England* (Oxford: Oxford University Press, 1999), 44. Kamensky refers to John Cotton, "Gods Promise to his Plantations: As it was Delivered in a Sermon," London: Printed by William Jones for John Bellamy, 1630. Early English Books 1475–1640 Series; microform, 1421:5; John Winthrop, "Letter to Margaret Winthrop, 15 May 1629," Winthrop Papers 2:92.

7. Sacvan Bercovitch, *The American Jeremiad* (Madison: University of Wisconsin Press, 1978).

8. Eliot, *Learned Conjectures*, 21–22.

9. Thomas Shepard, *The Clear Sun-shine of the Gospel* (London: J. Bellamy, 1648), in *The Eliot Tracts: With Letters from John Eliot to Thomas Thorowgood and Richard Baxter*, ed. Michael P. Clark (London and Westport, CT: Paeger, 2003), 120.

10. *See* Basso, *Wisdom Sits in Places*; Cronon, *Changes in the Land*; Leavelle, "Geographies of Encounter."

11. Shepard, *Clear Sun-shine*, 115.

12. Ibid., 116.

13. Mary Louise Pratt, *Toward a Speech Act Theory of Literary Discourse* (London and Bloomington: Indiana University Press, 1977), 113.

14. Ibid., 113.

15. Shepard, *Clear Sun-shine*, 120.

16. Samuel Eliot Morison, *Harvard College in the Seventeenth Century*, part 1. (Cambridge, Massachusetts: Harvard University Press, 1936), 48.

17. Perry Miller, *Orthodoxy in Massachusetts, 1630–1650: A Genetic Study* (Cambridge, MA: Harvard University Press, 1933), 298. For Miller's fuller account of New England in the seventeenth century, see his *The New England Mind: From Colony to Province* (Cambridge, MA: Harvard University Press, 1953). See also Janice Knight, *Orthodoxies in Massachusetts: Rereading American Puritanism* (Cambridge, MA: Harvard University Press, 1994), rpt. 1997.

18. "The Cambridge Synod and Platform 1646–1648," *The Creeds and Platforms of Congregationalism*, ed. Williston Walker (New York: Charles Scribner's Sons, 1893), Internet Archive, http://archive.org (accessed April 4, 2013) 215.

19. Perry Miller, *Orthodoxy in Massachusetts*, 262.

20. Pratt, *Toward a Speech Act Theory of Literary Discourse,* 113.

21. Shepard, *Clear Sun-shine,* 120.

22. William Kellaway, *The New England Company 1649–1776: Missionary Society to the American Indians* (Westport, CT: Greenwood Press, 1975), 11; Morison, *Harvard College in the Seventeenth Century,* 46–48, 342–43.

23. John Eliot, *A Further Accompt of the Progresse of the Gospel Amongst the Indians of New England* (London: Printed by M. Simmons, 1659), in Clark, *Eliot Tracts*, 353.

24. "John Winthrop to Robert Boyle, November 3. 1663," in *Correspondence of Hartlib, Haak, Oldenberg and Others of the Founders of the Royal Society, with Governor Winthrop of Connecticut, 1661–1672.* ed. Robert C. Winthrop (Boston: Press of John Wilson and Son, 1878), 17.

25. *New England's First Fruits.* (London: Printed by R. O. and G. D. for Henry Overton, 1643), rpt. in *The Eliot Tracts: With Letters from John Eliot to Thomas Thorowgood and Richard Baxter*, ed. Micheal P. Clark (London and Westport, CT: Praeger, 2003), 67. Samuel Eliot Morison suggests that the hall was used for lectures, disputations, exercises, prayers, and dining, similar to the practice of medieval universities on which it was based. *See* "Governing Boards in 1671, *C.S.M.*, xi, 339–40," in Morison, *Harvard College in the Seventeenth Century*, 49.

26. Morison, *Harvard College in the Seventeenth Century*, 278.

27. "Commissioners of the United Colonies to Robert Boyle, 13 September 1665," in *The Correspondence of Robert Boyle*, ed. Michael C. W. Hunter, Antonio Clericuzio, and Lawrence M. Principe, vol. 2, 1662–1665 (London and Burlington, VT: Pickering and Chatto, 2001), 529.

28. Morison, *Harvard College in the Seventeenth Century,* 357.

29. Ibid., 356–57.

30. Eliot, *Day-Breaking*, 79–100.

31. Ibid., 91–92.

32. Ibid., 88.

33. Ibid., 81.

34. Ibid., 87.

35. . Ibid., 91.

36. Ibid.

37. Ibid., 96.

38. John Eliot and Thomas Mayhew Jr. *Tears of Repentance, Or, A further Narrative of the Progress of the Gospel Amongst the Indians in New-England* (London: Peter Cole, 1653), rpt. in Clark, *Eliot Tracts*, 258.

39. Ibid., 272.

40. Ibid., 266–67.

41. Ibid., 268.

42. Ibid., 292.

43. Eliot's account of the foundations of his town, *see* Henry Whitfield, *The Light Appearing More and More Towards the Perfect Day* (London: J. Bartlet, 1651) in Clark, *Eliot Tracts*, 201. For comprehensive analysis of the praying towns, *see* Lisa Brooks, *Common Pot*; Richard Cogley, *John Eliot's Mission to the Indians Before King Philip's War* (Cambrdige, MA: Harvard University Press, 103–71); Dane Morrison, *A Praying People: Massachusetts Acculturation and the Failure of the Puritan Missions, 1600–1690* (New York: Peter Lang, 1998).

44. Aspirations placed on the praying towns particularly during the 1650s could not have been higher: the layout of Natick, the first praying town, had implications for New England's millennial pretensions, all of which had been carefully encoded in John Eliot's *The Christian Commonwealth, Or, The Civil Policy of the Rising Kingdom of Jesus Christ* (London: Printed for Livewell Chapman, 1659). James Holstun's study, *A Rational Millennium: Puritan Utopias of Seventeenth Century England and America*, argues that from Eliot's point of view the

physical layout of Natick reflected the eschatological implications of the praying town. (New York: Oxford University Press, 1987, 123–24).

45. Whitfield, *Strength out of Weakness*, 231.

46. Shepard, *Clear Sun-shine*, 114–16.

47. Recently, an unpublished collection of confessions by Mashepog penitents has been recovered by J. Patrick Cesarini. Although Eliot transcribed these confessions and sent them to the Corporation, they were never published as part of the official promotional tracts. Nor was Eliot directly responsible for the penitents' religious education or conversion; rather, on this occasion Richard Bourne, a fellow missionary, tutored all seven penitents and led them to church membership. These confessions, which were uttered and recorded in 1666 are equally significant to the negotiation of faith as experienced by Christian Indians in seventeenth-century New England, and it is more by chance and timing than by design that they were not published as previous confessions had been. J. Patrick Cesarini who has examined the previously unpublished accounts of the conversion narratives of Mashepog penitents at Mashpee in the Plymouth Colony provides a comprehensive commentary and a reprint of the original manuscript. J. Patrick Cesarini, "Sources and Interpretations: John Eliot's 'A History of the Mashepog Indians' 1666," *William and Mary Quarterly* 65, no. 1 (2008): 101–35. The original manuscript, "'A brief History of the Mashepog Indians,' and their conversion on 11 May 1666," is held in the archive collections of the Royal Society, London, RB/1/11/11 or, previous numbers, BP 11, fols. 279–84.

48. Eliot and Mayhew, *Tears of Repentance*, 268–69.

49. David Thomson, "The Antinomian Crisis: Prelude to Puritan Missions," *Early American Literature* 38, no. 3 (Fall 2003): 419.

50. Eliot and Mayhew, *Tears of Repentance*, 271.

51. Ibid.

52. Eliot, *A Further Accompt*, 333.

53. John Eliot, *A Further Account of the Progress of the Gospel Amongst the indians in New England* (London: Printed by John Maacock, 1660), rpt. in Clark, *Eliot Tracts*, 394.

54. Eliot and Mayhew, *Tears of Repentance*, 272.

55. No copies of *Psalms* or *Matthew* are known to exist. For Genesis, see Wilberforce Eames, *The Discovery of a Lost Cambridge Imprint: John Eliot's Genesis, 1655* (Boston: Merrymount Press, 1937).

56. Eliot, *A Further Accompt*, 336–37.

57. Eliot states in a postscript to the transcribed confessions: "They have none of the Scriptures printed in their own Language, save Genesis, and Matthew, and a few Psalmes in Meetre, and I blesse the Lord that they read them, and improve them, which putteth my soule into an earnest longing that they might have more zeal." (Ibid., 339–40).

58. John Eliot, *The Logic Primer* (Cambridge, MA: Maramaduke Johnson, 1672), rpt. (Cleveland: The Burrows Brothers Company, 1904), n.p.

59. Eliot, *A Further Accompt*, 334–35.

60. For Example, *see* Thomas Shepard *Confessions*, ed. George Selement and Bruce C. Woolley, vol. 58 (Boston: Publication of the Colonial Society of Massachusetts, 1981); and John Fiske, *The Notebook of the Reverend John Fiske, 1644–1675. Publication of the Colonial Society of Massachusetts*, vol. 47 (Boston: Colonial Society of Massachusetts, Anthoensen Press, 1974).

61. Craig White extends this analysis of language and metaphor in relation to several praying Indians in: "The Praying Indians Speeches as Texts of Massachusett Oral Culture," *Early American Literature* 38, no. 3 (Fall 2003): 437–67.

62. Jane Kamensky, *Governing the Tongue: The Politics of Speech in Early New England* (Oxford: Oxford University Press, 1999), chapter 5, "Saying and Unsaying."

63. Ibid., 131.

64. Joseph Roach, "Culture and Performance in the Circum-Atlantic World," in *Performativity and Performance*, ed. Andrew Parker and Eve Kosofsky Sedgwick (London: Routledge, 1995), 46. Roach quotes Richard Schechner, *Between Theater and Anthropology* (Philadelphia: University of Pennsylvania Press, 1985).

65. Thomson, "Antinomian Crisis," 425.

66.   John Eliot, *Indian Dialogues: A Study in Cultural Interaction* (Cambridge, MA: Printed by M. Johnson, 1671), rpt. ed. Henry W. Bowden and James P Ronda, vol. 88 (Westport, CT: Greenwood Press, 1980), 131.

67.   Ibid., 143.

68.   John Eliot, *The Dying Speeches of Several Indians* (Cambridge, MA: Printed for Samuel Green, c. 1685), Early American Imprints, 1st ser., Evans 1639–1800, microform, 2. Also available online: *Readex, Archive of Americana*, www.newsbank.com/readex/.

69.   Ibid., 7.

70.   Ibid.

71.   Ibid.

72.   Ibid., 7–8.

73.   Ibid., 7.

74.   Craig White, "Praying Indians Speeches as Texts of Massachusetts Oral Culture," 457.

75.   Shepard, *Clear Sun-Shine*, 137.

76.   Ibid., 137–38.

77.   Douglas L. Winiarski, "Native American Popular Religion in New England's Colony, 1670-1770," *Religion and American Culture* 15, no. 2 (2005): 166.

78.   White, "Praying Indians speeches as Texts of Massachusetts Oral Culture," 455.

79.   Bragdon cited in White, "Praying Indians speeches as Texts of Massachusetts Oral Culture," 454; see Kathleen J Bragdon, *Native People of Southern New England* (Norman: Univ. of Oklahoma Press, 1996), 219–20.

80.   For commentaries on King Philip's War, see Benjamin Church, "Entertaining Passages Relating to King Philip's War, 1716," in *The Literatures of Colonial America: An Anthology*, ed. Susan Castillo and Ivy Schweitzer (Oxford and Malden, MA: Blackwell Publisher, 2001), 299–307; William Hubbard, *A Narrative of the Indian Wars in New England* (Brattleborough, VT: William Fessenden, 1814), Early American Imprints, 2nd ser., microform, 31766; and Nathaniel Thomas, "Letter From Nathaniel Thomas, on the Expedition against Philip, to Governor Winslow;" *Swanzey, 25th June, 1675,* in *Massachusetts Historical Society Collections* (hereafter cited *MHSC*), 1st ser., vol. 4 (Boston: Massachusetts Historical Society, 1799), 86–87. For contemporary analysis, see Jill Lepore, *The Name of War: King Philip's War and the Origins of American Identity* (New York: Vintage Books, 1999).

81.   "A Petition from Reverend John Eliot against selling Indians for slaves," 13th of the 6th, '75." *New England Historic and Genealogical Register* (hereafter cited *NEHGR*), July 1852: 297.

82.   Eliot, *Dying Speeches*, 1.

83.   Bross, *Dry Bones and Indian Sermons*, 339.

84.   Eliot, *Dying Speeches*, 4.

Chapter Four

Christian Indian Women in Seventeenth-Century New England

In the opening dedication to *New England's Prospect*, William Wood names Sir William Armyne, Knight and Baronet, as his generous and noble patron. Significantly, he also extends his compliments to Armyne's wife, Lady Mary Armyne, whom he describes as William's "very good lady" and "vertuous Consort."[1] Lady Mary Armyne became a supporter of Eliot's missionary enterprise in the decades which followed, but in this context it is Lady Armyne's fleeting presence in the dedication which offers the first hint that Wood perceives his audience to be divided along gendered lines. In the narrative which follows, Wood details the usual array of flora, fauna, and cultural encounters, which readers would expect from this type of travel narrative or promotional pamphlet, but at the end of the narrative he makes a deliberate attempt to address female readers. In the final section of the narrative, "CHAP. XIX. Of their women, their dispositions, employments, usage by their husbands, their apparell, and modesty," Wood states:

> To satisfie the curious eye of women-readers, who otherwise might thinke their sex forgotten, or not worthy a record, let them peruse these few lines, wherein they may see their owne happinesse, if weighed in the womans ballance of these ruder *Indians*, who scorne the tuterings of their wives.[2]

In this early, representative promotional pamphlet, Wood discusses the domestic role of Indian women and also offers some indication of their role in the intricate lineage of tribal leadership, whereby women hold positions of power and can control the transference of power to their children. Wood's description of Indian women corresponds with other, later observations, including those of Roger Williams in *A Key to the Language of America*, where

he also offers the dual role of women as domestic laborers and tribal leaders.[3] Aside from the obvious interest in the customs and concerns of the
Native people of the Massachusetts Bay area which the pamphlet offers,
Wood's specific and direct invitation to female readers in England to examine the experiences of tribal women confirms that when he wrote this pamphlet he imagined that his observations would hold different interests for male
and female audiences. Moreover, he implies in a rather patronizing tone that
women's interests might be relegated to women's experiences but, more
importantly perhaps, this in turn suggests that women's experiences, regard-
less of culture, religion or social organization, might easily speak to each
other in a separate, gendered, sphere of comparison.

While we might doubt the validity of this binary, Anglo-centric framework, it remains a significant fact that Wood was one of the first commentators of colonial New England to identify a female community of readers,
curious about colonial American encounters. With reference to Eliot's mission in particular, this chapter will investigate the more subtle and intrinsic
ways in which Eliot too imagined his audiences to be divided along gendered
lines. It will consider the role native women played in the religious conversion of tribal families and argue that wives and mothers formed a distinct and
effective reception community for Eliot's religious teachings.

In contrast to other studies of gender in colonial New England, which
either consider the ways in which Native and colonial women adjusted to
their new environment while maintaining their original systems of beliefs[4] or
consider the ways in which white and native women were constructed by
colonialist discourses,[5] this chapter examines the experiences of Native
women who made dramatic changes to their lives when they converted to
Christianity. There is no doubt that in Eliot's publications women are often
perceived to be peripheral to the missionary endeavor: of the confessional
narratives which are recorded and transcribed for English audiences in *Tears
of Repentance*, for example, there are no sustained traces of female confessions. Yet, as I intend to demonstrate, women were a distinct and important
reception community for Eliot's missionary endeavor, and this chapter
argues that a female reception community was constructed and embraced by
colonial missionaries. Specifically, it analyses the female reception community through the transcribed utterances of Christian Indian women, principally from Eliot's *Tracts*, the fictional creation of Kinswoman from *Indian
Dialogues*, and the words of one Christian Indian woman in her desperate
response to King Philip's War.

DEFINING A FEMALE RECEPTION COMMUNITY

The influence of women over their families' faith is notable from the earliest of Eliot's accounts of tribal life. Indeed, one of Eliot's first female penitents was a mother responsible for the conversion of her children. In a revealing digression about an eleven-year-old boy's entreaties to his parents to join the church as a direct result of John Eliot's teaching, Gookin states: "The parents who were well inclined, especially the mother, and being also very affectionate to their child, as the Indians generally are, did seriously ponder the child's reiterated intreaties: and not long after, first the mother, and then the father of the child, joined to the church. Soon after the lad was baptized."[6] Notably, it is the mother who takes the lead in the family's religious conversion. More anonymous conversions would follow, and, in 1670, Daniel Gookin records that in Natick there were thirty to forty male and female communicants,[7] demonstrating that women did not simply observe, support, or facilitate the conversion of their husbands but they actively participated in religious conversion themselves. Again, in his summary of the praying towns in Massachusetts Bay, Gookin estimates the population of each town by counting the number of nuclear families, which he defines as a mother, a father, and three children in each family. We can derive from a town like Hassamesitt, where James Printer lived, that there are twelve Christian women in this town because there are twelve families, but more than this Gookin is very clear that the sixteen individuals in full communion are made up of both men and women.[8] Other towns include: Pakemitt or Punkapaog, with an estimated twelve Christian women and families, Wamesit had fifteen, Nashabah, ten, Magunkaquog, eleven, Manchage, twelve, Maanexit, twenty, Quantisset, twenty, Wabquissit, thirty, Pakeckoag, twenty and, finally, in Nantucket, according to John Cotton Jr.'s accounts, there were ten women in church fellowship.[9]

Therefore, despite their often physical separation at fast and lecture days—"In all these acts of worship . . . the menkind [are seen to be] sitting by themselves and the womenkind by themselves"[10]—women were still expected to declare their religious confession, either in public or in private, before they could be admitted to church fellowship. In 1648, John Cotton's "The Way of Congregational Churches Cleared" defended the principles of public confession and examination, so when his son accounts for exactly ten women in full church membership at Nantucket in the early 1670s, we have to assume that they were accepted into the church through the same performances of religious utterance that men were expected to perform.[11] A further piece of evidence clearly demonstrating the common practice of female confession is Thomas Shepard's collection of confessions from settlers at Cambridge. This collection of confessions includes the transcription of speeches from several women from different social classes: alongside the confession of Barbary (or Barbara) Cutter, the wife of Elijah Corlet who was remembered by Cotton Mather as the celebrated schoolmaster in Cambridge, is the first-person confession of Katherine, who is described as the maid of Cambridge residents, John and Elizabeth Russell. [12]

Even from the very limited range of evidence provided by Eliot, in the very first of his accounts in *New England's First Fruits*, we know that Native women practiced spoken confession in a similar way to the penitent women of Thomas Shepard's Cambridge parish. Two anonymous women feature in a list of five named converts: in addition to the women, this list also includes Sagamore John, William, and Wequash, as well as various Indian children. [13] Accepting Kristina Bross's contention that this tract "invents rather than reports a policy of evangelism" and that Indian encounters with Christianity are anecdotal, I would argue that the gender balance recorded in these initial narratives of conversion give us cause to value these anecdotes more highly: firstly, because women become even less prominent in the *Tracts* as the mission forges ahead and, secondly, because of the clarity of the conversion process in rhetorical and practical terms. [14]

Initially, Eliot records that the "Indian maid" from Salem would respond to the sermons and lectures by "crying out with abundance of teares, concluding that she must burne when she die" and that she is likely to be "miserable for ever, unlesse free Grace should prevent it." Her conversion and her transformation from this emotional behavior is as sudden at it is complete: "after this [she] grew very careful of her carriage, proved industrious in her place, and so continued." [15] That is, once the woman has adapted her social appearance and her emotional behavior to the reserve and self-reflection of virtuous and pious Puritan women, then her religious conversion is seen to be complete. [16]

The second female Christian experience extends beyond the rhetoric of behavior and civility in the presentation of religious conversion and provides as well a methodical and deliberate overview of the practical steps required to enter into full church fellowship. [17] The "Blackmore maid" demonstrates very little of the emotional turmoil present in the account of the Salem woman; therefore to some extent she appears already formed in terms of specific codes of civility which always precede religious conversion in Eliot's missionary work. In a similar way to some of the colonial women Shepard identifies, the Blackmore maid is "tried" in private: that is, she is questioned on her knowledge of the Bible and principles of Christianity probably by the Dorchester minister and at least one other senior, male church elder. She is then required to make a full public confession, where she would have contextualized the working of God's grace in her own life through reference to specific scriptural text and, finally, she is sponsored by a member of the church who provides a report of her good character and commitment to her faith. Even more significant from a gendered perspective is the fact that she is represented as a central focus of social change and an axis around which others might be prompted to change their religious views and convert to Christianity:

> [W]e have heard her much admiring Gods free grace to such a poore wretch as she was; that God leaving all her friends and Kindred still in their sinnes, should cast an eye upon her, to make her a member of Christ, and of the Church also: and hath with teares exhorted some other of the *Indians* that live with us to embrace *Jesus Christ*, declaring how willing he would be to receive them, even as he had received her. [18]

Eliot would go on to exploit this aspect of women's role in society when he foregrounded the caregiving and healing roles of mothers and wives in his representations of women. From the very beginning of Eliot's missionary practice, women, through specific constructs of femininity as nurturers, healers and caregivers, were regarded as influential members of the community and were represented as such in the pamphlets and letters which followed.

The role of caregiver and influential social presence hints at the reasons why Algonquian women, who had been familiar with matrilineal social systems, might be attracted to the comprehensively patriarchal structures of Christianity. By taking a close, comparative look at the lives and experiences of native women and colonial women, my intention is to establish a framework through which the attractions of Christianity can be analyzed. This discussion also considers the effects which Christianity had on shared and contested understandings of women's roles in society. Conclusions can be drawn from an exploration of the ways in which Christian Indian women were represented in the textual representation of their utterances: these traces of speech are found in Eliot's Tracts, the fictional *Indian Dialogues* and Eliot's letters.

In relation to Eliot's Tracts and other historical accounts from Daniel Gookin and Experience Mayhew, four strands of the conversion experience will be examined. Firstly, a consideration of the woman as the axis around which a community or a family revolve; secondly, a comparative account of women's roles in Native and colonial societies; thirdly, an analysis of women's responses to powerful oratory; and finally, an account of the gendered implications of creation narratives from Christian and Algonquian belief systems.

THE CENTRAL AXIS

Despite the fact that women's confessions were not recorded to the same extent as their male counterparts, wives and mothers remained influential members of the nuclear family unit and the larger community. In their role as caregivers, educators and healers, we can examine the ways in which Eliot grafts Anglo-centric and Christian-centric notions of femininity on to the identities of penitent Indian women.

Only in one facet of colonial life did women, for a short time, dominate their male counterparts, and this is through medicine and healing. One key example from Daniel Gookin, will serve to illustrate the significance of this role to colonial communities: In May 1674, John Eliot attended a court meeting at Pawtucket with Daniel Gookin and in that town lived a young Algonquian woman who, thanks to the care and attention of an older colonial woman, had survived a brutal attack by a small band of Maquas only four years earlier:

> [In 1670] a young maid of about fourteen years old was taken, and the scalp of her head taken off, and her skull broken, and left for dead with others. Some of the Indians escaping, came to their fellows; and with a party of men, they went forth to bring off the dead bodies, where they found this maid with life in her. So they brought her home, and got Lieutenant Thomas Henchman, a good man, and one that hath inspection over them by my order, to use means for her recovery; and though he had little hope thereof, yet he took the best care he could about it; and as soon as conveniently he could, sent the girl to an ancient and skilful woman living at Woburn, about ten miles distant, called Goodwife Brooks, to get her to use her best endeavours to recover the maid: which, by the blessing of God, she did, though she were about two years or more in curing her. I was at Goodwife Brooks' house in May, 1673, when she was in cure; and she showed me a piece or two of the skull, that she had taken out. And in May last, 1674, the second day, I being among the Indians at Pawtuck-ett, to keep court, and Mr. Elliot, and Mr. Richard Daniel, and others, with me, I saw the maid alive and in health. [19]

Gookin's account of a young woman's survival weaves together the contesting and violent forces at work in colonial New England: intertribal warfare had always been part of life. But, new civil and religious changes transported by colonial settlers brought new tensions to bear between praying Indians who lived in close proximity to the "English houses," and Indians who resisted colonial rule and were losing ground to colonial settlers. At the same time, Gookin explores the miracle of healing as God's "wonders" appear to be channeled through the hands of an "ancient and skilfull woman," Goodwife Brooks of Woburn, and in doing so constructs a familiar opposition between violent Natives and God-fearing white settlers. In the event, Goodwife Brooks removes bone fragments which had been imbedded in the young woman's head and then nurses the girl back to health. That the healing process took two years suggests that Goodwife Brooks and presumably a larger network of female caregivers in the community did in fact hold a strong commitment toward the girl, as well as a strong commitment to their role as healers in colonial New England. [20]

Given the dominance of women in this story of physical and spiritual healing we might well wonder why Eliot's name has been dropped into this account. In one sense the presence of Eliot and Richard Daniel offer a means of corroboration as to the health and welfare of the victim, the inclusion of specific details of whom, why, and where, fits well with the reportage style of history that Gookin is writing. Another, more subtle reason for Eliot's alignment with this event is to associate him with the act of healing; Gookin's rhetorical alignment of Eliot's visit and the girl's full and hearty recovery confirms to the intended reader of these *Historical Collections* that Eliot, more than any other missionary on the mainland, has apparently brought God's miracles of healing to the spiritually and physically wounded Indians of Massachusetts Bay. This, however, can only be a rhetorical gesture since it is a white woman's commitment to an Indian girl that brings about these miracles, highlighting both the gendered and racial complexities implicit in the spread of Christianity among Algonquians of Massachusetts Bay.

The female sphere of medical healing is a notable element in the success of Eliot's mission: acts of healing as well as the application of medicinal remedies provide some evidence of female autonomy and influence that might bring us to understand what Indian women had to gain or maintain from Puritan culture. As Robert S. Grumet highlights in "Sunksquaws, Shamans and Tradeswomen," Algonquian society boasted powerful women healers, commonly referred to as shamans or powwows (pawwaus), and they often held the same position of authority and power as their male counterparts.[21] Indeed, Gookin, Eliot, and Roger Williams are among the few people who record this role for women in their publications. Gookin in particular states: "There are among them certain men and women, whom they call powows. These are partly wizards and witches, holding familiarity with Satan, that evil one; and partly are physicians, and make use, at least in show, of herbs and roots, for curing the sick and diseased."[22] On some occasions, according to Grumet, the influence of the shaman would complement that of the mother when so-called "love doctors" would attempt to influence the marriage with potions and sacred rights. The success of these "potions" aside, the fact that women were accorded such influence over sacred and political matters in coastal Algonquian societies is important, and they may well have interpreted the role of women as mothers, healers, and matchmakers in colonial New England as having similar social status and responsibility. Algonquian women would have had the added benefit of not having to share these powers with their male counterparts.[23]

When the power of the powwows, male and female, began to wane as disease and gunpowder took their toll on indigenous people, women as well as men, one has to assume, searched for another kind of healing power or medicine. The fact that colonial women appeared to be the healers in local colonial communities may well have been an attractive prospect to local

Algonquian women who could envisage a continuation of at least one aspect of their identity and social role. This would be especially relevant to the role of women as midwives, a role exclusively dominated by women and by the knowledge which women had accumulated in both societies and passed on through generations.

One instance of a dangerous and protracted childbirth in Martha's Vineyard around 1649 engages with conflicting religious and medicinal healing powers. However, rather than demonstrate the role of women as midwives in colonial or Algonquian societies, the centrality of the women's position in this story is used to secure her husband's and her family's religious fate:

> [T]his woman, the wife of Hiacoomes, was, as I said, in sore labour and travail
> in child birth several days, and could not be delivered; insomuch that nothing
> less than death was expected by herself and husband. In this strait, several of
> their carnal and unconverted kindred and relations applied themselves unto
> Hiacoomes and his wife, pressing them to send for a powow, and use that help
> for release. But both husband and wife utterly refused their temptation; the
> man being willing to submit to God's disposal, and lose his wife, though he
> loved her dearly, rather than take assistance from the devil and his instruments,
> whom he had renounced; and the woman, who was the sufferer, yet, through
> the grace of God, was endowed with such Christian fortitude, that she also
> utterly refused this method for her deliverance, and would rather lose her life
> than seek help that way. [24]

After a day of fasting and prayer Hiacoomes's wife safely gives birth to a daughter. Mayhew doesn't mention any other specific women in relation to the success of the delivery, but it is unimaginable that she would have been left isolated with no Native or colonial midwife helping her in the days of pain which she endured. Evidence from Experience Mayhew suggests that in the mid to late seventeenth century, Algonquian Christian women, Abiah Paaonit, for example, were identified by their communities as capable midwives who could provide spiritual and practical support to women in labor. [25] Alternatively, in Algonquian society, help would have been sought through traditional remedies, and as a last resort a shaman would have been called, a possibility which Gookin notes in his account. [26] However, the lack of comment on any other kind of help is perhaps more suggestive of the patriarchal and Puritan motives behind Gookin's publication which were, in the main, intended to celebrate the paths to conversion of many Algonquian penitents. In the event, the experience of this woman's hard labor becomes part of the male conversion experience.

In an examination of Hiacoomes's religious convictions in 1651, he was asked if God ever answered his prayers, and his positive response was to relate the story of his wife's difficult but successful labor. [27] The role of women and specifically the female experience of childbirth are used to high-

light and secure the faith of men, establishing the female presence in the text
as the core around which other conversions narratives rotate.

From these two examples, the scalped injured woman and the woman in
labor, we can begin to asses the ways in which the female experience was
mapped onto missionary endeavor; different aspects of female health and
healing became significant markers in the success of the mission as women's
experiences became a focal point around which husbands and sometimes
children proclaimed their faith. This was significant on two counts: firstly, it
demonstrated that the mission was succeeding in changing social practices
which were perceived to be barriers to a complete Christian lifestyle; and,
secondly, they knew that by successfully altering the tribal practices in wom-
en's lives, powwowing for example, they were much more likely to convert
whole families. Women had to be convinced that their roles in the social
organization of Christian Indian living would be secure, and Eliot was at
pains to highlight the caring, nurturing, and healing roles that would be
sustained by women after religious conversion. Women were represented as
central points to each nuclear family; John Eliot's own account in 1648 of
one of his first female penitents is a case in point.

> (S)he called her children to her, especially two up-grown daughters, which she
> had before she married this man, and said to them, *I shall now dye, and when I
> am dead, your Grand-Father and Grand-mother, and Unckles, &c. will send
> for you to come live amongst them, and promise you great matters, and tell
> you what pleasant living it is among them; But doe not beleeve them, and I
> charge you never hearken unto them, nor live amongst them; for they pray not
> to God, keep not the Sabbath, commit all manner of sinnes and are not pun-
> ished for it: but I charge you live here, for here they pray unto God, the Word
> of God is taught, sins are suppressed, and punished by Lawes; And therefore I
> charge you live here all your dayes.* [A precious dying speech of an Indian
> woman to her children.][28]

This is one of the very few occasions where a woman's voice is communicated in the first person. Similar to the *Dying Speeches of Several Indians* which
circulated in Massachusetts in 1685, this speech is perhaps not a verbatim
account of the actual words spoken, but the very fact that Eliot wants to
present the illusion of a woman's dying speech is significant. After all, Eliot
tells us that women should properly speak through their husbands, and we
know from the examples above that women's experience of trauma, due to
injury or childbirth, is most often mediated through male accounts and their
names, let alone their beliefs or experiences, are rarely recorded. This speech
is important because it allows readers of this letter to imagine their own
direct engagement with the female voice and Christian Indian women's experience. Equally significant is the space which Eliot accords this woman's life
experience in what is a relatively short letter (approximately one page of six

is given over to this one account). We learn from this letter about her daughters, we know that she has outlived at least one husband, she has re-married, she is diligent in her domestic duties, and we also understand that she converted to Christianity with her second husband. We learn that she has made and traded goods, including baskets, and spun cotton, demonstrating her industrious nature. Finally, we are told that she died through a complication in childbirth, not an unusual experience in colonial society or, indeed, English society, where this story is finally communicated as part of *The Glorious Progress of the Gospel*, the fourth of Eliot's Indian tracts. Indeed, it is the story's final destination that really defines its purpose: Eliot is aware that the letter will be included in the promotional pamphlets collated by the Corporation and printed for metropolitan and churchgoing regional audiences. Reception communities in England, especially ordinary female readers or listeners, would have understood the pressures placed on the woman as a mother and a wife, a widow or "deputy husband,"[29] and as a contributor to the economic welfare of the family and community.

As the Indian woman adopts a colonial identity in her conversion to Christianity, both her diligence and her endeavor would have struck a chord with ordinary English women who went on to contribute to the mission in parishes across England.[30] At the very least Eliot is exploiting an Anglocentric construction of femininity which he imposes on Christian Indian women in an effort to make them more familiar to English audiences. Eliot's nameless penitent woman's concern with the importance of a family environment, together with the education and fate of her children, is one which recurs in a variety of colonial women's narratives, as well as in the experiences of women from Martha's Vineyard. Elizabeth Cutter and Ann Errington, both of whom were members of Thomas Shepard's Cambridge parish, had previously gone to live with other families and gained religious and social benefit from the experience. Elizabeth Cutter's confession states that she was born into a "sinful place where no sermon preached" and was sent to a "godly family."[31] As well, Ann Errington remembers that as a child she "lived in ignorance" until "she came to Newcastle to a godly family."[32] In Martha's Vineyard, we know that Rachel Amos was sent as a child to live with Thomas Mayhew (Sr.) to be educated and instructed Christian religion.[33]

The practice of sending children to "godly" parents, as in the case of Elizabeth Cutter and Ann Errington, was common in England, familiar to colonial families, and practiced in small pockets by Algonquian Christians. As the anonymous woman's dying wish is made sometime in 1648, she would have been one of the first native women in the area to recommend this fate for her own children. Just as Mary Griswald of Thomas Shepard's parish remembers hearing her mother say that she must be "born again,"[34] so too does Eliot's penitent dying woman use her last words to recommend this religious path to her children. The sentiments and concerns of the woman in Eliot's letter are typical of seventeenth-century Christian women of New England, and it is likely that the other women whose existences are only barely traced in Eliot's and Gookin's letters and publications accommodated these sentiments too. Even in death, Christian Indian women were the axis around which children were asked to shape their lives.

In an earlier letter which was published by the Corporation in *The Clear Sun-shine of the Gospel*, the apparent benefits for Indian women when they become part of the Christian community are, again, predicated on their roles as wives and mothers and their supposed vulnerability in face of violence and rebellion from the men in their families. Specifically Wampoowas, from Concord, beats his wife, and Cutshamaquin's son refuses to accept his parent's punishment after a drunken binge. In each case the so-called sinners are male, but the effects of violence and rebellion are more damaging to the women involved. Wampoowas's wife is protected by a new law which fines violent behavior: as one of twenty nine "conclusions and orders" agreed upon by "Sachims and Other principall men" at Concord in 1646, it is notable that "Whosoever beats his wife shall pay 20s" is among the list.[35] Eliot is pleased that Wampoowas saw fit to blame only himself, leaving his wife's character without blemish, and his renewed protective instinct toward his wife is much more in keeping with the gendered foundation of colonial order: the new civil laws and social responsibilities at Concord reflect Christian and colonial insistence on monogamy and, following that, their insistence that nuclear family was the stabilizing bedrock of civility.[36]

In this new civil structure, a man could have only one wife, adultery was punishable by death, and fornication outside of wedlock would be fined (men would have to pay twice as much as women). The intention was to mirror the roles and expectations that were placed on women in colonial society: women's behavior should be controlled, but they should also be protected if that control become violent.[37] That Wampoowas bears his punishment with tears and repentance allows Eliot to imply that the success of the new gendered hierarchies is located in the strength of a man's character, his ability to repent, and his wife's ability to forgive.

Cutshamaquin's wife is also a silent central focus around which the stories of a drunken son and sinful father revolve. Indeed, her part in this tale of wrongdoing is articulated through absence:

> Cutshamaquin the Sachim having a son of about 14. or 15. yeers old, he had bin drunk, & had behaved himself disobediently, and rebelliously against his father and mother, for which sinne they did blame him, but he despised their admonition. And before I knew of it, I did observe when I catechized him, when he should say the fift Commandement, he did not freely say, *Honor thy father*, but wholly left out *mother*, and so he did Lecture day before, but when this sinne of his was produced, he was called forth before the Assembly and

> hee confessed that what was said against him was true, but hee fell to accuse
> his father of sundry evils, as that hee would have killed him in his anger, and
> that he forced him to drink Sack.[38]

The father is called to confess so that the son might follow suit, and after
much persuasion the son "humbles" himself by asking for forgiveness. It is
only after these male penitents have been brought to repentance that the
mother makes her crucial appearance as she completes the family unit. To
add another layer of complexity to the story, this wife has quite recently been
admonished by Eliot for speaking of "worldy matters." Notably, on this
earlier occasion, she shows herself to be an eloquent speaker as she debates
with her teacher, Nabantons, the supposed "evil" of such talk, and counter-
accuses him of encouraging such discussion through his "discourse in the
publick meeting."[39] However, it is a reformed and silent woman who is
brought in at the end of this later performance of repentance to weep with her
husband and son and enable the emergence of the perfectly repentant Puritan
family unit. By the end of the story, her presence has become symbolic of
New England wives and mothers who, silently for the most part, sustained
the domestic backbone of the colony.

This image of the strong, archetypal family unit is repeated in the story of
Hiacoomes and his wife, who are presented as exemplary Christians when
they lose a five-day-old baby and "carry" themselves as an "excellent" example of Christian mourning to fellow Algonquian Christians: "here were no
black faces for it as the manner of the Indians is, nor goods buried with it, nor
hellish howlings over the dead, but a patient resigning of it to him that gave
it."[40] The death of children is a feature of colonial women's narratives too. In
Shepard's collected *Confessions* "Brother Crackbone's wife," for example,
notes the death of one of her children and near death experience of another,
as significant events on the road to her own spiritual salvation.[41] Rarely,
however, do such events feature in the narratives of English or colonial men.
In praying Indian communities, female experience of childbirth, domestic
violence, outspoken rebellion, bereavement, are not just applicable to wom-
en; rather, they are reported in such a way as to demonstrate the strengthening of the resolve of male penitents and encouraged the impression of a
strong nuclear family unit, which easily unravels without the presence of an
influential wife and mother.

A COMPARATIVE APPROACH

In contrast to other parts of British North America, in New England the
colonies of Plymouth and Massachusetts were founded by families. Wives
and mothers arrived with their husbands, or were sent for not long after
arrival, to settle their new lives and communities together. Many commu-

nities of coastal Algonquian women would, therefore, have witnessed different kinds of domestic chores and social status accorded to colonial women, and it is through this comparative framework that we might understand some of the reasons why Algonquian women were attracted to Christianity. Edmund S. Morgan's *The Puritan Family* and Laurel Thatcher Ulrich's seminal *Good Wives: Image and Reality in the Lives of Women in Northern New England 1650–1750* remain the most significant contributions to date demonstrating the complex lives of colonial women in early New England.[42] Through these studies we begin to understand that women's lives were anything but straightforward as they mediated their responsibilities in domestic and public spheres.[43]

Domestic and public life became intermingled and the home became the center of community communications; women often became the conduits of business information as well as gossip on family matters. Indeed the division of public and private spaces was perhaps not as clearly defined in the seventeenth century as it was in later centuries. In an economy which was largely agrarian, Timothy Stephen suggests, "there was no separate productive sector supplying an alternative social context apart from the home. For the most part, one worked alongside those with whom one lived and married someone whose beliefs and behavior were not likely to be distinctive within the homogenous social framework of the tradition-centered colonial community."[44] In colonial communities, where families worked and lived together, it is important to note that although women did live under a strict patriarchal order, they played a crucial domestic, legal, and economic role in the maintenance of social and religious order.

In their day-to-day existence colonial women negotiated the limits of patriarchal order and became conduits of communication because their role in New England life was so diverse. These were the women with whom coastal Algonquian women watched and, presumably, interacted, so it is important that we remember the freedoms, limitations, and negotiations of powers which permeated the civil and religious environment in which colonial women lived.

In contrast to colonial settlements, Algonquian society provided a combination of matrilineal, matrilocal, and patriarchal forms of social organization which have been identified most notably by Robert S. Grumet, John A. Strong, and Kathleen M. Brown.[45] Grumet maps the sociopolitical organization of the coastal Algonquian women from the clan, which he describes as the smallest unit in the structure, to the confederacy, the largest, and the one which Europeans recognized and cultivated most often. The building blocks of Algonquian social organization through the clan system were matrilineal and matrilocal: "All domestic affairs were regulated by the matriclan. Decisions concerning subsistence, social life, and family religious obligations were made by the corporate kingroup."[46] The influence of these women could be felt at village, district, and tribal level of organization and, as several contemporaneous writers have identified, many women also assumed positions of civil and military leadership, perhaps most famously, Weetamoo, mentioned in Mary Rowlandson's narrative, a Pocasset sunksquaw (female leader) and commander of over three hundred warriors at the time of King Philip's War.[47]

Following Grumet's analysis, Strong provides documentary evidence of women as civil and military leaders throughout the seventeenth century through to the nineteenth century: they were equally responsible for drawing up agreements and signing legal documents on the sale of land, they negotiated alliances with other tribes and with the English, and they also led warriors in battle.[48] Notable female leaders not mentioned elsewhere in this chapter include: Awashonks, sunksquaw of the Sakonnets (Wampanoag), who made a peace treaty with the English at Massachusetts Bay, confirming her alliance to them in 1671, and Quaiapen, sunksquaw of the Niantic, who led warriors against the English in alliance with Metacom or, King Philip.[49] More importantly perhaps, Strong also makes the case that women would assume these positions of authority either through the death of their husbands or by inheritance from either one of their parents' lineage. Strong provides details of the Montaukett sunksquaw as a case in point: Wyandanch, leader of the Montaukett in 1659 died, leaving his wife (who is never referred to by name in the records) in charge of the tribe since the son was too young to accept the role of leader. Following the son's death due to an outbreak of smallpox, her daughter, Quashawam, becomes leader of the Montaukett, tribe when the mother also succumbs to this fate.[50] The flexibility of inherited leadership along gender lines is telling: Wyandanch's wife becomes leader through the death of her husband, but Quashawam's role as leader is bestowed by her mother.

At around this time, and perhaps even earlier, in other parts of colonial America, Kathleen M. Brown notes that male Algonquian leaders, specifically Powhatan in the Chesapeake area, began to integrate the patriarchal structures of the English colonizers in a deliberate attempt to increase their power base.[51] With the impact of patriarchal, European forms of social and civil organization being felt across the region, it is important to consider the response of Algonquian women to Christianity, particularly in Puritan New England, where civil and ecclesiastical structures provided little or no opportunity for women to become influential leaders in political or religious aspects of life. The evidence suggests that in the process of colonization Algonquian women were set to lose their position as clan leaders, civil leaders, military leaders and, perhaps more importantly for ordinary women, their defining role in the lineage of the clan, village, and tribe. Some of them, like Weetamoo and Quaiapen, fought to resist these cultural changes, but other women, many of them left nameless in the records, like Wyandanch's wife, as well as the Salem and Blackmore maid, did take the decision to embrace religious conversion and, with that, significant changes in their social status. In Martha's Vineyard, Dinah Ahhunnut, who died in 1684, and is a near contemporary of Weetomoo and Quaiapen, is hailed by Experience Mayhew as a praying Indian who successfully occupied a domestic role and was praised for her complete assimilation of female colonial attributes, specifically her dedicated attention to household duties as a daughter, wife, and mother.[52] In a world where patriarchal structures were encroaching on pre-existing matrilinear and matrilocal structures, there may well have been some attraction in being a social conduit or deputy husband; women might be persuaded that they were, or could be, a vital center around which family and social matters, as well as matters of health and spiritual well-being, cohered.

Eliot acknowledges that it is through a grassroots approach that the success of the mission will rise or fall: Indian mothers, like the ones described above, were central to the continuance of Christian communities as they dominated the upbringing and education of their children, but so too were colonial women. Colonial women were in a position to be practically involved in the grassroots approach to the social and religious conversion of native communities, and in 1650 Eliot highlights the experience of one woman who is asked to take on the role of 'mother' to Algonquian children of Martha's Vineyard:

> It is a great ground of doubt of the truth of grace in that mans heart, when he hath not an heart to take care to traine up his children in the truth and in the practise of all godliness, but this care is in them, and it is a pity it should not be furthered by all meanes; I have intreated a woman living neer where they dwell, to do that office for their children, and I pay her for it; but when they go to their plantation, we shall be in a streight for help that way; the Indians so well like the parties who performeth that service, that they intreat them to go with them, which I look at as a finger of God.[53]

He completes the story by reckoning that "the care of their (Algonquian children's) schooling may be among the chiefest cares."[54] Childhood education from a maternal source becomes more than a natural domestic circumstance which maintained the social and religious equilibrium of the colony but, in fact, was a tradable commodity and sanctioned, it appears, by the "finger of God," as noted above. This schooling is a rather somber precursor to the orchestrated removal of children from their communities which became prevalent in the nineteenth century, but, in relation to seventeenth-century life, the work of this anonymous white woman offers a glimpse of the significance and value placed on the silent, hidden, and godly mothers and their work in the maintenance of social and religious order in New England.[55]

Algonquian women, especially Christian Algonquian women, had to negotiate these changes to the gendered environment with which they had been familiar, adapting to the changing nature of their civil roles and social status. The case of Sarah Ahhaton's adultery requires a comparative approach to gender politics because it exposes the expectations of Algonquian and Puritan onlookers and demonstrates the conflicting expectations on married Christian Indian women and two very different approaches to sexuality. Ahhaton was discovered to have had an affair with a native man called Joseph and was called to repent in the Massachusetts way: she was sentenced to "stand on the gallowes after the lecture in Boston, with a roape around hir necke one hower. & that then the marshall generall shall cause her to be tooke doune & returned to prison & committed to the Indian constable of Naticke, who on publick day, by order from Capt. Gookin, shall severely whip her, not exceeding thirty stripes..."[56] Notably, her own parents and Joseph's parents counseled Sarah on her relationship with Joseph, and Joseph's mother was apparently proactive in attempting to fulfill the match in marriage. Ann Marie Plane's study on Sarah's trial and punishment demonstrates different colonial and pre-contact approaches to marriage and sexuality and the role of older women in the policing of these matters:

> While the older Indian women possibly protected Sarah from the abuses of her husband, they also actively encouraged and abetted her "adultery." From English eyes they may have fulfilled their role as protectors, but certainly failed to check sinful or unlawful behaviour.[57]

The choice of sexual partners and husbands would have had implications for the social fabric of Algonquian clans and tribes; it is also the case that women were instrumental in matching and policing suitable unions. However, the legal proceedings and punishments in which Sarah Ahhaton found herself were alien to Algonquian custom. Marriage was political in many cases but not in the same way that Puritans would have it. As Grumet has identified, marriage and family provided structural continuance for Algonquian civil leadership: a civil leader might take several wives, but the first one would always come from a neighboring group in order to maintain "strong and reciprocal relationships with other lineages," since the children of those marriages were legitimate future leaders of the maternal lineage.[58] Yet, with these traditions on the wane or, at the very least, being eroded in the face of Puritan colonization of the area, some women chose to convert to Christianity. As noted above, male Algonquian leaders, specifically Powhatan in the Chesapeake area, began to integrate the patriarchal structures of the English colonizers in a deliberate attempt to increase their power base. Kathleen M. brown notes:

Women were not without their bases of power in Algonquian society, however; their important roles as agriculturalists, reproducers of Indian culture, and caretakers of lineage property kept gender relations in rough balance. . . . By no means equal to men, whose political and religious decisions directed village life, Indian women were perhaps more powerful in their subordination than English women.

Even before the English sailed up the river they renamed the James, however, Indian women's power may have been waning, eroded by Powhatan's chiefdom-building tactics. During the last quarter of the sixteenth century, perhaps as a consequence of early Spanish forays into the region, he began to add to his inherited chiefdom, coercing and manipulating other coastal residents into economic and military alliances. Powhatan also subverted the matrilineal transmission of political power by appointing his kinsmen to be *werowances* of villages recently consolidated into his chiefdom.[59]

One instinct to convert might have been made on the basis that it offered women a secure role in society, one which accommodated their power to heal, to educate, and to nurture familial bonds and the collective bonds of the community in a different but sustainable way. If we can assume that Eliot presented their role as Christian wives and mothers to them in the same way that he represented these women to his English audiences in the tracts, then they understood that their role was to embrace tensions in families and communities and provide a strong central axis around which children and husbands would revolve. Before contact, Algonquian women were central to the social cohesion of the tribe and the kinship ties which allowed for its continuance; Eliot uses this pre-existing structure to persuade his female audience of the potential similarities between Algonquian and Puritan models of womanhood. Whether or not there was any truth in this cozy fit is beside the point, since it is Eliot's decision to target and persuade his audience in a gender-specific way which remains crucially important. He deliberately constructs a female audience and attends to their concerns, building his missionary project with a gendered audience in mind.

GENDER AND ORATORY

This understanding of a gendered audience also played a part in the tradition of oratory which Puritan preachers brought with them to the colony. Amada Porterfield has argued that in the seventeenth century New England women made up two-thirds to three-quarters of church communicants, and they were attracted to Puritan teachings through a combination of charismatic Puritan preachers as well as the "erotic satisfaction and emotional security" offered by repeated imagery of "Christ as a ravishing Bridegroom and God as an omnipotent Father which in turn 'answered women's desires for powerful love objects.'"[60] Examples of this argument can be found in the confessional narratives of women in Thomas Shepard's parish in Cambridge. The narratives of Joanna Sill, Mary Angier, Alice Stedman, Katherine (maid), Brother Jackson's maid and Mary Griswald, to name just a few, all make reference to the power and influence of moving sermons from specific ministers, rather than simply personal revelation through reading scripture, as key factors in the course of their religious transformation.[61] In particular, Mary Angier notes that her decision to move to New England and her journey to this spiritual confession is influenced by what she hears from Reverend John Wilson.[62]

Another notable example is Jane Holmes, who names John Cotton and Thomas Weld as providing influential and guiding sermons. Her assertions confirming the influence of powerful oratory are echoed in her husband's confession: Robert Holmes, another of Shepard's congregation at Cambridge, notes that while he slept through sermons when in Northumberland, his "heart melted all sermon time" when he heard John Cotton's sermons in New England.[63] This begs the question of whether or not Algonquian women (and men) really did experience the same kind of attraction to powerful orators. Perhaps. After all, their own male and female leaders were graced with similar powers of oratory. Grumet points out that in coastal Algonquian communities, the authority of a civil leader rested on his or her ability to persuade: "Unable to arbitrarily order action, those in leadership positions were provided an opportunity, rather than a mandate, to authority; power depended on the power of persuasion rather than the persuasion of power."[64] Of the thin shreds of evidence of female penitents in Eliot's Indian Tracts, we know that oratory played a part in the spiritual negotiations of women's experiences. In the case of one anonymous woman, which I will develop more fully below, Eliot notes that hearing the preacher's spoken word is a key part of conversion: "After I began to preach unto them, her husband and she did quickly come in; and after she came, she was a diligent hearer."[65]

On Porterfield's second point regarding erotic imagery, Barbary (Barbara) Cutter's confession demonstrates the intertwining of oratory and emotional fulfillment: "And then hearing Matthew 25, Christ would come as a glorious bridegroom to church."[66] This attention to colonial women's interpretation of sexual metaphors from sermons and liturgical readings might also lead us to ask if Algonquian women experienced these readings in the same way. This is debatable since Algonquian women did not live under the same powerful legislative framework of monogamy, nor did they have the same complex of guilt associated with the Christian understanding of original sin that led to the necessary acquisition of such "love objects." The closest Christian Indian women are seen to come to such an emotional response to Christ as "glorious bridegroom,"[67] is through ecstatic prophetic visions of the afterlife. In Martha's Vineyard at the beginning of the eighteenth century, Abiah Paaonit experiences a vision of light, come from heaven directed to her alone.[68] Experience Mayhew comments that this vision confirms Abiah's faith, and she later refers to the Light as a "Glimpse of the Glory of the Heavenly World" and that the "Rays of that Glorious Light" are those which "the saints in Light do enjoy."[69] Other spiritual interventions include that of Abigail Kesoehtaut, who dreamed that she heard a "Voice from Heaven by the Ministry of Angels," and the daughter of Abigail or Ammapoo, who was also the sister of Caleb Cheshchaamog, who claimed to witness a vision of her mother's spiritual guardians: "saying something to her Mother of what she had seen, she replied, *This is what I said to you, God taketh Care of me.* She also, as I am informed, told another Person before she dy'd, that her Guardians were already come for her."[70]

These visions are, to some extent, predicated on sermons and teachings from Christian ministers, but much is also made of women and girls being taught to read the Bible themselves; therefore we cannot locate these spiritual interventions and visions purely through the voice of eloquent and charismatic preachers. Instead, these visions which Christian Indian women and girls experience (and we should note that Christian Indian men and boys of Martha's Vineyard are not recorded as having the same wealth of sensory spiritual experiences) are more closely linked to Anne Hutchinson's revelatory, prophetic pronouncements of God's grace than with ordinary godly women who cling to the metaphors of sexual union as explicated by their preacher. Mayhew clearly envisages some potential misgivings in endowing these experiences with too much credibility, since he cautions the reader about granting spiritual interventions through dreams with more significance than a "common dream."[71] Still, the parallels with Hutchinson are revealing: all of these women, Hutchinson and Christian Indian women of Martha's Vineyard, control and activate their own sensory spiritual experiences since it is through their own mind and soul that God speaks to them. Alternatively, the sensory experience of ordinary Puritan women in the colony was not within their own control to the same extent: they wait for their bridegroom and they rely on the words of their preacher to allow them to feel spiritual grace. Therefore, it is within this physical and sensory experience of spirituality that differences between Puritan and Algonquian Christian women are most clearly defined, suggesting that Native women, like their male counterparts, actively sought to negotiate and define their own spiritual identities. This community of female penitents did not simply assimilate Puritan models of spiritual femininity; instead, they blended what they already knew with what Eliot and other missionaries were preaching. This expression of a hybrid female identity, one which was located in the middle-ground between pre-contact and colonial identities, may well be routed in the differences between the creation narratives of each cultural tradition.

GENDER AND CREATION

One of the key challenges to Puritan missionaries in North American was the prevalence of so many founding creation narratives belonging to Native American tribes, including the Algonquian tribes of New England, which refused the sense of guilt or shame that the biblical narratives of Genesis promulgated. Rather than riddle their founding narratives with gender hierarchies, sin, repentance, and punishment, in many cases woman's fertility is featured as a necessary and positive catalyst to creation. According to Gookin's firsthand accounts, some Algonquian tribes in the region believed that

> there were two young squaws, or women, being at first either swimming or wading in the water: The froth or foam of the water touched their bodies, from whence they became with child; and one of them brought forth a male; and the other, a female child; and the two women died and left the earth: So their son and daughter were first progenitors. [72]

Relatively relaxed attitudes toward sexuality would be comprehensively challenged in Algonquian communities in New England during the seventeenth century, and the gendered framework of original sin is just one of the sites where this new understanding of sexuality was encoded. Antony, one of Eliot's key Algonquian penitents, opens his final confession by stating, "I confess that in my Mother's Womb I was conceived in sin," [73] and at around the same time Monotunkquanit, another of Eliot penitents, explores his conversion to Christianity and the concept of sin in relation to Eve's temptation in the Garden of Eden: "I heard that *Satan came and tempted Eve*, and cozened her, and she tempted the man." [74]

The role of women in creation narratives remained central, but her function was no longer linked exclusively to fertility; rather, she had come to embody mankind's inherently sinful nature. The creation story of Genesis linked women, sin, and sexuality together in a way that challenged indigenous creation stories and inverted the life-giving force women had previously enjoyed. Instead, native communities were instructed to be ashamed or guilty about sexual desires which, according to Puritan belief, would lead to eternal damnation if left unchecked. While Edmund S. Morgan provides persuasive evidence that Puritans were much more open about sexuality than we might imagine (he cites a variety of sermons, commonplace books, and political publications to support his claim about the intrinsic relationship between the spiritual and sexual bonds of marriage), it is also true that sexual behavior was controlled by strict legal and religious scrutiny which was alien to native traditions. [75] The case of Sarah Ahhaton, detailed above, is representative of this kind of control.

Alternatively, Native wives and mothers, who had no other role of leadership in the community except through marriage, were still significant enablers of intertribal political ties. They demonstrated their influence in several ways: when they married into a neighboring clan, when their children combined the allegiances of both groups with claims leadership over their mother's clan, and when they chose suitable partners for their own children. This day-to-day maintenance of social order strikes a similar chord with the New England housewife that Ulrich describes; after all, women were the primary caretakers of children, maintained and policed social, familial, and kinship bonds, and in the case of Wyandanch's wife who, as Strong comments, "took over her husband's role in negotiations over land sales and whaling rights,"[76] they also had in common the responsibilities of deputy husbands. However, the tradition of a matrilineal framework of inheritance and lineage is a very distinctive difference and one which women would have been loath to relinquish. And, yet, the evidence from Daniel Gookin and the case of Sarah Ahhaton, as well as the documentary evidence provided by John Eliot, tells us that this is exactly what some of them did.[77] When Native women chose to convert to Christianity they did so in the expectation that at least some of the pre-existing roles in society would be sustained within a new religious model. As a unique community of believers, Native women shaped their own sense of religious identity but this was not without its own social tensions. These tensions are played out in John Eliot's rendering of "Kinswoman," the archetypal Algonquian woman, a doubtful traveler on the path to religious conversion.

ARCHETYPAL NATIVE WOMAN: CONSUMING FICTIONS AND KINSWOMAN'S DOMESTIC CONCERNS

John Eliot's fictional re-creation of Indian missionaries in *Indian Dialogues* features the voice of only one woman, Kinswoman, whose journey from so-called heathen to penitent is mapped in the first encounter. While her husband, Kinsman, is already teetering on the point of conversion, Kinswoman's function in this spiritual exchange is to champion tribal practices, establishing her final conversion as a powerful instructional tale. No other women are named in this missionary manual and, as her name suggests, Kinswoman is an archetype, representative of her culture and her gender. If Eliot intended these *Dialogues* to be read or used by English missionaries or Native missionaries, as he claims, then he intended that women would respond to this representation of a tribal domestic scene. The fact that Eliot makes no attempt to convey a realistic setting is not really the point; rather, it is his desire to attract a specifically female audience to his mission, through what he assumes to be gender-specific roles, that makes Kinswoman so important. In

a way similar to William Wood's nod to his female readers, Eliot is consciously identifying and addressing what he perceives to be the concerns and
common experience of a female reception community.

As noted in the previous chapter, the domestic space of religious conversion offered Puritans a way to codify in spatial terms small civilized or
civilizing spaces, which would lead to full, religious conversion. When the
domestic space is linked with the female experience in *Indian Dialogues*, it is
defined as a space of conflict, particularly in relation to cultural expectations
of hospitality.

Kinswoman's first words are uttered in her own home, which is described
in the text as a busy place full of "friends" and people "standing around in
every place," who have come by quite by chance and hear Piumbukhou's
"good discourse."[78] She welcomes her cousin to her lively and joyful household and is only sorry that he has missed a chance to take part in the merri-
ment. After greeting Piumbukhou, Kinswoman immediately observes social
niceties by asking after his wife and asks about her experiences as a Christian
wife:

> KINSWOMAN. And I pray cousin, how doth your wife, my loving kinswom-
> an, is she yet living? And is she not yet weary of your new way of praying to
> God? And what pleasure have you in those ways?
>   PIUM [Piumbukhou]. My wife doth remember her love to you. She is on
> good health of body, and her soul is in good condition. She is entered into the
> light of the knowledge of God, and of Christ. She is entered into the narrow
> way of heavenly joys, and she doth greatly desire that you would turn from
> these ways of darkness in which you so much delight, and come taste and see
> how good the Lord is.[79]

That women are sensitive to the concerns of other women is perhaps not
surprising but, more importantly, what Eliot displays here is a contrast between the outspoken, bold, native woman and the silent, modest Christian
woman whose husband speaks for her. Not for the first time are women
asked to speak through their husbands. In 1647, Thomas Shepard noted the
questions of two women in particular, Wampooas's wife and Tother-
swampe's wife, whose concerns are re-directed in the most elaborate way to
prevent them from speaking a word in the public meeting.[80]

Kinswoman's outspokenness, then, is the first sign of her non-Christian
representation. Despite her cheerful welcome, Kinswoman's hospitality is
rejected in terms which diminish her role as a good homemaker, and she is
presented as a rude reflection of her Christian Indian sisters:

> PIUM. . . . you wish I had come sooner, to have shared with you in your
> delights of this day. Alas, they are no delights, but griefs to me, to see that you
> do still delight in them. I am like a man that have tasted of sweet wine and

honey, which have so altered the taste of my mouth, that I abhor to taste of your sinful and foolish pleasures, as the mouth doth abhor to taste of the most filthy and stinking dung, the most sour grapes, or most bitter gall. Our joys in the knowledge of God, and of Jesus Christ, which we are taught of in the Book of God, and feel in our heart, is sweeter to our soul, than honey is unto the mouth and taste. [81]

Rather than stay silent, Kinswoman enters into a debate with Piumbukhou and appeals to her audience, other members of the household who duly cheer her on, as she counters Piumbukhou's visceral accusations. In this domestic setting, bodily and spiritual appetites provide a metaphorical basis for religious conversion: when Kinswoman wants to silence Piumbukhou's religious teachings she states that "our best answer is to stop your mouth, and fill your belly with a good supper, and when your belly is full you will be content to take rest yourself, and give us leave to be at rest from these gastering and heart-trembling discourses." [82] But even here, in what Kinswoman imagines is a neutral space of human need, "a good supper," Piumboukhou uses the consumption of food as a further battleground of conflicting spiritual views:

> PIUM. . . . I am hungry and weary, and willing to eat. God hath appointed food to be a means of sustaining, relieving and repairing our spent strength. This being a work above the power of the food we eat, or of ourselves that eat it, and only in the power of God himself to bless it, for such great uses. Therefore, God hath taught us, and it is our custom, among all that are godly, to pray to God for a blessing before we eat and therefore I entreat you to have so much patience and compliance, as to give me that quiet liberty to pray to God before we eat. . . .
> . . . We are poor worms under thy feet, thou feedest every living creature, and makest our food to be like a staff to sustain out faint and weary bodies. [83]

This first performance of prayer takes place in a domestic setting: consuming food becomes bound up with consuming a new religion and, in Piumbukhou's teaching, to accept bodily sustenance requires thanks and prayer for continuance of God's spiritual sustenance. Piumbukhou prays over the food and after the meal a prayer of thanksgiving is performed. Piumbukhou teaches Kinswoman about the reasoning behind prayer and presents a three-point explanation, detailing that God should be thanked for his mercy, for his protection, and for the good health which he secures for Christian Indians. Rather than placing the emphasis on theological and even spiritual implications of prayer, by far the most prominent aspect of the explanation is the physical sustenance provided by the food which is prayed over:

> While we sleep our food is boiled up within us, and digested into all parts of our body, and new spirits are extracted out of our food, and sent up both to our head, heart, and all parts of our body, so that we are fresh and strong in the

morning after a good night's rest. Now all this is the special work of God, beyond the power and skill of man to perform for us, and therefore it is great reason to pray for this blessing when we go to rest. [84]

There is no doubt that the logic of the text creates an opposition between Kinswoman's and Piumbukhou's responses to food and eating. This is more concretely asserted when Piumbukhou finally makes the link between the physical and spiritual appetite: "The body is fed by food, the soul is fed by the word of God, and prayer. You that pray not to God, you feed your bodies only." [85] The trope of eating therefore extends into the religious dialogue as Piumbukhou tries to convert Kinsman and other tribal members. When Sontim ponders what pleasures might be lost in his conversion to Christianity, Piumbukhou responds without ambiguity, and again uses food and eating habits to distinguish between the "soul food" [86] of Christian and tribal practice:

> If foolish youths play in the dirt, and eat dung, and stinking fish and flesh, and rotten corn for company's sake, their sachem makes this law: if you come forth from that filthy place and company, and feed upon this wholesome and good food I have provided, then you shall be honoured and well used all your life time. But if you so love your old company, as that you choose rather to feed on trash, and venture to perish among them, then perish you shall, and thank yourself for foolish choice. [87]

The opposition between tribal and Christian practice is clearly demarcated in the *Dialogues*: tribal dancing, sacrifice, play, and apparently gluttonous appetites for "stinking" food are contrasted with prayer and the Christian properties of food which apparently sustain the spiritual and physical appetite. The logic of the text steers the reader toward accepting the Christian viewpoint and consequently the reader is also forced to make a value judgment on tribal practices and tribal domestic settings, largely considered to be a specifically female domain. In the local performances of prayer and the Sabbath the *Dialogues* deal most directly with domestic concerns and every day activities and pleasures, a world where the woman's role as homemaker and her provision of good wholesome food is the contested site of opposing spiritual practice. Experience Mayhew's historical accounts of Martha's Vineyard demonstrate that the provision of food in an orderly household continued to be a telling indicator of a woman's Christian demeanor. Hannah Ahhunut (d. 1704), for example, is described as being literate, providing advice and charity to the community and a moral education for young people. She attended the sick and she also attended women experiencing difficult labors, where she is said to have had "remarkable" results. Moreover, and more pertinently, she was a "diligent provider and dresser of foods" and had an "ordered table." [88] Kinswoman certainly falls short of these colonial standards.

In the following three dialogues female voices fade but their presence does not evaporate entirely, and in dialogue three, the most politically motivated and perhaps the most confrontational of the dialogues, where Eliot challenges Native and Roman Catholic religious practices, the experience and 'sins' of one woman in particular, Sarah Ahhaton, are carefully encoded into the discussion. In the third dialogue, as Philip hovers on the brink of conversion, his concerns are defined through physical, spiritual, and medicinal consumption: "I am a sinful man as well as others, but if I must be admonished by the church, who are my subjects, I know not how I shall like that. I doubt it will be a bitter pill, too hard for me to get down and swallow."[89] The trope of consumption extends its reach into European clashes of culture: anti-Catholic and anti-monarchical views are characterized by excesses of wealth and power through the voice of William (Ahhaton). In this discussion of lusts, sinfulness, and licentious behavior, the case of William Ahhaton's adulterous wife, Sarah, and Joseph, her confessed lover, can hardly be far from the surface.

In his representations of Kinswoman and Philip (Metacom), religious conversion can be viewed through the lens of consumption: from a domestic household setting where the nature of personal, spiritual well-being is explored through the excessive consumption of food, to a transatlantic setting where European religious conflicts are explored in the excesses of lust, adultery and bastard children. In *Indian Dialogues* the housewife and the military leader of the Wompanoag are allied in their resistance to Christianity, and with the shadow of Sarah Ahhanton hinting at the consequences of women's vulnerability to licentious excesses, we can begin to understand the implications of gender in this instructional guide to religious conversion.

Housewives are required to be faithful, obey their husbands and provide a moral and spiritual education for their children, thereby sustaining the spiritual framework of the nuclear family so important to a unified colonial society.[90] The shadow of a woman's vulnerability to sexual excesses and adultery in Philip's conversion is telling: the implication of the *Dialogues* is to suggest that to be tribal is to be weak and vulnerable to the attractions of physical or sexual excess, in a way similar to women like Sarah Ahhaton. Eliot's rather negative view of femininity is not surprising but, crucially, Eliot's audiences remain gendered. He deliberately constructs a dynamic of male and female readership where female readers learn from a female role model in Kinswoman or Piumbukhou's silent and absent wife, and his male readers are asked to consider that tribalism harbors a shade of vulnerability and weakness, directly associated with femininity, one which he assumes tribal men would want to reject.

ONE WOMAN'S WAR: A LETTER FROM JOHN ELIOT

One of the most striking representations of a Christian Indian woman, and probably the last which Eliot records, occurs in a letter sent to Robert Boyle lamenting the "great sufferings" of the mission and the plight of 350 "soules" "put upon a bleake bare Iland" (Deer Island) without adequate food, clothes, and warmth to cope with the harsh winter weather.[91] All of these "soules" removed to Deer Island were Native casualties of King Philip's War. It is the wounded mother of a dead child who articulates the despair of the hundred or so people that Eliot estimates have survived an attack and have now returned from the woods:

> [T]he occasion of theire flight was, because some ungodly & unrulely youth, came upon them, where thei were ordered by Authority to be, called them forth theire houses, shot at them, killed a child of godly parents wounded his mother & 4 more. the woman lifted up her hands to heaven & saide. *Lord thou seest that we have neither done or saide anything against the English th[at] thei th[us dea]le with us (*or words to that effect).[92] (emphasis added)

In this letter Eliot relates to Boyle the mixed fates of praying Indians at various sites across the region: residents of Concord, Pautuket, Martha's Vineyard, Nantucket, and the Nipmuck who fled to Connecticut, are all mentioned. In this moment of crisis and in the midst of King Philip's war the words of one woman are recorded and sent to England. Her performance expresses the unprovoked and barbarous nature of the event, but her words and actions are also the only authoritative Indian account recorded by Eliot in his correspondence in relation to this major conflict in the colony's short history. Moreover, this mother's account is the only Indian testimony included in Eliot's correspondence about the conflict, which has the experiential authority or "autopsy" which Anthony Pagden has argued was central to the reporting of events in the New World.[93]

That a Christian Indian woman might be included in this process of establishing truth through eyewitness accounts is rare; that the truth she lends her voice to is the fact that Indians are being unfairly persecuted by a band of "ungodly and unruly" English youths, is remarkable. Eliot uses this woman's experience to further encourage Boyle that the mission, although faltering, was not "buryed" and with the correct guidance and support might "rise again."[94] This woman's utterance, her articulation of the loss and despair experienced by fellow Christian Indians, becomes a platform for renewal. After all, she does not address her words to Eliot; she does not question the existence of the Christian God, as well she might. Rather, her words are presented as a rhetorical extemporaneous plea. This plea is directed to God and asks that her personal loss and the loss of the safety and security of her whole community might be explained. That one woman's plea might be accorded such authority perhaps says something of the crisis and disruptions caused by the violent and prolonged nature of this colonial and intertribal conflict, where the usual classifications of authority were not easily delineated. On the one hand, Philip led Wampanoag, Narragansett, Nipmuck and some Mohegan tribes in this brutal conflict against colonial settlers in the Massachusetts Bay area; on the other hand, Uncas, leader of the Mohegans, provided safety for Christian Indians who were allied with the English but were also subject to attack from colonial settlers as well as Philip's warriors. Indian was pitted against Indian, English against Indian, and on an ideological level at least, English against English when Eliot and Gookin presented their petition to the Massachusetts court as a formal complaint concerning the treatment of captive Indians in Deer Island by colonial authorities. In the context of this chaos of authority, a rare and revealing moment of female utterance emerges through the cracks of a strained social order.

In the years which followed, the experiences of a white colonial woman, Mary Rowlandson, would also disrupt the patriarchal control of text and utterance as her captivity narrative provided the most compelling authoritative eyewitness account of this intercultural and intertribal warfare. She too saw her child die and did not question her Christian values; instead, like her anonymous Native counterpart her religious beliefs throughout her trial were the very platform for her strength, continuance, and recovery. This is not to suggest that easy, common bonds over shared experiences exist between colonial and Native women in New England. In relation to Rowlandson's narrative in particular, Tiffany Potter has perceptively observed that Rowlandson "re-creates" her identity *against* representations of Algonquian culture and of Weetamoo in particular, who also lost a child, in an attempt to preserve distinct racial difference.[95] Specifically, Potter suggests: "Rowlandson writes gender not as a shared identity, but as a basis of difference and hierarchy even among those of the same sex."[96] Christian Indian women, like the one in Eliot's letter, had to distinguish themselves from tribal women like Weetamoo to confirm their Christian identities, but they would never be able seek commonality with women like Rowlandson, who used racial difference to establish different types of femininity within social and religious hierarchies. For Christian Algonquian women, the process of constructing a spiritual identity was far from easy: constructions of this new Christian Indian identity rested on the ability to negotiate new patriarchal religious beliefs and social structures with the matrilineal traditions of the tribe. Christian Indian women re-created their identities in relation to the Puritan colonial sisters, but in doing so they accepted a unique and difficult position in a gendered and racial hierarchy.

The voices of Christian Indian women are buried deeply in the documents, letters, and narratives of colonial ministers and missionaries. However, despite Eliot's focus on male penitents throughout the Tracts, Algonquian women were consciously constructed as a separate and influential reception community for his religious teachings. Eliot knew that native women needed to accept Christianity if his mission was to be successful and he adopted a gendered approach to his audience of penitents, successfully engaging with his female reception community, in far more subtle ways than William Woods' earlier promotional tract. After all, female native penitents did not fit easily into contemporaneous and current constructions of femininity. Undeterred by these complexities, Eliot set about mediating an Anglo-centric representation of womanhood to his female reception community. For their part, Native women negotiated this model of womanhood as a way of maintaining their roles as educators, caregivers, and social conduits. They were defined by their race, their culture, and their gender, arriving at their new spiritual identity via a process of negotiation which had to take account of these concomitant, determining factors. Women's peripheral status in the documents of colonial New England disguises the fact that New England missionaries, Eliot in particular, recognized and courted their unique influence on the life of the mission.

NOTES

1. William Wood, *New England's Prospect* (London: Thomas Cotes, 1634), n.p., in *Early English Books Online* at http://eebo.chadwyck.com/home (accessed April 4, 2013).

2. Ibid., 94. William Wood was not the first or the last colonial writer to comment on the apparent drudgery of Native women's lives. David D. Smits provides a comprehensive account of seventeenth and eighteenth century colonial literature which perpetuates this kind of this Euro-centric interpretation of native women's lives. David D. Smits, "The 'Squaw Drudge': A Prime Index of Savagism," *Ethnohistory* 29, no. 4 (Autumn 1982): 281–306.

3. Roger Williams, *A Key to the Language of America* (London: Printed by Gregory Dexter, 1643), in *Publications of the Narragansett Club*, vol. 1 (Providence, RI: Providence Press Co., Printers, 1866).

4. *See* Kathleen M. Brown, "The Anglo-Algonquian Gender Frontier," in *American Indians*, ed. Nancy Shoemaker (Oxford and Malden, MA: Blackwell, 2001), 48–62; Edumnd S. Morgan, *The Puritan Family: Religion and Domestic Relations in Seventeenth Century New England* (London: Harper Perennial, 1966); John A. Strong, "Algonquian Women as Sunksquaws and Caretakers of the Soil: The Documentary Evidence in Seventeenth-Century New England," in *Women in Native American Literature and Culture*, ed. Susan Castillo and Victor M. P. da Rosa (Porto: Fernando Pessoa University Press, 1997), 191–214; Laurel Thatcher Ulrich, *Good Wives: Image and Reality in the Lives of Women in Northern New England, 1650–1750* (New York: Alfred A Knopf, 1982).

5. Rebecca Blevins Faery, *Cartographies of Desire: Captivity, Race and Sex in the Shaping of an American Nation* (Norman: University of Oklahoma, 1999); Tiffany Potter, "Writing Indigenous Femininity: Mary Rowlandson's Narrative of Captivity," *Eighteenth-Century Studies* 36, no. 2 (Winter 2003): 153–67.

6. Daniel Gookin, "Historical Collections of the Indians in New England, 1674," in *Collections of the Massachusetts Historical Society,* vol. 1, 1792 (Boston: Munroe and Francis, 1806), 182 (hereafter cited *MHSC*).

7. Ibid., 182.

8. Ibid., 185.

9. Ibid., 184–192, 207.

10. Ibid., 183.

11. See "The Way of Congregational Churches Cleared, 1648" in, *John Cotton on the Churches of New England,* ed. Larzer Ziff, (Cambridge, MA: Belknap Press of Harvard University Press, 1968). For Ziff's account of Cotton and Church governance, see "The Social Bond of Church Covenant," *American Quarterly* 10, no. 4 (Winter 1658): 454–62; and, *The Career of John Cotton: Puritanism and the American Experience* (Princeton, NJ: Princeton University Press, 1962).

12. Thomas Shepard, *Confessions,* ed. George Selement and Bruce C. Woolley, vol. 58 (Boston: Publication of the Colonial Society of Massachusetts, 1981), 89, 99. Thomas Shepard published his confessions as a way of demonstrating that a community of believers existed in Cambridge, Massachusetts. See also *God's Plot: Puritan Spirituality in Thomas Shepard's Cambridge,* ed. Michael McGiffert, rev. ed. (Amherst: University of Massachusetts Press, 1972); George Selement, "The Meeting of Elite and Popular Minds at Cambridge, New England, 1638–1645," *William and Mary Quarterly* 41, no. 1 (January 1984): 32–48.

13. *New England's First Fruits.* London: Printed by R. O. and G. D. for Henry Overton, 1643. Reprinted in *The Eliot Tracts: With Letters from John Eliot to Thomas Thorowgood and Richard Baxter,* ed. Micheal P. Clark (London and Westport, CT: Praeger, 2003)

14. Kristina Bross, *Dry Bones and Indian Sermons: Praying Indians in Colonial America* (London and Ithaca, NY: Cornell University Press, 2004), 7–8.

15. *New England's First Fruits,* in Clark, *Eliot Tracts,* 60.

16. For analysis of the "good" Christian colonial women, see: Laurel Thatcher Ulrich *Good Wives* and "Vertuous Women Found: New England Ministerial Literature, 1668–1735," *American Quarterly* 28, no. 1 (1976): 20–40.

17. *New England's First Fruits,* in Clark, *Eliot Tracts,* 61.

18. Ibid.

19. Gookin, "Historical Collections," 163.

20. Even John Eliot's wife Ann was known to be a trusted healer with some knowledge of medicine and surgery and, according to Patricia A. Watson, this was not especially unusual since medicine was not a closed profession and, as she goes on to document, people like Cotton Mather encouraged it as a "laudable" enterprise for a "gentlewoman." Patricia Watson, "The 'Hidden Ones': Woman and Healing in Colonial New England," in *Medicine and Healing,* ed. Peter Burns (Boston: Boston University Press, 1992), 26.

21. Robert Steven Grumet, "Sunksquaws, Shamans and Tradeswomen: Middle Atlantic Coastal Algonkian Women during and 17th and 18th Centuries," in *Women and Colonisation: Anthropological Perspectives,* ed. Mona Etienne and Eleanor Leacock (New York: Preager Publications, 1980), 51.

22. Gookin, "Historical Collections," 154.

23. Grumet, "Sunksquaws, Shamans and Tradeswomen," 53–54.

24. Gookin, "Historical Collections," 155.

25. Experience Mayhew, *Indian Converts; or Some Account of the Lives and Dying Speeches of a Considerable Number of the Christianized Indians of Martha's Vineyard in New England.* (London: Printed for Samuel Gerrish, Bookseller in Boston, 1727, rpt. Whitefish, MT: Kessinger Publishing), 159. Ann Marie Plane notes that childbirth practices were more social in colonial communities, whereas Algonquian mothers would leave their villages alone or with just a few women to give birth to their children. However, women did stay in close proximity to the village and Plane is clear to point out that they were not isolated despite their physical removal from the village. Plane, "Childbirth Practices Among Native American Women of New England and Canada, 1600–1800," in *Medicine and Healing,* ed. Peter Burns (Boston: Boston University Press, 1992), 13–24.

26. Plane, "Childbirth Practices Among Native American Women," 15.

27. Henry Whitfield, *Strength out of Weaknesse, Or, A Glorious Manifestation of the Further Progresse of the Gospel among Indians in New England. London* (Printed by M. Simmons for John Blague and Samuel Howes, 1652), rpt. in *The Eliot Tracts: With Letters from John Eliot to Thomas Thorowgood and Richard Baxter,* ed. Michael P. Clark (London and Westport, CT: Paeger, 2003), 245.

28. Edward Winslow, *The Glorious Progress of the Gospel Amongst the Indians in New England.* (London: Printed for Hannah Allen, 1649), rpt in Clark, *Eliot Tracts,* 151–52.

29. Ulrich uses this phrase throughout *Good Wives*.

30. English women made up significant part of church congregations and if collections in England were to be fully successful women too would have to be convinced that their money should be handed over in support of the mission. In the receipts collected by the New England Company, ordinary women from local parishes are named, alongside men, as contributors to the missionary cause: Magdalen Whittington of Walburton parish in Sussex gave 4d; in Clapham, 1656, Mary (Albany) gave 6d; Widow and Elizabeth (Slawld?) gave 1d and 6d respectively; and married couple, An Stand and her husband gave 3s; in Hitton, Elizabeth Williams contributed 6d; in the parish of Alderbury in Wilts a cross-section of the parish are represented as Mrs. Elizabeth Done tops the list with a contribution of £3, Widow Beard gives 1s, and Ann Howard servant also gives 1s. There are other female contributors but in some case names of people and parishes are difficult to decipher. *New England Company Archives*, Bodleian Library, Oxford, Rawlinson Collection, C943, 54–73 .

31. Shepard, *Confessions*, 144.

32. Ibid., 184.

33. Experience Mayhew, *Indian Converts*, 152.

34. Shepard, *Confessions*, 188.

35. Shepard, *Clear Sun-shine*, 116.

36. See Morgan, *Puritan Family*.

37. See Ulrich, *Good Wives*, 94.

38. Shepard, *Clear Sun-shine*, 127

39. Ibid., 126.

40. Whitfield, *Light Appearing*, 183.

41. Shepard, *Confessions*, 139–40.

42. Other important contributors to the field include: Nancy Shoemaker, *Negotiators of Change: Historical Perspectives on Native American Women* (London: Routledge, 1995); and Rebecca Faery Blevins, *Cartographies of Desire: Captivity, Race and Sex in the Shaping of an American Nation* (Norman: University of Oklahoma, 1999).

43. Morgan's analysis of the role of women is embedded in a religious framework, specifically the fifth commandment, "honor thy father and mother," which he claims demonstrates that the family structure was the bedrock of social and ecclesiastical organization. (Morgan, *Puritan Family*, 12) Women were wives, mothers, caregivers, and the formative educators of their children, and in each role they were afforded responsibilities and some protection. Widows, for example, could also drive a hard bargain in relation to prenuptial contracts which might allow them to retain some of their land and wealth from their previous marriage. (Morgan, *Puritan Family*, see in particular chapter 2, "Husband and Wife.") In seventeenth-century Cambridge, Massachusetts, Joanna Sill, a member of Thomas Shepard's church, did not remarry after the death of her husband, John Sill, and managed the family estate on her own. As well, in 1653 she was appointed to Susan Blackiston, to work as her lawyer to recover debts which she was owed by some local traders. (Shepard, *Confessions*, 49) Joanna Sill's combined role as a wife, mother, lawyer, manager of the family estate and owner of property demonstrates the complex role of women as caregivers and providers in both private and public life. Laurel Thatcher Ulrich refers to women like Joanna Sill as deputy husbands who had power of attorney in legal and financial matters (Ulrich, *Good Wives*). For comment on the family and marriage in New England. See also Gerald F. Moran and Maris A. Vinovskis, "The Puritan Family and Religion: A Critical Reappraisal," *William and Mary Quarterly* 39, no. 1 (January 1982): 29–63; Chilton L. Powell, "Marriage in Early New England," *The New England Quarterly* 1, no. 3 (July 1928): 323–34.

44. Timothy Stephen, "Communication in the shifting Context of Intimacy: Marriage, Meaning and Modernity," *Communications Theory* 4, no. 3 (2006): 202.

45. Grumet, "Sunksquaws, Shamans and Tradeswomen"; John A. Strong "Algonquian Women as Sunksquaws and Caretakers of the Soil: The Documentary Evidence in Seventeenth Century New England," in *Women in Native American Literature and Culture*, eds., Susan Castillo and Victor M. P. da Rosa (Porto: Fernando Pessoa University Press, 1997); Brown, "Anglo-Algonquian Gender Frontier."

46. Grumet, "Sunksquaws, Shamans and Tradeswomen," 46.

47. Ibid., 51.
48. Strong "Algonquian Women as Sunksquaws and Caretakers of the Soil," 206–10.
49. These leaders are listed in Grumet's, "Sunksquaws, Shamans and Tradeswomen."
50. Strong "Algonquian Women as Sunksquaws and Caretakers of the Soil,"193–94.
51. Brown, "Anglo-Algonquian Gender Frontier," 52.
52. Experience Mayhew, *Indian Converts*, 138–40.
53. Whitfield, *Light Appearing*, 206.
54. Ibid., 206.
55. In Experience Mayhew's eighteenth-century historical account of the "Religious Women" of Martha's Vineyard, he would use this indicator of Christian motherhood to venerate Assannooshque, or Old Sarah, a widow, who adopted many orphaned children and fed and educated them alongside her own children, as well as Abigail Kesoehtaut, who home-schooled her children. (Experience Mayhew, *Indian Converts*, 143–45).
56. "The Trial of Sarah Ahhaton in Massachusetts, 1668," in *Major Problems in American Women's History*, ed. Mary Beth Norton and Ruth M. Alexander, 2nd ed. (Lexington, MA: D. C. Heath and Co, 1996), 22.
57. Ann Marie Plane, "'The Examination of Sarah Ahhaton': The Politics of 'Adultery' in an Indian Town of Seventeenth-Century Massachusetts," in *Algonkians of New England: Past and Present*, Dublin Seminar for New England Folklife Annual Proceedings (Boston: Boston University Press, 1991), 18.
58. Grumet, "Sunksquaws, Shamans and Tradeswomen," 47–48.
59. Brown, "Anglo-Algonquian Gender Frontier," 52.
60. Amanda Porterfield, "Women's Attraction to Puritanism," *Church History* 60, no. 2 (1991): 196, 198.
61. See the confessions of: Joanna Sill, Mary Angier, Alice Stedman, Katherine (maid), Brother Jackson's maid, and Mary Griswald (Shepard, *Confessions*, 52, 67, 102, 99, 119, 187).
62. Ibid., 66.
63. Ibid., 76–80, 143.
64. Grumet, "Sunksquaws, Shamans and Tradeswomen," 48.
65. Winslow, *Glorious Progress of the Gospel*, 151–52.
66. Shepard, *Confessions*, 91.
67. Ibid.
68. Experience Mayhew, *Indian Converts*, 160.
69. Ibid.
70. Ibid., 150.
71. Ibid., 148.
72. Gookin, "Historical Collections," 146–47.
73. John Eliot, *A Further Account of the Progress of the Gospel Amongst the Indians in New England* (London: Printed by J. Macock, 1660), in Clark, *Eliot Tracts*, 382.
74. Ibid., 372.
75. Edmund S. Morgan, "The Puritans and Sex," *New England Quarterly* 15, no. 4 (December 1942): 607.
76. Strong, "Algonquian Women as Sunksquaws and Caretakers of the Soil," 194.
77. More overwhelming evidence of pious Christian Indian women of Martha's Vineyard is also notable but as James P. Ronda has argued, indigenous culture and Christianity were allowed to coexist more easily under the direction of three generations of Mayhews. James P Ronda, "Generations of Faith: The Christian Indians of Martha's Vineyard," *William and Mary Quarterly* 38, no. 3 (July 1981): 369–94.
78. John Eliot, *Indian Dialogues: A Study in Cultural Interaction* (Cambridge, MA: Printed by M. Johnson, 1671), rpt. ed. Henry W. Bowden and James P Ronda, vol. 88 (Westport, CT: Greenwood Press, 1980), 69.
79. Ibid., 69.
80. Shepard, *The Clear Sun-shine*, 117.
81. Eliot, *Indian Dialogues*, 69–70.
82. Ibid., 72.
83. Ibid., 73.

84. Ibid., 79.

85. Ibid., 84.

86. Ibid., 87.

87. Ibid., 86.

88. Experience Mayhew, *Indian Converts*, 141.

89. Eliot, *Indian Dialogues*, 128.

90. Morgan, *Puritan Family*.

91. "Eliot to Boyle, 17th December 1675," in *The Correspondence of Robert Boyle,* ed. Michael C. W. Hunter, Antonio Clericuzio, and Lawrence M. Principe, vol. 2, 1662–1665 (London and Burlington, VT: Pickering and Chatto, 2001), 400.

92. Ibid., 401.

93. Anthony Pagden, *European Encounters with the New World: From Renaissance to Romanticism* (New Haven, CT: Yale University Press, 1993), 51.

94. "Eliot to Boyle, 17th December 1675," in Hunter, Clericuzio, and Principe, *Correspondence of Robert Boyle*, 4:400.

95. Potter, "Writing Indigenous Femininity," 161.

96. Ibid., 155.

Chapter Five

A Reading Comunity

Praying Indians and the Written Word

As noted in chapter 1, on March 19, 1683, sixteen praying Indians appended their names and marks to a letter which found its way to the New England Company.[1] The markers and signatories, all of whom resided in Natick, include: Olt Waban, John Maqoof, Daniel Takawompait, Thomas Tray, Nemiah, Nataniel, John Moquah, Olt Nuomont, Olt Jetro, Olt Nosauwunna, Olt Maquis, Nellem Hahatun, Jams, John Awaquin, Thomas Waban, and Simon Betoqkom. The letter asks that Eliot might use his influence with the Corporation in London in two ways. Firstly, he is asked to encourage the commissioners in New England to support Daniel Gookin so that he might develop his linguistic skills and preach in Massachusett. Secondly, the letter urges that "noble pious and worthy patriots in England" might contribute more for Gookin's annual allowance.

This letter is ostensibly about the financial priorities of the mission's treasurers and plans for a replacement for the aging John Eliot. But the letter is also about language. David Cressy has noted that Protestants and Puritans placed more and more significance on the written word, especially due to their iconoclastic, antisymbolic, antivisual, religious beliefs.[2] For a Puritan colonial missionary like Eliot the cultural and religious conversion of indigenous people was reflected in his creation of the built environment of the praying towns, but it was also reflected through his passion for literacy and the reception of the Algonquian written word and Word. This chapter explores the ways in which the oral language of Algonquian was transcribed into written forms, and it seeks to address the ways in which Algonquian communities adapted to and negotiated written forms of communication.

A PRAYING INDIAN LETTER

The very existence of the praying Indian letter asks us to consider the relationship between reading and writing in praying Indian communities in New
England and, in particular, it asks us to consider that there was a functioning
scribal community of praying Indians in New England. An initial survey of
anecdotal evidence supports this idea: In Eliot's financial accounts there are
references to the purchase of paper, ink, and inkhorns for use in the colonies
from 1654 and 1657, and some years later in 1678 Thomas Mayhew Sr.
records the ability of several emissaries from Martha's Vineyard to put together a written account of their experiences of Nantucket.[3] More conclu-
sively, Matthew Mayhew, in his *A Brief Narrative*, alludes to a lost letter
written by praying Indians living on the west of Martha's Vineyard at the
time of King Philip's War, which notes their refusal to surrender their weap-
ons to the English:

> [T]hey were unwilling to deliver their Arms, unless the English would propose
> some mean for their safety and livelihood: with this return they drew a *Writing*
> in their own Language, which I have often read, and would have *Verbatim*
> inserted, but cannot at present find it; the Substance was, that as they had
> Submitted to the Crown of *England*, so they resolved to *Assist the English* on
> these Islands against *their* enemies.[4]

Notably the letter was written in Algonquian and according to Mayhew's
paraphrasing, those who put their name to this letter were highly experienced
political operators who simply used a new form of communication to practice pre-existing negotiating skills.

   In addition to these isolated letters, individual male students who attended
Harvard, including Joel and Caleb, were accomplished linguists and scribes;
Eliot's own translators, Cockenoe, John Sassomon, Job Nesutan, Monequas-
son, and especially James Printer, who set type on the press at Cambridge,
were certainly able to read in both English and in Massachusett. Further,
throughout the official records of the colony, there are marks and signatures
of many indigenous leaders: in 1644 Weetowish, a Narragensett leader, put
his mark to a document which agreed a period of peace with Uncas, Sachem
to the Mohegans.[5] In the same year, a letter marked by Pessicus and Colouni-
cus details the Narragansetts' "voluntary subjection" to King Charles and the
governing laws and customs of England.[6] Later, in 1664, the marks of six
Narragansett are recorded below a land sale agreement: Sam Elridge, Newcome, Awashous, Quissoquus, Neneglad, and Scuttup of the Narragansett all
signed the sale agreement for what is described as "our whole Countrey" for
"five hundred and ninety five fatham of wampum."[7] Finally, even before
Metacom, or King Philip, engaged in the conflict of 1675 he too used traces
of written language as a valuable communicative tool: the name "Philip alias

Metacome" appears alongside his mark, "P," on a deed dated 1672 beside the signature of Benjamin Church.[8] And, during the conflict, pens, ink, and paper were sent to him to facilitate the end of the hostage siege.[9] Even in Eliot's fictional re-creation on Philip in *Indian Dialogues*, Philip is seen learning to read.[10]

From the academic excellence of the college students to the marks of Narragansett leaders, the spectrum of literacy in Native communities in the Massachusetts Bay area was great indeed, making any unequivocal assertion that there was a scribal or literate community fraught with difficulties. More specifically, the interpretation of marks in place of signatures compounds this difficulty. Studies of colonial literacy, as well as studies of seventeenth-century English literacy rates, generally note that many more people in the colonies and in England were able to read than could write and that more men than women were able to write.[11] Lockridge and Cressy contend that being able to write one's own name on a legal document, a will for example, was roughly comparable with recognized levels of literacy but a mark alone reflected illiteracy.[12] Native American communities who were dealing with official documents were in a position somewhat similar to nonliterate English men or women in New England who relied on official or unofficial scribes and friends to allow them access to legal documents and written correspondence.[13] More recent research differs in the interpretation of marks and signatures, and E. Jennifer Monaghan has argued that due to the very structure of the educational system, which was imported to the colonies from England and demanded that reading skills be mastered before writing skills were introduced, the mechanism of using signatures rather than marks to measure rates of literacy is problematic. It was wholly possible that a marker could read but not write.[14]

In relation to the praying Indian letter, the signatures and marks of sixteen Natick praying Indians demonstrate a determined effort to engage with scribal culture, but I would suggest that there is more at work here than the adoption of one form of communication over another. Instead, given the collective nature of the signatures, the letter presents the collective voice of a community who valued its own survival. I would go so far as to extend Hilary Wyss's assessment of the Wampanoag on Martha's Vineyard to these sixteen men of Natick. Wyss argues that by collective signatures the Wampanoag "appropriated the tools of the dominant culture" to continue the "traditional Wampanoag emphasis on consensual decision-making."[15] In this light, the letter, which conveys a collective sentiment rather than an individual point of view, is perhaps just as significant a marker in Algonquian engagement with Eliot's mission as the building of the praying towns and the publication of the Algonquian bible, which are more commonly noted as Eliot's major and lasting achievements. The adaptation of manuscript culture to express and secure traditional collective identity is equally remarkable and the remainder of this chapter considers the gradual development of Native literacy, together with an account of the flexibility of Native culture to adapt to scribal and printed text.

ROOTS OF LITERACY IN MASSACHUSETTS BAY

To understand the roots of praying Indian engagement with scribal culture, we need to return to the beginnings of the mission. There is no doubt that literate Indians (and to a lesser extent non-literate Indians) contributed to written documents related to legal, religious, educational, and civil matters from the 1650s, and the fascination with literacy began even earlier, in 1643–1644, when Algonquian boys and girls were taken into English households and were taught to speak and read in English as a prerequisite to religious conversion.[16] This was exemplified by Waban, who sent his eldest son to be educated by a colonial schoolmaster.[17] The emergence of an Indian reading and scribal community relied on two basic elements: formal and informal education, as well as the creation of an Algonquian orthography. From the very early accounts and correspondence related to the guiding principles of the mission, schooling for children and adults is interlinked with the publication of Algonquian language primers and religious texts. In 1651, a letter regarding the progress of the mission from William Steele, the treasurer of the Corporation, prompts a response from the commissioners, detailing the allocation of funds, as well as the individuals involved in programs of education and language acquisition.[18]

The links between education and print culture as they developed in the missionary endeavor are fairly well established. William Wallace Tooker, one of the first commentators on Eliot's translators, suggests that Cockenoe, Eliot's first interpreter, was also a teacher of Algonquian.[19] Hilary Wyss also refers to the crucial role of James Printer and Job Nesutan in teaching and translating for Eliot, as well as their role in the publication of the Bible.[20] It is important, then, to establish an understanding of Indian readers and the impact of literacy in an integrated context: firstly, by establishing the educational framework and evidencing readers and writers in praying Indian communities and, secondly, by considering the growing number of Algonquian-language publications.

EDUCATION

Norman Earl Tanis suggests that Eliot was "condemned by the Protestant Ethic to become an adult educator"[21] and that his first foray into the education occurred in 1646 when he met with Waban and several other "chiefs" in Waban's "principall" wigwam and began praying, preaching, and responding to their questions and queries about this new religion.[22] This was an event which involved all sections of the community: "many more *Indians*, men, women, children, gathered together from all quarters round about, according to appointment, to meet with us, and learne of us."[23] Over the course of the next few decades, and as the praying towns became more firmly established, children were taught in the meeting houses, which often doubled as school-houses, and from a letter dated 1653 it is evident that the fruits of these very early endeavors began to pay off. A letter from the commissioners to the Corporation detailed the immanent printing of the *Primer and Catechism* but also the prospect of sending six young Indian scholars to Harvard:

> what you propound from the honorable corporation about six hopful Indians to bee trained vp in the collige vnder some fitt Tutor that p'seruing theire owne Languige they may Attaine the knowlidge of other toungues and disperse the Indian tounge in the college wee fully approue as a hopfull way to further the worke ; But the college being alreddy to strate for the English Students wee shalbee forced to raise some building there for the conveniencye of such Indians wherin probably wee shall expend att least an hundred pounds desire-ing the building may bee stronge and durable though plaine ; But wee haue neither yett agreed with any workmen nor are wee come to any full resolution about the mannor of building or charge Mr Eliot is preparing to print a Catti-chisme in the Indian langwige which wee shall further (as wee may) by dis-bursing the charge of paper and printing out of the stock but by some due allowance shall Indeavor to Incurrage Thomas Stanton to assist in the worke.[24]

These hopeful youths were educated at the expense of the Corporation, and from the Commissioners accounts there is clear evidence of a significantly-sized educational system in operation: in 1657, Eliot spent £50 on five Indian interpreters and Schoolmasters, an English Schoolmaster who made use of two Indian interpreters was paid £20 and the interpreters £10 each.[25] In keeping with an English tradition that encouraged only male students in the art of writing and access to formal education,[26] in 1657 one or two of the "Indian Boyes att Rocksbery that can read and write" were offered as inter-preters and scribes to Mr Blindman, Mr Newman, and Mr Leverich, "who were willing to apply themselves to the Indian worke."[27] In order to gain the best advantage, it was also recommended that the youths who were being schooled by Mr Wells should be removed to a Grammar School, presumably Elijah Corlet's Grammar School in Cambridge, for their "farther improve-ment."[28]

As noted in chapter 3, by 1656 Harvard had erected the Indian College to which some of these young scholars were admitted with the expectation that they would become Christian leaders in their own communities.[29] Not much is known of the actual curriculum, but it is clear that the same religious imperatives were fundamental to the pedagogical vision: just as Harvard produced ministers for New Englanders, so the Indian college would produce missionaries or ministers to help convert Native American communities. As already illustrated, again in chapter 3, in this sense it was an undoubted failure. Few students lived long enough to realize the founders' dream, and those who did were not inclined to the religious life.[30] The loss of Caleb and Joel was perhaps felt most keenly by those who shared Eliot's vision of the college producing Native ministers for the next generation. In 1658, like their fellow New English scholars, Caleb and Joel were called before president Charles Chauncy and examined on their linguistic, rhetorical, and reasoning skills. In addition to this, however, they are also credited with composing *written* addresses to benefactors in England.

Of these addresses, only Caleb Cheeshateaumauk's letter, "Honoratissimi Benefactores," (1663) survives.[31] In this letter we read of Orpheus, a symbol of education and regeneration, who duly transformed the "nature of barbarians" as well as the "trees, rocks and brute beasts" of uncultivated land. Caleb quickly conflates the regenerative role of Orpheus with that of the benefactors to whom he addresses the letter: just as Apollo gave Orpheus the lyre, Caleb speaks to his benefactors and suggests that God "delegated you to be our patrons" so that "you might perform the work of bringing blessings to us pagans."[32] Quite fittingly for Caleb's educational experience, the letter demonstrates knowledge of western classical tradition overlaid with Christian tradition.

As the editors of this letter suggest, there is very little opportunity in this letter to identify any kind of hybrid, Native Christian identity. Indeed, Hochbruck and Dudensing-Reichel argue that Caleb either did not write the letter himself and it was dictated to a scribe or, at worst, the whole document was falsified.[33] For the latter to be the case, John Winthrop Jr., who sent the letter to Robert Boyle at the Royal Society, would be guilty of misleading Boyle and the royal society for the purpose of blatant fundraising. Given Winthrop Jr.'s close correspondence with Boyle and the royal society on matters of natural history and scientific observations, it seems highly unlikely that he would risk his reputation with such an astounding ruse. On the issue of Caleb simply not writing the letter himself, Hochbruck and Dudensing-Teichel provide evidence of narrative inconsistencies to prove this point. This argument is not watertight, and it seems equally likely that young scholars who are still learning new languages and new literary traditions could easily make the kind of syntactical errors which Hochbruck and Dudensing-Teichel find so problematic. As the editors point out, Caleb's use of Homeric tradition and its transition into Christian salvation is not entirely appropriate for the subject matter, and this may also point to the rather naive or superficial understanding of young scholars in relation to the texts they read and the literary forms which they employed.

Despite Hochbruck and Dudensing-Reichel's rather negative claims, it seems reasonable to suggest that Caleb's letter demonstrates that Native literary achievements were used by colonial New England to promote their missionary agenda, certainly, but they also provide evidence of highly literate Indian readers in Massachusetts Bay. This is not to argue that these texts offer a positive indictment of the education of Indian youths at Harvard's Indian college or, indeed, evidence of hybrid Indian-Christian identity. Instead, these documents demonstrate the intellectual rigor of Indian scholars as they assessed their place in a colonial environment and new literary and spiritual traditions.

The experience of students like Caleb was in some way exceptional, and they were not representative of the average, literate praying Indian who would have read the Algonquian translation of Genesis and the Gospel According to Matthew. These texts were circulating in 1655 and featured strongly in the public confessions made by praying Indians in the late 1650s and early 1660s, suggesting that these texts were read by a small community of private readers. They may also have been read aloud to praying Indians in places like Waban's wigwam or the Natick meetinghouse. Unfortunately, no copies of Eliot's earlier biblical translations survive, unlike the complete Algonquian bibles which, as I will highlight below, were read and annotated by generations of private readers, especially in Martha's Vineyard.

Compelling anecdotal evidence of examples of education and literacy are sprinkled throughout the tracts. As mentioned already, in 1643 there is evidence of children reading and being educated in English homes,[34] and in following years this informal educational framework develops into small local schools, two of which Eliot mentions in a letter dated 1647, published in *The Clear Sun-shine of the Gospel* (1648). Two years later, in 1649, the donations for schooling were being sent from London: of a ten pound donation, five pounds were given to a "grave woman in Cambridge, who taught the Indian children" and the other five was given to the School master at Dorchester who was responsible for the education of several "capable" children.[35] In the same year, Eliot appealed publicly for an annual allowance of ten pounds per student from donations made in England, which would "maintaine one Indian youth at Schoole."[36] At around this time both Thomas Mayhew and Eliot were proposing schools on Martha's Vineyard and Massachusetts Bay.[37] In Eliot's case, in around 1651, this aim was complete and the religious motivation for educational instruction was put into practice:

> I know not whether I have yet mentioned our Schoole, which through the Lords mercy we have begun, though wee cannot yet be constant in it, wee have two men in some measure able to teach the youth with my guidance, and inspection. And thus wee order the Schoole: The Master daily prayeth among his Schollers, and instructeth them in Catechisme for which purpose I have

compiled a short Catechisme, and wrote it in the Masters booke, which he can
reade, and teach them; and also all the Copies he setteth his Schollers when he
teacheth them to write, are the Questions and Answers of the Catechisme, that
so the Children may be the more prompt and ready therein: wee aspire to no
higher learning yet, but to spell, reade and write, that so they may be able to
write for themselves such Scriptures as I have already, or hereafter may (by the
blessing of God) translate for them; for I have no hope to see the Bible
translated, much lesse printed in my dayes. Therefore my chiefe care is to
Communicate as much of the Scriptures as I can by writing: and further, my
scope so to traine up both men and youths, that when they be in some measure
instructed themselves, they may be sent forth to other parts of the Countrey, to
traine up and instruct others, even as they themselves have been trained up and
instructed.[38]

Eliot's motivation for instruction in reading and writing is perhaps not so
surprising, but it does show that Eliot's rather ambitious aim was to establish
a situation where Christian Indians would spread their skills and knowledge
to others to create a constant and increasing wave of literacy and Christian
understanding. As more and more schools were established in the praying
towns in the next few decades this plan did have at least some success:
Monequassun, a schoolmaster by around 1652, specifically mentions his desire and later ability to read as a key part of this conversion;[39] John Wilson
provides an account of an Indian schoolmaster who "read out of his Booke
one of the *Psalmes* in meetre, line by line, translated by Mr *Eliot* into *Indian*,
all the men and women, &c singing the same together in one of our ordinary
English tunes melodiously."[40] These small successes were replicated in the
praying towns, but it was far from the wave of change that Eliot perhaps
envisaged and which he would continue to idealize in his fictional account of
Indian proselytizing in *Indian Dialogues*.

A more revealing aspect of Eliot's description of the educational instruction is his focus on the circulation of handwritten scriptures. Due to a lack of
printing facilities, Eliot's only option was to write out part of the scriptures in
longhand and, he claims, these were read by those scholars attending the
school. Although instruction manuals and primers for reading and writing
were available in English before this, and Eliot asks for more to be sent from
England at this time,[41] the Algonquians' engagement with written traces of
their own language were handwritten, suggesting that their understanding of
Algonquian text began in scribal form. The process of writing and producing
manuscript text was embedded in these scholars' education before the printed
text of Algonquian was mechanically produced for their reception. One wonders if they saw value or ownership in the handwritten word at this time. As
demonstrated above, marks and signatures on legal documents concerning
land sales and loyalty to the English crown demonstrated an ability, maybe
even a desire, to engage in the colonial political system through scribal

means, and, by 1683, the letter signed by sixteen Indians hints that they had become far more politically aware of the power of epistolary forms. From this evidence alone, it is apparent that Christian Indians came to value hand-written documents and were not ignorant of the potential political expediency of such documents.

THE HANDWRITTEN WORD AND THE ALGONQUIAN BIBLE

Beyond the political, nation-building intentions behind the Algonquian bible, as described in chapter 2, Eliot primarily intended his bibles to be read by Algonquian-speaking Indians, and the marginal notes, which have been re-corded and translated by Kathleen Bragdon and Ives Goddard, confirm that Algonquian Indians owned, wrote on, and read Eliot's bibles well into the eighteenth century.[42] Domestic use is further emphasised by the fact that the New Testaments and both editions of the complete Bible were distributed in New England without a dedicatory address, something peculiar to the copies circulated in England, and the reprinting of the Bible in 1685 was provoked by the loss of so many during the destruction of King Philip's War.[43]

Through the marginalia in English-owned and praying Indian bibles, one of the most significant adaptations of Algonquian tradition occurs. The unique nature of native appropriations of the handwritten text had a decisive impact on their ability to renew and adapt their traditional forms of oral communication; English, colonial, and Native individuals who read and an-notated Eliot's Algonquian bible did so in demonstrably different ways. English and colonial owners, including Lady Armyne and Thomas Shepard (the son of the Reverend Thomas Shepard), sign and date their books typically on the first page or the title page. Since books were a relatively rare commodity, Morison comments: "Your seventeenth-century scholar was fond of seeing his name in writing, and a book-label gave him the thrill of seeing it in print. He had a keen sense of possession, which he was wont to spend in Latin formulae, often including the date (which enables us to ascertain that it was bought when in college) and the price."[44]

Indian signatures also determine ownership, but differ in that they appear on various, random pages.[45] Bragdon and Goddard have compiled a reliable transcription of Indian owners, typically: "I Mantooekit (x) This is my hand," or "James I wrote it, [I] this times, this 25th of June, 1695."[46] The Bibles seem to have been a shared commodity and in the Library of Philadelphia copy,[47] one Indian reader writes: "This is Joseph's. And this is his book. And I am Moses Papenau. All people, know it to be so, that he is God in heaven who created us and everything in this world."[48] This notion of collective ownership is not so discernible in colonial society in New England and is certainly not the case with the signed books of the Harvard students. Although Harvard students did share rare books the concept of individual ownership was never questioned. The written trace of the Indian experience in marginal notes and cover pages demonstrates that the book became a way to communicate the thoughts of the reader, whether he is the owner or not. Therefore, through these handwritten inscriptions a hybrid form of ownership emerges: this notion of ownership borrows from the individual ownership typical of an English or European model and collective ownership which was most commonly practiced in tribal communities.

Resistance to full acceptance of this European form of ownership is implicit in the dialogues which emerge in the marginal notes of the bibles. A direct example of this is recorded in The Congregational Society Library copy.[49] Next to the opening of the Book of Daniel, "In the third year of the reign of Jehoiakim king of Judah came Nebuchadnezzar king of Babylon unto Jerusalem, and besieged it," (Daniel I: 1), is written: "You, Thomas, remember: do not fornicate."[50] This seems to be advice from another reader, but why this particular passage is the source of these words of wisdom is not clear.[51] Some marginal notes respond more clearly and directly to the text, and this is true of the George W. Pratt copy.[52] Alongside 2 Samuel 1:1-2, which describes the deaths of Saul and his son Jonathan, the notes read: "Saul and Jonathan [were] lov[ed]."[53] In the same Bible, next to Judges 4:1, 5:1, and 6:1, there is a record of the deaths of the writer's, or writers', family or acquaintances, respectively, "Ephraim Naquatta died on July 7, 1731," "Joshua Seiknouet died January 22, 1716," and "Peapsippo died August 9th, 1715."[54] Through these inscriptions, there is a clear indication that the Indian bibles were read, given the commentary on the Books of Samuel and Daniel, but they were also used to record important events in the lives of these particular readers for their own reference, and that of the wider reading community. These written traces, at the very least, reflect the level of acceptance with which Christian Indians of New England approached the written word, but, through this scribal method of communication, they also reflect an intention to address and sustain their collective identity as a community.

The written inscriptions in the book, in this case the Bible, became a site of dialogue, exchange, and perhaps resistance. James Axtell notes that the Jesuit missionaries continued to encourage the objectification of the Bible in a deliberate attempt to perpetuate the myth of the shamanic qualities of the book and those who could read from it.[55] In contrast, the Christian Indians of Massachusetts wrote on and conversed in the margins of these texts succeeding, to some extent, in incorporating their "living voices"[56] into the written traces of their thoughts, advice, and personal loss. In this way, Indian appropriation of the Bible is somewhat disruptive. The marginal voices exist autonomously without colonial interruption or explanation and, through Eliot's attempts to capture the living voice of the Massachusetts dialect in a phonetic orthography, Algonquians reclaim their voices through written communication. The potential of handwritten text was certainly realised by the early eighteenth century when many of these written traces were penned, and I would argue that the possibilities of harnessing Algonquian living voices through these written traces was prefigured in the scriptural manuscripts which Native scholars were introduced to in the early 1650s.

As bibles passed through generations, Algonquian Christian Indians adapted a tradition of oral communication to establish a new form of dialogue or silent conversation in the written traces of the margins. With the introduction of manuscripts and the printed text, Christian Indian readers in particular adapted their oral communicative practices to develop a new communicative practice as a way to record their lives and experiences for fellow readers and for posterity. William H. Sherman's *Used Books: Marking Readers in Renaissance England* notes a similar tendency in Renaissance readers to mark books, not necessarily to demonstrate any connection with the text, but to place the book in "the reader's social life, family history, professional practices, political commitments, and devotional rituals."[57] More particularly, with reference to scriptural texts, annotations were often interpretive comments on the content of the text which allowed the reader to join "the community of godly readers."[58] Native readers and writers of Massachusetts and Martha's Vineyard would not have been familiar with the practices of Renaissance readers, but their attempts to document and place themselves and the book in a particular community and in a particular "time and space" are similar.[59] From the very early experiences of the scribal forms in Eliot's early praying communities to these more sophisticated interactions with text in the eighteenth century, changes in the communicative practice allowed Christian Indians to bridge oral traditions and scribal culture and establish a "community of the text," similar to the one which Sherman describes in relation to ordinary but engaged Renaissance readers.[60] Through very particular uses of scribal culture, Christian Indians made a significant attempt to negotiate and maintain a new hybrid identity.

PRINT CULTURE: ALGONQUIAN SPEECH AND ALGONQUIAN ORTHOGRAPHY

Once the printing press had been established in Cambridge, Eliot made full use of its potential to further his educational and missionary project. At the same time that Eliot was hearing and recording public confessional narratives, and at the same time as Caleb and Joel were impressing their examiners at Harvard, Eliot was piecing together what would later be known as the Indian Library: a collection of twelve Algonquian language texts, including instructional language primers, *Indian Grammar Begun*, *The Logic Primer* and "*our Indians ABC*," as well as scriptural texts, principally, the complete

Bible.[61] The publication of language instruction manuals and religious texts in Algonquian occurred in conjunction with the formal education of adults and children in praying towns. Eliot understood that it was not only talented scholars or individuals who could gain from reading; any penitent, like Monequassun above, who was to have a relationship with God in the Protestant, Puritan tradition, needed to be able to read and/or interpret the Bible on his or her own and to that end he set about publishing manuals to help maintain this literacy project.

In 1654 John Eliot published *Primer and Catechism,*[62] the first of his attempts to formalize in print a language which previously had only been spoken. *The Indian Primer*, which is the 1669 reprint of this original text book and the only edition extant, is a very small object, easily held in the palm of a hand and as such portable. It lists letters and textual formations of sounds to help with the pronunciation of the Roman alphabet; it also includes the Lord's Prayer and the Creed, in English and Algonquian, and each of these is expounded in Algonquian. It contains the Catechism in Algonquian in a long and short version, and has lists of numbers in Roman numerals, European numbers (1, 2, 3, . . .), as well as in words up to one hundred fifty: significantly, the purpose for this insertion was to "serve for the ready finding of any chapter, Psalms and verse in the bible, or elsewhere."[63] This was an instructive text, bringing together necessary literacy and numeracy skills, with the aim of successful religious conversion through text-based education.

Closely following the *Primer and Catechism*, Eliot published *The First Book of Moses called Genesis,*[64] *The Gospel of Matthew,*[65] and *The Psalter,*[66] and a metrical translation of the Psalms into Massachusetts, which was appended to both editions of Eliot's Algonquian bible: *Mamvsse Wunneetupanatamwe Up-Biblum God*, 1663 (1685). By far, Eliot's most sustained attempt to harness the spoken dialect of Massachusetts into a grammatical form which would be recognizable to a European audience, and certainly his most sophisticated language primer, is *The Indian Grammar Begun* (1666).[67]

Eliot was not a lone voice in this linguistic project, and *Indian Grammar* is part of a small tradition of linguistic and cultural transcriptions. William Wood's "Small Nomenclator," which was appended to *New England's Prospect* (1634), is considered to be the first attempt to trace an Algonquian dialect, Naumkeag, in print. Wood included his vocabulary to complement his broader description of the Naumkeags from northern Massachusetts.[68] The overall purpose of Wood's pamphlet was to promote the relatively new colony and encourage further emigration to New England. Nine years later, Roger Williams published *A Key to the Language of America* (1643), which was a more sustained account of the language and traditions of the Narragansett tribe. Williams' *Key* is often characterized as a cultural encounter, a text through which not only a language can be understood but also customs and traditions. To an extent this is true, and in some senses Williams presents a fair account of the Narragansett to his London audience and even goes so far as to state: "Boast not proud English, of thy birth & blood, / Thy brother Indian is by birth as Good."[69] However, the question of audience presents an alternative purpose for this cultural and linguistic encounter. The manuscript was written as Williams sailed back to England to secure a charter for Providence Plantation in Narragansett Bay, and the publication of the *Key* was to engage the interest of the authorities and promote his own cause. To this end it seems somewhat opportunistic and perhaps culturally voyeuristic as he attempts to disclose some "Rarities concerning the Natives themselves, not yet discovered."[70]

Where Wood and Williams transcribed the language and recorded the traditions of indigenous New England tribes for an English audience, in later years, with the publication of Abraham Pierson's *Some Helps for the Indians* (1658) and Eliot's *Indian Grammar*, the purpose and audience changed substantially. The printing history of Pierson's *Some Helps for the Indians* hints at a complexity of purpose which we do not find in Williams's *Key*. Although *Some Helps for the Indians* was printed in the colony for the purpose of teaching Indians who could read the lessons of the Scriptures, especially the Ten Commandments, Pierson's Catechism, which he rewrote in 1658, was sent to England and published in *A Further Accompt of the Progresse of the Gospel*, 1659, as part of the Corporation's effort to persuade the English audience of the success of the missionary work in New England. While this tactical promotional motivation should not be minimized, in Pierson's case his primary audience was a local audience made up of colonial missionaries and praying Indians who might use his manual to promote and enable religious conversion.

Although Pierson and Eliot enjoyed recognition and praise for this work in England, as well as financial reward through the Corporation for Propagating the Gospel and latterly the New England Company, they were motivated by their desire to proselytize. For Eliot more than anyone, the written word represented another vehicle through which this end could be achieved, hence, the publication of Eliot's *The Indian Primer* (1669) and republication of *The Christian Covenanting Confession* (1660–1661 and 1670). In the *Covenanting Confession*, as well as Pierson's *Some Helps for the Indians*, Algonquian and English are interlinear and the subject is typically a catechism, or instructions on the practice of conversion. By the mid to late seventeenth century there was a growing body of Algonquian-language texts,[71] but it was John Eliot who, more than any other translator or missionary in New England, promoted the continuance of the Algonquian language in large print productions.

Thomas Thorowgood, a contemporary of Eliot and an admirer of his work, suggested that although Algonquians did not practice a written language comparable with the European model, symbolic or hieroglyphic traces were part of Algonquian communicative practice. In *Jews in America* he includes examples of Native signatures: the signatures of Pessicus, Conaunicus, Mixon, Auwashoose, and Tomanick are reprinted. [72] These written traces were not part of Eliot's plan to transcribe Massachusett and he endeavored to replace this communicative practice with phonetic transcriptions of Algonquian using the Roman alphabet. On the one hand, Eliot refuses existing textual communication but, importantly, he is determined to ensure the survival of the sound of Massachusett in its written form.

THE LIVING VOICE AND THE WRITTEN WORD

Throughout his career Eliot pursued his desire to harness the "living voice" of speakers in his written texts. [73] For example, in his transcription of Indian conversion narratives and dying speeches, as well as his translations of religious instruction manuals, Eliot imagines that the voice of the speaker remains transparent and immediate. As noted already, in one of his later tracts, *A Further Accompt*, Eliot glosses over issues of translation and transcription in relation to Indian conversion narratives, stating "let the work it selfe speake," while he remains "silent," giving the illusion of the transparency, which he believes the written trace of direct speech offers. [74] This is repeated in his accounts of the *Dying Speeches*, where each speech is purported to be a translation and transcription "in the Language as they were spoken." [75]

Further, in the Puritan texts Eliot chooses to translate as religious "instruction manuals" for Algonquian readers, it is the voice of the preacher during his sermon which dramatizes and characterizes the text. His pursuit of the authority of the living voice of the preacher is detailed in a letter to Richard Baxter. Eliot states: "I believe it will not be unacceptable to you, that the Call of Christ by your Holy Labours [*Call to the Unconverted*, 1664], shall be made to speak in their Ears, in their own language, that you may preach unto our poor Indians." [76] Therefore, when he translates Richard Baxter's *A Call to the Unconverted* (1664, 1688), an abridged version of Lewis Bayly's *The Practice of Piety* (1665, 1685) and, finally, Thomas Shepard's *The Sincere Convert* (1689), he is conscious of the need to harness the strategic qualities of the "living voice" of speech as well as the "permanence and stability" of text. [77]

It is difficult to determine how Eliot's translations into Massachusett of the religious tracts by Baxter, Bayly and Shepard were received by Christian Indians. Originally written for English audiences and, presumably, incorporating a certain amount of assumed knowledge about that audience and their religious understanding, these texts contained considerable cultural and religious differences which separated them from their new reception community. However, Neal Salisbury does indicate that of all Eliot's publications, his translations of Baxter and Bayly's work were the most often reprinted.[78] Baxter's and Bayly's texts went through a second reprint in Cambridge press, which suggests that they were distributed and read by praying Indian communities either in private by individual readers or, through group readings where one member of the community might read the work aloud. We can also be sure of the fact that Eliot was drawn to texts which continued to develop the instructive nature of his overall linguistic project. To this end, he needed to familiarize Massachusett Indians with the Christian God, demonstrate how religious conversion should be practiced or performed and, finally, maintain the living voice of the preacher within the bounds of the written text.

Bayly's *Practice of Piety*, as the title suggests, is the most overtly instructive of the three manuals as it directs the pious Christian on how to pray and meditate on given occasions: for example, at meal times, when sick, and when in despair. From Bayly's point of view the power of the written word is all-encompassing and the relationship between the reader and the text is characterized as an inextricable bond. Not only does the text provide essential, enlightening instruction, even if the reader rejects that instruction, the bond between text and reader remains fierce:

> Whoever thou are that lookest into this Book, never undertake to read it; unlesse thou first resolvest to become from thy heart, an unfained *Practitioner of Piety*. Yet reade it, and that speedily, least before thou has read it over, God (by some unexpected death) cut off, for thine inveterate Impiety.[79]

Bayly anticipates that his book will provoke the *practice* of prayer and meditation and the link between the written word and action, or reaction, remains; according to Bayly's hyperbole, this has rather fatal consequences for the "impious" reader.

Shepard and Baxter extend this dynamic between the written word and the anticipated active response by adding speech to the existing relationship between word and action. Baxter's *A Call to the Unconverted* familiarizes the reader with the Christian God whom Baxter characterizes as a forgiving deity who embraces the penitent sinner. Alternatively, Shepard focuses on a vengeful God and with reference to Revelation 21:8[80] describes the fate of the unrepentant soul:

> The never-dying worm of a guilty conscience shall torment thee, as if though had swallowed down a living poysonfull snake, which shall lie gnawing and biting thine heart for sin past, day and night. . . . A thousand such bites will this worm give at thine heart, which shall make thee cry out, O time, time! O Sermons, Sermons! O my hopes and my helps are now lost that once I had to save my lost soule![81]

With reference to the sermon at this desperate point of repentance, Shepard confirms that conversion is most often inspired by the spoken words of the preacher. This belief culminates in Shepard imagining that "every creature" is a "loud preacher" to the truth of God's creation in "the stately theater of Heaven and Earth."[82] The very fact of being is both a proclamation (by a "loud preacher") and a performance (in the "stately theater") of Christianity. Thus, in this written text, a strong link is established between the spoken word, the written word and the enactment of conversion. Eliot's fascination with the living voice in textual form should not be forgotten or minimized in a study of his orthographic project.

Indeed, as the orthography developed, the sounds of Algonquian speech in the ears of European scribes had a crucial effect on the written traces which were produced. In the nineteenth century Du Ponceau observed certain assumptions linked with Eliot's phonetic orthography. By comparing Eliot's orthography of Massachusett, which is mediated through English speech, and Zeisberger's vocabulary of the Delaware dialect, which is mediated through German, Du Ponceau notes that apparent differences in Massachusett and Delaware vocabulary can in fact be traced to the phonetic register of the scribe.[83]

The transcription of the Massachusett dialect was inevitably shaped by the language of the original scribe, but this is not the only consequence of colonial transcription. Further inconsistencies emerge with variations in grammar: for example, Eliot noted that the Massachusett dialect did not have an equivalent of the substantive verb, "to be."[84] In the following century, Jonathan Edwards (Jr.) comments on the impact that the absence of this verb has on English ears. In relation to the Mohegan language, he suggests: "The circumstance that they have no verb substantive, accounts for their not using that verb, when they speak English. They say *I man, I sick, &c.*"[85]

Edwards' observation highlights certain cultural assumptions and appropriations which are directly related to the transcription of Native speech patterns. Rather than acknowledge grammatical differences, the lack of a substantive verb in the transcription of Indian voices is left unexplained in colonial texts. For example, the transcription of direct speech in *New England's First Fruits* (1643) illustrates the cultural implication of verbatim transcription. As discussed earlier, Wequash, a Pequot Indian, addresses himself in the third person as he discusses the process of his conversion: "*Wequash, no God, Wequash no know Christ.*"[86] Because he speaks in pidgin English (following Ives Goddard's use of the term) and demonstrates unusual grammatical construction, the voice might appear "uneducated" and even childlike to an English audience, and this was no doubt the point.[87] Peaceful penitent Indians were a far more powerful political tool in the promotion of the colony compared with the image of dangerous and violent Natives which characterized accounts of the Pequot war in the 1630s. This reception, however, misses a larger point: the example of Wequash shows that Algonquian speakers of English were engaging with a cross-cultural understanding of language which incorporated English vocabulary and Algonquian grammatical constructions.

Eliot never acknowledged this hybrid form and instead set about responding to this grammatical problem by importing it from the Delaware dialect. [88] This linguistic borrowing has obvious consequences for the codification of Massachusett into written text, since it creates distance between the spoken Massachusetts dialect and Eliot's orthography. Linguistic assimilation between different Algonquian dialects was provoked and quickened by the existence of the printed text, the Algonquian bible in particular. Experience Mayhew writes:

> I am obliged to tell you, That the Martha's Vineyard Indian Dialect, and that of Natick, according unto w[ch] last Mr. Eliot translated the Indian Bible, are so very much a Like, that without a very Critical Observation, you would not see y[e] difference. . . . Indeed the difference was something greater than now it is, before our Indians had vse of y[e] Bible and other Books translated by *Mr. Eliot*, but since that the most of y[e] Litle differences that were betwixt y[m], have been happily Lost, and our Indians Speak, but especially write much as those of Natick do. [89]

Bragdon and Goddard confirm this phenomenon, suggesting that Eliot's bible helped to standardize dialects in the region: "Some documents from the islands of Martha's Vineyard and Nantucket, generally those of a relatively late date, use the spelling *ohke* of Eliot's bible translation for the word 'land,' apparently replacing the earlier *ahkuh*, a spelling not found on the mainland."[90] Eliot grafts existing linguistic structures onto an Algonquian language but, as is less often observed, his aim is to maintain linguistic diversity and acknowledge the Algonquian language, in speech and text, as a language of religious and civil discourse. In response to the inter-dialectal borrowings and the unusual cultural clashing between Algonquian sounds and English grammar, and vice versa at times, Wyss correctly concludes: "Eliot fluctuates between envisioning his project as the description of an already existing language and the creation of a new one."[91]

THE EFFECTS OF TEXT

Indian Grammar was probably the first concerted effort to teach English missionaries the Massachusett dialect of Algonquian.[92] It is a peculiar text because it cannot be categorized as a cultural ethnography, like that of Wood and Williams, nor can it be characterised as a substitute preacher, as is the case with Pierson's language primer. Its motives may have been to encourage religious conversion, as the full title suggests, *The Indian Grammar Begun: or, An essay to bring the Indian language unto Rules, For the help of such as desire to learn the same, for the furtherance of the Gospel among them*, but the content is not always spiritual.[93] In the preamble to an extensive analysis of verbs, Eliot uses the actions, "I eat, sleep, piss &c"[94] to highlight the fact that not all verbs in Massachusetts can be formed or 'used' in the same way. These basic human requirements are mirrored in his attempts to elaborate on the building blocks of language: Eliot begins by categorizing the sounds of consonants and vowels ("vocals"),[95] diphthongs and double sounds,[96] and then focuses on parts of speech: pronoun, noun, verb, "adnoun" (adjective), adverb, conjunction and interjection.[97] The largest part of the text is Eliot's analysis of verbs in their various modes, which is not particularly unusual, although it does reflect his attempt to force Algonquian into a classical grammatical framework.

Particularly fascinating are the verbs used to create this framework: "to be wise," "to pay," and "to keep."[98] Wisdom, money, and ownership become the basis on which the language is transcribed and understood. While the importance and respect for wisdom can be traced in both cultures, Eliot also imposes European ideas of "payment" rather than exchange, and a clearly articulated sense of individual ownership, including the ownership of land, property, and people, onto another culture. Interestingly, when Eliot discusses the verb in its substantive passive mode with "I am kept," Noowadchanit, he suggests in a preamble that "Wadchanittuonk,"[99] the Massachusetts word for salvation, might be treated in a similar way. He does not take this analogy any further, and while there is a trace of the negative mode, "I am not kept,"[100] there is never a written trace of "I am not saved." Therefore, while the concept of individualism is promised, in the context of this text, there is no option but to be spiritually saved, since there is no written trace of I am not saved. In this instance, the printed text fixes religious and ideological motivations of the missionary-colonizer, and the printing press plays its role in the codification of language, religion, and culture for its readers, Algonquian and English. Far from objective linguistic analysis, as might be expected, Eliot's *Indian Grammar* reflects his own religious motives to a certain degree but, usually for Eliot, more clearly formalizes European notions of monetary exchange, trade, and ownership into a new language and new culture.

Through the process of transcribing speech into text, Eliot makes no apology for inscribing into that written trace the economic and social interests of the colonizer. There is no evidence to suggest that Eliot intended to address, or even understood, the ethnological relationship of language and culture, an issue that Roger Williams's *Key*, with its focus on the traditions and customs of the Narragansett tribe, engages fairly successfully. Williams concentrates on traditions such as Native practices of "Salutation," "Eating and Entertainment," "Sleep and Lodging," "Hunting," and "Death and Burial," for example.[101] Therefore, while Roger Williams takes Narragansett traditions and customs to England, Eliot transports European social and economic structures as well as religious traditions to Massachusetts.

Like most missionary-colonizers, Eliot wanted to replace Native religious, social, and political practice with a Puritan, congregational model; however, given the extent of Eliot's Indian Library, he is set apart from most other missionary-colonizers in his desire to place the written trace of Massachusett at the center of his missionary project. Quite apart from many of his contemporaries, he truly believed that tribal languages could be languages of Christianity. With this vision in mind and with the educational parameters and instructional manuals loosely in place, the physical nature of the Algonquian language book had a significant effect on native reception communities.

Key to this analysis of Eliot's orthographic methods and the consequences of transcribing an oral language into written text is an assessment of the ways in which Indian readers received these publications. Even before Algonquian texts were available, a significant amount of emphasis was placed on the book as a material object and cultural signifier. As early as 1644 Hiacoomes carried around with him a copy of an English primer[102] and while the book was probably used for its intended purpose (Hiacoomes did learn to read, after all) it was used to symbolize his close relationship with the English settlers on the Vineyard and hints at the material representation of colonial spiritual authority which books came to provide. Before the Bible was fully translated and printed in Algonquian, the indigenous people of Massachusetts Bay were already reckoning with the symbolism of books and authority.

The dream of one Indian clearly signals the power of this material object on a nonliterate culture:

> That about two yeeres before the *English* came over into those parts there was a great mortality among the *Indians*, and one night he could not sleep above half the night, after which hee fell into a dream, in which he did think he saw a great many men come to those parts in cloths, just as the *English* are now apparelled, and among them there arose a man all in black, with a thing in his hand which hee now sees was all one *English* mans book.[103]

The arrival of the Englishman's book (or the Bible) is significant in two ways. On the one hand, this story justifies the Puritan New Englander's place in the colony, since the dream allows the missionary to imagine himself as fulfilling a prophecy. On the other hand, the dream acts as a way for the Indian speaker to write himself into the history of the colony, and perhaps to define a place in its future, thus incorporating the material object, which remains mysterious but powerful, into his own narrative of cultural survival.

Over several more years and after the mysteries of this unfamiliar object, the Bible, began to be revealed to penitent Indians, one asks: "*Can one be saved by reading the book of the creature?*" A strange question by all accounts, which is partially explained by Eliot: "This question was made when I taught them, That God gave us two books, and that in the book of the creature, every creature was a word or a sentence, &c."[104] The question, then, is a spiritual one, and the use of animate, living things to describe the Bible is incredibly suggestive. Eliot adopts a descriptive register which is akin to Native spirituality, where animals often represent powerful spirits. For example, in *The Day-Breaking*, Mayhew describes the "election" of a pawwaw: an Indian falls into a "strange dreame" where the apparition of a serpent signifies the choice of pawwaw, and "for two dayes after the rest of the Indians dance and rejoyce for what they tell them about this Serpent, and so they become their Pawwaws."[105] A similar picture emerges in the dreams of another pawwaw:

> One of them did then discover the bottome of his witchcraft, confessing that at first he came to be a *Pawwaw* by Diabolical Dreames, wherein he saw the Devill in the likeness of foure living Creatures; one was like a man which he saw in the Ayre. . . . Another was like a Crow. . . . The third was like to a Pidgeon. . . . The fourth was like a Serpent, very subtile to doe mischiefe, and also to doe great cures, and these he said were meer Devills, and such as he had trusted to for saftie, and did labour to raise up for the accomplishment of any thing in his diabolicall craft but now he saith, that he did desire that the Lord would free from them, and that he did repent in his heart, because of his sinne.[106]

Mayhew encodes the dream to function as a story of good overcoming evil but, that aside, this account and the one above provide unmistakeable evidence that *creatures*, good or evil, were the physical manifestation of spiritual power. So when Eliot describes the Bible as a 'creature' he is incorporating Native processes of symbolizing spirituality in material or physical forms. In this way he mediates and negotiates a cultural understanding between two religious practices; although he would not accept the validity of tribal spirituality, he certainly appreciates the usefulness of comparative explanation and as such invites, albeit inadvertently, Native penitents to draw significant parallels between Christianity and tribal spirituality. Ultimately, he allows them to re-shape rather than reject their existing systems of belief.

CONCLUSION

Eliot's final publication and final transcription of praying Indian speech acts did not and was not meant to travel across the Atlantic. The print run was small and intended for a local audience; Eliot writes in the opening dedication that the speeches have been collected and printed "not to so much for Publishment" but because it was easier than handwriting copies "for those that did desiere them."[107] There is no evidence that any were sent to England. As already noted in chapter 3, in *The Dying Speeches of Several Indians* (1685) the oral performances of the dying speeches can be interpreted as a hybrid speech act which preserves parts of traditional cultural as well as incorporating elements of Puritan tradition.

By piecing together the gradual emergence of a community of readers and writers, it becomes possible to gauge the effect that these new skills had on native collective identity. While I have argued that Eliot's interest in the living voice is an important context for his translations, and that the written traces in the margins of the Algonquian bibles are important for the reclamation of the living voice, in the reprint of Eliot's *Indian Grammar* this process of reclaiming and recovering spoken Algonquian has taken a surprising turn. In the foreword to the *Grammar* (reprinted 2001), *Caring Hands*, Touohko-muck Silva Clan Sachem Natick Praying Indians writes:

> Many colonists were interested in understanding the native language, which prompted Eliot to pen a grammatical representation. Eliot had no written reference for this complex language other than his own Bible translation and aptly entitled this new work *Indian Grammar Begun*. Although the original text was written for English speaking non-natives, today many Algonquian Natives utilize Eliot's works for their language reaffirmation and / or spirituality. . . . Kuttabotomish to the Reverend John Eliot, whose gifts to our people have spanned over 350 years and continue to reach his beloved Praying Indians.[108]

In this final appropriation of Eliot's text, descendants of Algonquians from Massachusetts Bay learn and reclaim their language, but, according to the Foreword, they are also finding a way back to their spirituality. Although Eliot wished to separate native language and native culture, it seems that in the past and the present the written trace of Algonquian provided opportunities to resist linguistic and cultural assimilation.[109] In its most recent incarnation, Eliot's language primer is appropriated to meet the political and cultural needs of present-day Natick descendants.

NOTES

1. The original letter is held in the Guildhall Library in London: "From 16 Indians at Natick, Massachusetts, to the Rev John Eliot, 19th March 1683," *New England Company Archives*, Guildhall Library, London, ms. 07957.
2. See David Cressy, *Literacy and the Social Order: Reading and Writing in Tudor and Stuart England* (Cambridge: Cambridge University Press, 1980).
3. *Records of the Plymouth Colony, Acts of the Commissioners of the United Colonies of New England, 1643–1651 and 1653–1678-9*, ed. David Pulsifer, vol. 2 (New York: AMS Press, 1968) (hereafter cited as *RPC1* and *RPC2*); "An Envoyce of such goods . . . for the Indians by the Corporation," September 1654, *RPC2*, 133; "Accounts for the Indians in New England; is

debt; since the last account dated at Boston the 19th of September 1657," September 1658, *RCP2*, 205; "Letter from Thomas Mayhew to the Commissioners of the United Colonies, 24:6:78," *RPC2*, Appendix, 404–6.

4. Matthew Mayhew, *A Brief Narrative of the Success which the Gospel hath had, among the Indians of Martha's Vineyard (and Places Adjacent) in New-England* (Boston, 1694) 35.

5. "September, 1644," *RPC1*, 30.

6. "Letter of Pessicus and Collounicas, Naheganset May 24th 1644," *RPC1*, Appendix, 416.

7. "September 7th, 1664, Appendix," *RPC1*, 449.

8. "July 5, 1851," *New England Historical and Genealogical Register*, 358.

9. *Massachusetts Archive Collection*, Massachusetts Archive, Boston, 68:193, quoted by Hilary E. Wyss, *Writing Indians: Literacy, Christianity, and Native Community in Early America* (Amherst: University of Massachusetts Press, 2000), 39.

10. John Eliot, *Indian Dialogues: A Study in Cultural Interaction* (Cambridge, MA: Printed by M. Johnson, 1671), rpt. ed. Henry W. Bowden and James P. Ronda, vol. 88 (Westport, CT: Greenwood Press, 1980), 134.

11. David Cressy, *Literacy and the Social Order: Reading and Writing in Tudor and Stuart England* (Cambridge: Cambridge University Press, 1980); Kenneth A. Lockridge, *Literacy in Colonial New England: An Enquiry into the Social Context of Literacy in the Early Modern West* (New York: W. W. Norton & Co., 1974); E. Jennifer Monaghan, *Learning to Read and Write in Colonial America* (Amherst and Boston: University of Massachusetts Press, 2005); E. Jennifer Monaghan, "Literacy Instruction and Gender in Colonial New England," *American Quarterly* 40, no. 1 (1988): 18–41; Margaret Spufford, *Small Books and Pleasant Histories* (Cambridge: Cambridge University Press, 1985).

12. Lockridge, *Literacy in Colonial New England*, 7; Cressy, *Literacy and the Social Order*, 42.

13. David Cressy, *Coming Over: Migration and Communication Between England and New England in the Seventeenth Century* (Cambridge: Cambridge University Press, 1995), 213–34.

14. Monaghan, *Learning to Read and Write in Colonial America*, 18–19.

15. Wyss, *Writing Indians*, 60.

16. *New England's First Fruits*. (London: Printed by R. O. and G. D. for Henry Overton, 1643), rpt. in *The Eliot Tracts: With Letters from John Eliot to Thomas Thorowgood and Richard Baxter*, ed. Micheal P. Clark (London and Westport, CT: Praeger, 2003), 59.

17. Thomas Shepard, *The Day-Breaking if not The Sun-Rising of the Gospel, With the Indians in New England* (1647), rpt. in *The Eliot Tracts: With Letters from John Eliot to Thomas Thorowgood and Richard Baxter*, ed. Micheal P. Clark (London and Westport, CT: Praeger, 2003), 83.

18. "Mr Wiliam Steele President of the Corporation for Propagating the Gospell in New England," Hartford, September 28, 1650, *RPC1*, 192–95; Response from the Commissioners of the United Colonies, Newhaven, September 10, 1651, *RPC1*, 195–96.

19. William Wallace Tooker, *John Eliot's First Indian Teacher and Interpreter, Cockenoe-de-Long Island and the Story of His Career from the Early Records* (New York: Francis P. Harper, 1896).

20. For a discussion on the role of the translator, *see also* Richard W. Cogley, *John Eliot's Mission to the Indian Before King Philip's War* (Cambridge, MA: Harvard University Press, 1999); Stephen Andrew Guice, "The Linguistic Work of John Eliot." PhD diss., University of Michigan, 1990 ATT9117819; David Murray, *Forked Tongues: Speech, Writing and Representation in North American Indian Texts* (Bloomington: Indiana University Press, 1991); Wyss, *Writing Indians*.

21. Norman Earl Tanis, "Education in John Eliot's Indian Utopias 1646-1675." *History of Education Quarterly* 10, no. 3 (Autumn 1970): 321.

22. Shepard, *Day-Breaking*, 83.

23. Ibid.

24. "September, 1653," *RPC2*, 105.

25. "September 1657," *RPC2*, 189.

26. For an analysis of gender and literary in England and colonial New England, see E. Jennifer Monaghan, *Learning to Read and Write in Colonial America*, American Antiquarian Society (Amherst and Boston: University of Massachusetts Press, 2005).

27. "September 1657," *RPC2*, 182.

28. Ibid., 190.

29. Samuel Eliot Morison, *Harvard College in the Seventeenth Century* (Cambridge, MA: Harvard University Press, 1936), 1:353.

30. Ibid., 1:356–57. Morison offers an account of the lives, patronage and education, as far as can be known, of the Indian scholars, and also accounts for their premature deaths, which occurred all too often. (Morison, *The Founding of Harvard College* [Cambridge, MA: Harvard University Press, 1935], 352–59). John Sassamon was Harvard's first Indian student, and his untimely death was used by the English to precipitate what became known as King Philip's War. Jill Lepore discusses the precarious position Sassamon experiences as a literate Indian in, Jill Lepore's "Dead Men Tell No Tales: John Sassamon and the Fatal Consequences of Literacy," *American Quarterly* 46, no. 4 (December 1994): 479–512.

31. Wolfgang Hochbruck and Beatrix Dudensing-Reichel,"'Honoratissimi Benefactors': Native American Students and Two Seventeenth Century Texts in the University Tradition," in *Early Native American Writing: New Critical Essays*, ed. Helen Jaskowski (Cambridge: Cambridge University Press, 1996), 5-6.

32. Ibid., 5.

33. Ibid., 5, 10–12.

34. *New England's First Fruits*, 59.

35. Edward Winslow, *The Glorious Progress of the Gospel* (London: Printed for Hannah Allen, 1649), rpt. in *The Eliot Tracts: With Letters from John Eliot to Thomas Thorowgood and Richard Baxter*, ed. Michael P. Clark (London and Westport, CT: Paeger, 2001), 58.

36. Henry Whitfield, *The Light Appearing More and More Towards the Perfect Day* (London: J. Bartlet, 1651), rpt. in *The Eliot Tracts: With Letters from John Eliot to Thomas Thorowgood and Richard Baxter*, ed. Michael P. Clark (London and Westport, CT: Paeger, 2003), 187.

37. Henry Whitfield, *Strength out of Weaknesse, Or, A Glorious Manifestation of the Further Progresse of the Gospel among Indians in New England* (London: Printed by M. Simmons for John Blague and Samuel Howes, 1652), rpt. in *The Eliot Tracts: With Letters from John Eliot to Thomas Thorowgood and Richard Baxter*, ed. Michael P. Clark (London and Westport, CT: Paeger, 2003), 241.

38. Whitfield, *Strength out of Weakness*, 225.

39. John Eliot and Thomas Mayhew Jr , *Tears of Repentance, Or, A further Narrative of the Progress of the Gospel Amongst the Indians in New-England* (London: Peter Cole, 1653), rpt. in *The Eliot Tracts: With Letters from John Eliot to Thomas Thorowgood and Richard Baxter*, ed. Michael P. Clark (London and Westport, CT: Paeger, 2003), 277.

40. Whitfield, *Strength out of Weakness*, 233.

41. Whitfield, *Light Appearing*, 206.

42. See also the evidence collected in *Native Writings in Massachusett*, ed. Kathleen J. Bragdon and Ives Goddard, 2 vols. (Philadelphia: American Philosophical Society, 1988).

43. After King Philip's War and after the removal of captured Indians to Deer Island, Eliot wrote: "When the Indians were hurried away to an Iland at half an hours warning, pore souls in terror yei left their goods, books, bibles, only some few caryed yr bibles, the rest were spoyled & lost. So yt wn the wares wr finished, & yei returned to yr places yei wr greatly impov'ished, but yei especially bewailed yr want of Bibles, ys made me meditate upon a 2d imprssion of or Bible, & accordingly tooke pains to revise the first edition." (*Roxbury Church Records* (Boston, 1881) 196), in James Constantine Pillings, *Bibliography of the Algonquian Languages* (Washington, DC: Government Printing Office, 1891), 154.

44. Morison, *Harvard College in the Seventeenth Century*, 151.

45. Morison notes that Harvard students also wrote on random pages in their own books, but the argument that they differ substantially from Algonquian readers remains, since individual ownership was not in question (Ibid.).

46. Bragdon and Goddard, *Native Writings in Massachusett*, 1:391 and 1:405.

47. Wilberforce Eames has recorded a list of owners in his contribution to Pillings' *Bibliography* (Pillings, *Bibliography*, 126–85). This specific Bible is designated no. 45 by Eames (Pillings, *Bibliography*, 165–66).

48. Bragdon and Goddard, *Native Writings in Massachusett*, 1:443.

49. This Bible is designated "Eames no. 16" (Pillings, *Bibliography*, 160).

50. Bragdon and Goddard, *Native Writings in Massachusett*, 1:377.

51. Hilary Wyss suggests that this might be written by Thomas himself. While there is no way of verifying this either way, it is just as likely to be written by someone else. Wyss, *Writing Indians*, 2.

52. Privately owned, "Eames no. 47" (Pillings, *Bibliography*, 166).

53. Bragdon and Goddard, *Native Writings in Massachusett*, 1:461.

54. Ibid., 1:459.

55. James Axtell, "The Power of Print in the Eastern Woodlands," *William and Mary Quarterly* 44, no. 2 (April 1987): 300–9.

56. For this understanding of the properties of the living voice that Eliot tries to incorporate, I am indebted to Sandra Gustafson's explanation, which I have referred to in chap. 3. Sandra M. Gustafson, *Eloquence is Power: Oratory and Performance in Early America* (London and Chapel Hill: Published for the Omohundro Institute of Early American History and Culture, Williamsburg, Virginia, by the University of North Carolina Press, 2000), xvi.

57. William H. Sherman, *Used Books: Marking Readers in Renaissance England* (Philadelphia: University of Pennsylvania Press, 2008), xiii.

58. Ibid., 72.

59. Ibid., 76.

60. Ibid.

61. William Kellaway uses this term, Indian Library, in his overview of the financing and printing of Eliot's translations, see William Kellaway, *The New England Company 1649–1776: Missionary Society to the American Indians* (Westport, CT: Greenwood Press, 1975). John Eliot's Algonquian language texts include: *A Christian Covenanting Confession* (Cambridge, Massachusetts, 1660); trans. *Mamvsse Wunneetupanatamwe Up-Biblum God. (The Holy Bible containing the Old Testament and the New)* (Cambridge, 1663); trans. *Mamvsse Wunneetupanatamwe Up-Biblum God*; (*The Holy Bible containing the Old Testament and the New*) rev. ed. (Cambridge, 1685); *Nehtuhpeh peisses ut mayut, A Primer in the Language of the Algonquian Indians* (Cambridge, 1684); *The Indian Grammar Begun*, 1666. (Bedford, MA: Applewood Books, 2001); *The Logic Primer* (Cambridge, MA: Maramaduke Johnson, 1672) rpt. (Cleveland, OH: Burrows Brothers Company, 1904) trans. *The Psalter*. 1658. Appended to *Mamvsse Wunneetupanatamwe Up-Biblum God* (Cambridge, 1685); trans. *Wusku Wuttestamentum Nullordumun Jesus Christ.* (New Testament) (Cambridge, 1661); *The Book of Genesis* (1655). Non-extant texts: Psalms (1658), and Matthew (1655).

62. John Eliot, *Primer and Catechism* (Cambridge, 1654). No longer extant.

63. John Eliot, *The Indian Primer* (Cambridge, Massachusetts, 1669), n.p.

64. *See The First Book of Moses called Genesis*, trans. John Eliot (Cambridge, 1655).

65. *The Gospel of Matthew* Trans. John Eliot (Cambridge, 1655) No longer extant.

66. *The Psalter*, trans. John Eliot (Cambridge, 1658). Only copies attached to editions of the Algonquian bible are extant. This was Eliot's second attempt to translate the Psalms. Eliot, along with Richard Mather and Thomas Weld together authored *The Bay Psalm Book* (Cambridge, MA: n.p., 1640), which was a translation of the Psalms from Hebrew to English. As coauthor of *The Bay Psalm Book*, Eliot can be credited, in part, with the authorship of the first published book in New England. Also, his bible was the first bible to be published in North America.

67. Kathleen J. Bragdon comments: "John Eliot's description of Massachusett, particularly in his *Indian Grammar Begun*, first printed in 1666, was a remarkably sophisticated study for its time. His analysis, based on work with skilled native bilinguals, approaches modern standards of language descriptions. He proceeded with the assumption that Massachusett, the language of 'these Sons of our Morning,' was in fact capable of being described according to a limited number of rules, as were the classical languages that formed the basis of his own education." Kathleen J. Bragdon, "Native Languages as Spoken and Written: Views from

Southern New England," in *The Language Encounter in the Americas, 1492-1800: A Collection of Essays*, ed. Edward G. Gray and Norman Fiering (Oxford and New York: Berghahn Books, 2000), 176–77.

68. Bragdon, "Native Languages as Spoken and Written," 175.

69. Roger Williams, *A Key to the Language of America* (London: Printed by Gregory Dexter, 1643) rpt. in *Publications of the Narragansett Club*, vol. 1 (Providence, RI: Providence Press Co., Printers, 1866), 141.

70. Ibid., Dedicatory Epistle, n.p.

71. In addition to Eliot's extensive Indian Library, see also Roger Williams, *A Key to the Language of America*, 1643; Abraham Pierson, *Some Helps for the Indians*, 1658. *Connecticut Historical Society Collections*, vol. 3 (Hartford: Published for the Society, 1895). Later texts of this nature include: Josiah Cotton, "Vocabulary of the Massachusetts (Or Natick) Indian Language, 1707–1708," in *Massachusetts Historical Society Collections*, 3rd. ser., vol. 2 (Cambridge, MA: E. W. Metcalf and Company, 1830); and Jonathan Edwards, *Observations on the Language of the Muhhekaneew Indians* (New-Haven, CT: Josiah Meigs, 1738, rpt. London: W. Justins, 1783).

72. Thomas Thorowgood, *Jews in America, Or, Probabilities* . . . (London: H. Brome, 1660), American Culture Series, microform, 6:62. For a survey of Native American orthographies, which include orthographies which use Roman and Russian alphabets, as well as symbolic systems created by indigenous scholars, *see* Willard Walker, "Native American Writing Systems," in *Languages of the USA*, ed. Charles A. Ferguson and Shirley Brice Heath (Cambridge: Cambridge University Press, 1981).

73. Gustafson, *Eloquence is Power*, xvi.

74. John Eliot, *A Further Accompt of the Progress of the Gospel Amongst the Indians in New-England* (London: Printed by M. Simons, 1659), rpt. in *The Eliot Tracts: With Letters from John Eliot to Thomas Thorowgood and Richard Baxter*, ed. Michael P. Clark (London and Westport, CT: Paeger, 2003), 332.

75. John Eliot, *The Dying Speeches of Several Indians* (Cambridge, MA: Printed for Samuel Green?, c. 1685), in Early American Imprints, 1st ser., Evans 1639–1800, microform, 1. Also available in a digitized version in *Readex, Archive of Americana*, www.newsbank.com/readex/.

76. George Parker Winship, *The Cambridge Press: 1638–1692. A Reexamination of the Evidence concerning the Bay Psalm Book and the Eliot Indian Bible.* (Philadelphia: University of Pennsylvania Press, 1945), 243.

77. Gustafson, *Eloquence is Power*, xvi.

78. Neal Salisbury, "Red Puritans: 'The Praying Indians' of Massachusetts Bay and John Eliot," *William and Mary Quarterly* 31, no. 1 (January 1974): 27–54, 44.

79. Lewis Bayly, *The Practice of Piety* (Cambridge: Printed for Samuel Green and Marmaduke Johnson, 1665, rpt. 1685), 1.

80. Revelation 21:8, "But for the fearful, and unbelieving, and abominable, and murderers, and fornicators, and sorcerers, and idolaters, and all liars, their part *shall be* in the lake that burneth with fire and brimstone; which is the second death."

81. Thomas Shepard, *The Sincere Convert: Discovering The Small Number of True Beleevers, And The Great Difficulty of Saving Conversion*, 1640. 5th edition. Corrected and amended (London: 1650), 93–95.

82. Shepard, *The Sincere Convert*, 3–4.

83. "Our author (Eliot) has, of course, made use of the *English* letters to express the sounds of the *Massachusetts* language; in consequence of which, it is sometimes difficult to recognize even the same words differently spelt by Zeisberger in the *Delaware*. Thus the latter writes *n'dee*, (*my heart*) which is to be pronounced as if spelt *n'day*, according to the powers of the *English* alphabet. Eliot, on the contrary, writes it *nuttah*. This makes it appear a different word, in which we scarcely perceive an analogy with the former. By the first syllable, *nut*, he means to express the sounds, which the *German* represents by *n'd* (perhaps *n't*, for the reason above suggested), the short *u* standing for the interval, or sheva, between the two consonants; which Zeisberger more elegantly represents by an apostrophe. The last syllable, *tah*, is the German *dee* or *tee*, (English *day* or *tay*,) the *a* being pronounced acute, as in *grace, face*. If our author had selected the dipthong (sic) *ay* to express this sound, and reserved the *a* to represent its

broad pronunciation in *far*, *car*, the student would have been much better able to perceive the analogy between the Massachusetts and its cognate idioms." Peter S. Du Ponceau, "Notes and Observations on Eliot's *Indian Grammar*. Addressed to John Pickering, Esq," *Collections of the Massachusetts Historical Society*, 2nd ser., vol. 9 (Boston: Steam Power Press Office, 1832), xi-xii.

84. For a concise discussion of Eliot verbs and verb formations, see Guice, "Linguistic Work of John Eliot," ATT9117819, chap. 6.

85. Edwards, *Observations on the Language*, 13.

86. *New England's First Fruits*, 62.

87. Ives Goddard further demonstrates this argument when she demonstrates unusual grammatical construction and omission of the substantive verb in her transcription of American Indian Pidgin English as it appears in Sarah Kemble Knight's *Journal*, 1704: "Noteworthy is the double use in 'all one speake, all one heart,' presumably meaning *the way he speaks is the way he feels*, with the syntax of 'like father, like son.'" Ives Goddard, "Some Early Examples of American Indian Pidgin English from New England," *International Journal of American Linguistics* 43, no. 1 (January 1977): 37–41, 38.

88. "I have only to add a remark respecting the verb *nutapip*, which, as Judge Davis observes, (in the Postscript to his letter), is used for *I am*, in Eliot's bible: '*Before Abraham was*, I AM-*Negonne onk Abrahamwi nutapip*. John viii. 58.' At the time when Judge Davis wrote to me, I could not explain the meaning of *nutapip*; but I am now able to do it. *N'dappin* is a Delaware verb, which signifies *to be* (in a particular *place*) *stare*; the preterite is *n'dappineep*, stabam, hic stabam. There can be no doubt but Eliot's *nutapip*, that is to say, *n'tapip* or *n'dapip*, is a contraction of the Delaware *n'dappineep*, and means, *I was there*." Du Ponceau, *Notes and Observations*, xxix.

89. Experience Mayhew, "To Paul Dudley, 20 March 1721–1722," in *Observations on the Indian Language* (Boston: Press of D. Clapp & Sons, 1884), 5.

90. Bragdon and Goddard, *Native Writings in Massachusett*, 19.

91. Wyss, *Writing Indians*, 23.

92. In a letter to Robert Boyle, which become a dedicatory epistle to the publication, Eliot states that he: "(complied) *a Grammar of this language, for the help of others who have an heart to study and learn the same, for the sake of Christ, and of the poor Souls of these Ruines of Mankinde* . . . ." Eliot, *The Indian Grammar Begun* (2001), A2.

93. Hillary Wyss comments that the full title of *Indian Grammar* shows that, "Eliot emphasized literacy as the core of true conversion" (Wyss, *Writing Indians*, 22).

94. Eliot, *Indian Grammar Begun*, 19.

95. Ibid., 2.

96. Ibid.

97. Ibid., 5–23.

98. Ibid., 24, 28, 17.

99. Ibid., 60.

100. Ibid., 62.

101. Williams, *A Key to the Language of America*. For recent analysis of Williams' language texts, see David Murray, "Using Roger Williams' *Key* into America," *Symbiosis: A Journal of Anglo-American Literary Relations* 1, no. 2 (October 1997): 237–53; Ivy Schweitzer, *The Work of Self-Representation: Lyric Poetry in Colonial New England* (Chapel Hill: University of North Carolina Press, 1991). For a comparison between Eliot's *Grammar* and Williams' *Key*, see Alison Stanley, "'To Speak With Other Tongues': Linguistics, Colonialism and Identity in 17th Century New England," *Comparative American Studies*, 7, no. 1 (2009): 1–17; Susan Castillo, *Colonial Encounters in New World Writing 1500–1776: Performing America* (London and New York: Routledge, 2006), esp. chap. 2.

102. Whitfield, *Light Appearing*, 177.

103. Shepard, *Clear Sun-shine*, 119.

104. Whitfield, *Light Appearing*, 193.

105. Shepard, *Day-Breaking*, 97

106. Whitfield, *Strength out of Weakness*, 239.

107. Eliot, *Dying Speeches*, n.p.

108. "Foreword" by Caring Hands, Touohkomuck Silva Clan, Sachem Natick Praying Indians. (Eliot, *Indian Grammar Begun*, 2001. n.p.)

109. Testament to this is a website created by Natick Praying Indians: "A. Richard (Dick) and Jill Miller of Natick are creating this Web page with help from a lot of friends, including the Natick Praying Indians under Caring Hands, their Clan Mother. We are delighted to find this small tribe of Native Americans still practicing the blend of Puritan and traditional teachings that their forefathers and John Eliot evolved 350 years ago!" 1651–2001 350th Anniversary of Natick, Massachusetts and the Natick Praying Indians. September 29, 2003, online at www.millermicro.com/natprayind.html (accessed March 28, 2013).

Bibliography

"An Act for the promoting and propagating the Gospel of Jesus Christ in New England, July 27, 1649." In *Acts and Ordinances of the Interregnum, 1642–1660*, edited by C. H. Firth and R. S. Raits, vol. 2, 197–300. London: Wyman and Sons, 1911.

Allen, Paula Gunn. *The Sacred Hoop: Recovering the Feminine in American Indian Traditions.* Boston: Beacon Press, 1986.

Alsop, George. *A Character of the Province of Maryland.* London: Printed by T. J. for Peter Dring, 1666. Reprinted in *Narratives of Early Maryland, 1633–1684*, ed. Clayton Colman Hall. New York: Charles Scribner's Sons, 1910.

Anderson, Virginia DeJohn. *New England's Generation: The Great Migration and the Formation of Society and Culture in the Seventeenth Century.* Cambridge: Cambridge University Press, 1991.

Arch, Stephen Carl. *Authorizing the Past: The Rhetoric of History in Seventeenth-Century New England.* Dekalb: Northern Illinois University Press, 1994.

Armitage, David, and Michael J. Braddick, eds. *The British Atlantic World 1500–1800.* New York: Palgrave MacMillan, 2002.

Armstrong, Catherine. *Writing North America in the Seventeenth Century: English Representations in Print and Manuscript.* Aldershot: Ashgate, 2007.

Aspinwall, William. *A Brief Description of the Fifth Monarchy, Or, Kingdom.* London: Printed by M. Simmons and are to be sold by Livewell Chapman, 1653.

Austin, J. L. *How To Do Things With Words.* 2nd ed. Edited by J. O. Urmson and Marina Sbisà. Oxford: Clarendon Press, 1975.

Axtell, James. *The Invasion Within: The Contest of Cultures in Colonial North America.* New York: Oxford University Press, 1985.

———. "The Power of Print in the Eastern Woodlands." *William and Mary Quarterly* 44, no. 2 (April 1987): 300–9.

Bachelard, Gaston. *The Poetics of Space.* Translated by Maria Jolas, with foreword by John R. Stilgoe. Boston: Beacon Press, 1994.

Bailyn, Bernard. *Atlantic History: Concepts and Contours.* Cambridge, MA: Harvard University Press, 2005.

Bailyn, Bernard, and Patricia L Denault, eds. *Soundings in Atlantic History: Latent Structures and Intellectual Currents, 1500–1830.* Cambridge, MA: Harvard University Press, 2009.

Basso, Keith H. *Wisdom Sits in Places: Landscape and Language among the Western Apache.* Albuquerque: University of New Mexico Press, 1996.

Baxter, Richard. *A Call to the Unconverted.* Translated into the Indian Language by John Eliot. Cambridge, MA: Printed for Samuel Green and Marmaduke Johnson, 1664. Reprint 2nd ed., 1688.

————. *A Holy Commonwealth.* Edited by William Lamont. Cambridge Texts in the History of Political Thought. Cambridge: Cambridge University Press, 1994.

Bayly, Lewis. *The Practice of Piety.* Translated into the Indian Language by John Eliot. Cambridge, MA: Printed for Samuel Green and Marmaduke Johnson, 1665. Reprinted 1685.

Bell, Colin, and Howard Newby, eds. *Community Studies: An Introduction to the Sociology of the Local Community.* London: George Allen and Unwin, 1971.

Bellin, Joshua David. "Apostle of Removal: John Eliot in the Nineteenth Century." *New England Quarterly* 69, no. 1 (March 1996): 3–32.

————. "John Eliot's Playing Indian." *Early American Literature* 42, no. 1 (2007): 1–30.

Benjamin, Thomas. *The Atlantic World: Europeans, Africans, Indians and Their Shared History.* New York: Cambridge University Press 2009.

Bercovitch, Sacvan. *The American Jeremiad.* Madison: University of Wisconsin Press, 1978.

————. *Horologicals to Chronometricals: The Rhetoric of the Jeremiad.* Edited by Eric Rothstein. 3rd ed. Madison: University of Wisconsin Press, 1970.

————. "Typology in Puritan New England: The Williams-Cotton Controversy Reassessed." *American Quarterly* 19, no. 2 (Summer 1967): 166–91.

————, ed. *Typology and Early American Literature.* Amherst: University of Massachusetts Press, 1972.

Bigge, Richard. "Richard Bigge's letter to William Cooke, treasurer for the County of Wiltshire, 21 May 1653," Bodleian, Ms.Rawlinson C934, f72.

Bozeman, Theodore Dwight. "John Eliot and the Civil Part of the Kingdom of Christ." In *To Live Ancient Lives: The Primitivist Dimension in Puritanism,* by Theodore Dwight Bozeman, 263–86. Chapel Hill: University of North Carolina Press, 1988.

————. *To Live Ancient Lives: The Primitivist Dimension in Puritanism.* Chapel Hill: University of North Carolina Press, 1998.

————. "The Puritans' 'Errand into the Wilderness' Reconsidered." *New England Quarterly* 59, no. 2 (June 1986): 231–51.

Bragdon, Kathleen J. "Linguistic Acculturation in Massachusett: 1663–1771." In *Papers of the Twelfth Algonquian Conference,* edited by William Cowan, 121–32. Ottawa: Carleton University Press, 1981.

————. "Native Languages as Spoken and Written: Views from Southern New England." In *The Language Encounter in the Americas, 1492–1800: A Collection of Essays. Eds. and Norman Fiering,* edited by Edward G. Gray and Norman Fiering, 173–88. Oxford and New York: Berghahn Books, 2000.

————. *Native People of Southern New England, 1500–1650.* London and Norman: University of Oklahoma Press, 1996.

Bragdon, Kathleen J., and Ives Goddard. *Native Writings in Massachusett.* 2 vols. Philadelphia: American Philosophical Society, 1988.

Brooks, Geraldine. *Caleb's Crossing.* London: Harper Collins Publishing, 2011.

Brooks, Lisa. *The Common Pot: The Recovery of Native Space in the Northeast.* Minneapolis: University of Minnesota Press, 2008.

Bross, Kristina. *Dry Bones and Indian Sermons: Praying Indians in Colonial America.* London and Ithaca, NY: Cornell University Press, 2004.

————. "Dying Saints, Vanishing Savages: 'Dying Indian Speeches' in Colonial New England Literature." *Early American Literature* 36, no. 3 (2001): 325–52.

Brown, Kathleen M. "The Anglo-Algonquian Gender Frontier." In *American Indians,* edited by Nancy Shoemaker, 48–62. Blackwell Readers in American and Social Cultural History Series 2. Oxford and Malden, MA: Blackwell, 2001.

Bumas, E. Shaskan. "The Cannibal Butcher Shop: Protestant Uses of las Casas's *Brevisima Relacion* in Europe and the American Colonies." *Early American Literature* 35, no. 2 (2000): 107–36.

Bush, Martha P. *John Eliot, the Apostle to the American Indians.* Philadelphia: American Sunday School Union, ca. 1820–1824.

Butler, Judith. *Excitable Speech: A Politics of the Performative.* New York: Routledge, 1997.

Caldwell, Patricia. *Puritan Conversion Narrative: The Beginnings of American Expression.* Cambridge: Cambridge University Press, 1983.

Calhoun, C. J. "Community: Toward a Variable Conceptualization for Comparative Research." *Social History* 5, no. 1 (1980): 105–29.

"The Cambridge Synod and Platform 1646–1648," *The Creeds and Platforms of Congregationalism*, ed. Williston Walker, 157–237. New York: Charles Scribner's Sons, 1893. *Internet Archive*, http://archive.org (accessed April 4, 2013).

Capp, B. S. *The Fifth Monarchy Men: A Study in Seventeenth-Century English Millenarianism.* London: Faber, 1972.

Caring Hands, Touohkomuck Silva Clan, Sachem Natick Praying Indians. "Foreword." In, *The Indian Grammar Begun.* N.p., Cambridge, MA: Johnson, 1666. Reprint Bedford, MA: Applewood Books, 2001.

Castillo, Susan. *Colonial Encounters in New World Writing 1500–1776: Performing America.* London and New York: Routledge, 2006.

Castillo, Susan, and Ivy Schweitzer. *The Literatures of Colonial America.* Oxford and Malden, MA: Blackwell, 2001.

Certeau, Michel de. *Heterologies: Discourse on the Other.* Minneapolis: University of Minnesota Press, 1986.

———. *The Practice of Everyday Life.* Translated by Steven F. Rendall. Berkeley: University of California Press, 1984.

Cesarini, J. Patrick. "Sources and Interpretations: John Eliot's 'A History of the Mashepog Indians' 1666." *William and Mary Quarterly* 65, no. 1 (2008): 101–35.

"The Charter of Massachusetts Bay." *The Avalon Project at the Yale School of Law.* 1629. http://avalon.law.yale.edu/17th_century/mass03.asp (accessed March 23, 2013).

Chartier, Roger, Alain Borneau, and Cécile Dauphin. *Correspondence: Models of Letter-Writing from the Middle Ages to the Nineteenth Century.* Translated by Christopher Woodall. Oxford: Polity Press, 1997.

Church, Benjamin. "Entertaining Passages Relating to King Philip's War, 1716." In *The Literatures of Colonial America: An Anthology*, edited by Susan Castillo and Ivy Schweitzer, 299–307. Oxford and Malden, MA: Blackwell Publisher, 2001.

Clark, Michael P. ed. *The Eliot Tracts: With Letters from John Eliot to Thomas Thorowgood and Richard Baxter.* Contributions in American History Series. London and Westport, CT: Paeger, 2003.

Clarke, John. *Ill Newes from New-England, Or, A Narrative of New-England's persecution . . . .* London: Printed by Henry Hills, 1652.

Cogley, Richard W. *John Eliot's Mission to the Indian Before King Philip's War.* Cambridge, MA: Harvard University Press, 1999.

Company for Propagation of the Gospel in New England and the Parts Adjacent in America, London, Experience Mayhew, and John W. Ford. In *Some Correspondence between the Governors and Treasurer of the New England Company in London and the Commissioners of the United Colonies in America the missionaries of the colony and others between 1657–1712.* London: E. Stock, 1897.

Cotton, John. "The Bloudy Tenent, Washed, and Made White in the Bloud of the Lambe." London: Printed by Matthew Symons for Hannah Allen, 1647. Early English Books 1641–1700 Series, microform, 136:14.

———. "Gods Promise to his Plantations: As it was Delivered in a Sermon." London: Printed by William Jones for John Bellamy, 1630. Early English Books 1475–1640 Series*;* microform, 1421:5.

———. "A Reply to Mr. Williams His Examination: The Bloudy Tenent, Washed, and Made White in the Bloud of the Lambe, London: Printed by Matthew Symons for Hannah Allen, 1647." Early English Books 1641–1700 Series, microform, 136:14.

———. "A Sermon Delivered at Salem, 1636." In *John Cotton on the Churches of New England*, edited by Larzer Ziff. Cambridge, MA: Belknap Press or Harvard University Press, 1968.

Cotton, Josiah. "Vocabulary of the Massachusetts (Or Natick) Indian Language, 1707–1708." In *Massachusetts Historical Society Collections.* 3rd. ser., vol. 2. Cambridge, MA: E. W. Metcalf and Company, 1830.

Cox, Virginia. *The Renaissance Dialogue: Literary Dialogue in its Social and Political Contexts, Castiglione to Galileo.* Cambridge: Cambridge University Press, 1992.

Cressy, David. *Coming Over: Migration and Communication Between England and New England in the Seventeenth Century.* Cambridge: Cambridge University Press, 1995.

———. *Literacy and the Social Order: Reading and Writing in Tudor and Stuart England.* Cambridge: Cambridge University Press, 1980.

Cronon, William. *Changes in the Land: Indians, Colonists, and the Ecology of New England.* New York: Hill and Wang, 1983.

Danforth, John. *" A Poem," Kneeling to God, At Parting with Friends.* Boston: Printed by B. Green and J. Allin, 1697.

Danforth, Samuel. "Errand into the Wilderness, 1670." In *American Sermons: The Pilgrims to Martin Luther King Jr.*, edited by Michael Warner, 151–71. New York: Library of America, 1999.

Davis, Thomas M. "The Traditions of Puritan Typology." In *Typology and Early American Literature*, edited by Sacvan Bercovitch, 11–45. Amherst: University of Massachusetts Press, 1972.

Dearborn, Henry A. S. *A Sketch of the Life of the Apostle Eliot, Prefatory to a Subscription for Erecting a Monument to His Memory.* Roxbury: Norfolk County Journal Press, 1850.

Decker, William Merrill. *Epistolary Practices: Letter Writing in America before Telecommunications.* London and Chapel Hill: University of North Carolina Press, 1998.

Deloria, Vine. *God Is Red: A Native View of Religion.* 2nd ed. Golden, CO: North American Press, 1994.

Derrida, Jacques. "Signature, Event, Context." In *Limited Inc.*, 1–23. Evanston, IL: Northwestern University Press, 1988. Reprint 1997.

"Documents of the Society for Promoting and Propagating the Gospel in New England." *New England Genealogical and Historical Register* 36 (1882) 371–76.

Du Ponceau, Peter S. "Notes and Observations on Eliot's Indian Grammar. Addressed to John Pickering, Esq." *Collections of the Massachusetts Historical Society*, 2nd ser., vol. 9. Boston: Steam Power Press Office, 1832.

Eames, Wilberforce. *The Discovery of a Lost Cambridge Imprint: John Eliot's Genesis, 1655.* Boston: Merrymount Press, 1937.

———, ed. *John Eliot and the Indians 1652–1657: Being Letters addressed to Rev. Jonathan Hanmer of Barnstaple, England.* Edited by Wiberforce Eames. New York: Adams and Grace Press, 1915.

Edwards, Jonathan. *Observations on the Language of the Muhhekaneew Indians.* New Haven, CT: Josiah Meigs, 1788. Reprint London: W. Justins, 1789.

Eliot, John. "An Account of Indian Churches in New England, in a letter written A.D. 1673." In *Massachusetts Historical Society Collections.* 1st ser., vol. 10, 124–34. Boston: Munroe, Francis and Partner, 1809. Reprint T. R. Marvin, 1857.

———. *A Brief Answer to a Small Book written by John Norcot, Against Infant Baptism.* Boston: John Foster, 1679.

———. *A Brief Narrative of the Progress of the Gospel amongst the Indians in New England.* London: Printed for John Allen, 1671. Reprinted in *The Eliot Tracts: With Letters from John Eliot to Thomas Thorowgood and Richard Baxter*, edited by Michael P. Clark, 397–407. London and Westport, CT: Paeger, 2003.

———. *The Christian Commonwealth, Or, The Civil Policy of the Rising Kingdom of Jesus Christ.* London: Printed for Livewell Chapman, 1659. In *Massachusetts Historical Society Collections*, 3rd ser., vols. 9–10, 127–164. Boston: Charles C. Little and James Bown, 1846–1849.

———. *Christiane oonoowae sampoowaonk = A Christian Covenanting Confession.* Cambridge, MA: sn. ca. 1670. http://opac.newsbank.com/select/evans/147 (accessed March 24, 2013).

———. *Communion of Churches, Or, The Divine Management of Gospel-Churches. . . .* Cambridge, MA: Printed by Marmaduke Johnson, 1665. *Early English Books Online* at http://eebo.chadwyck.com/home (accessed April 2, 2013).

——. *The Dying Speeches of Several Indians*. Cambridge, MA: Printed for Samuel Green?, ca. 1685. Early American Imprints, 1st ser., Evans 1639–1800, microform. It is also available in a digitized version, in *Readex, Archive of Americana*, www.newsbank.com/readex/.

——. "Eliot's Letters to Boyle, 1670–1688." In *Massachusetts Historical Society Collections*. 1st ser., vol. 3, 177–88. Boston: Munroe and Francis, 1810.

——. *A Further Account of the Progress of the Gospel Amongst the Indians in New-England*. London: Printed by J. Macock, 1660. Reprinted in *The Eliot Tracts: With Letters from John Eliot to Thomas Thorowgood and Richard Baxter*, edited Michael P. Clark, 355–396. London and Westport, CT: Paeger, 2003.

——. *A Further Accompt of the Progresse of the Gospel Amongst the Indians of New England*. London: Printed by M. Simmons, 1659. *The Eliot Tracts: With Letters from John Eliot to Thomas Thorowgood and Richard Baxter*, edited Michael P. Clark, 321–53. London and Westport, CT: Paeger, 2003.

——. "The Harmony of the Gospels." In *The Holy History of the* Humiliations *and* Sufferings *of Jesus Christ, From His Incarnation to his death and Burial*. Boston: Printed for John Foster, 1678.

——. *Indian Dialogues: A Study in Cultural Interaction*. Cambridge, MA: Printed by M. Johnson, 1671. Reprinted Contributions to American History Series, edited by Henry W. Bowden and James P Ronda, vol. 88. Westport, CT: Greenwood Press, 1980.

——. *The Indian Grammar Begun*. Cambridge, MA: Johnson, 1666. Reprint Bedford, MA: Applewood Books, 2001.

——. *John Eliot and the Indians, 1652–1657: Being Letters Addressed to Rev. Jonathan Hanmer of Barnstaple, reproduced from the original manuscripts in the possession of Theodore N. Vail*. Edited by Wilberforce Eames. New York: Adams and Grace Press, 1915.

——. *A Late and Further Manifestation of the Progress of the Gospel Amongst the Indians in New-England*. London: Printed by M. S., 1655. Reprinted in *The Eliot Tracts: With Letters from John Eliot to Thomas Thorowgood and Richard Baxter,* edited Michael P. Clark, 297–320. London and Westport, CT: Paeger, 2003.

——. "Learned Conjectures." In *Jews in America*, edited by Thomas Thorowgood, 2nd ed. London: Printed for Henry Brome, 1660.

——. "Letters of the Rev. John Eliot, The Apostle to the Indians." *New England Historical and Genealogical Register* 33 (1879): 62–65; 236–39; 295–99.

——. "A Letter of the Reverend John Eliot of Roxbury to the Reverend Thomas Shepard of Charleston, August 22, 1673, concerning the state of the gospel work among the Indians." Transcribed from manuscript by Robert E. Moody. January 18, 1952. American Antiquarian Society, Worcester, MA.

——. *The Logic Primer*. Cambridge, MA: Maramaduke Johnson, 1672. Reprint. Cleveland, OH: Burrows Brothers Company, 1904.

——. trans. *Mamvsse Wunneetupanatamwe Up-Biblum God*. (*The Holy Bible containing the Old Testament and the New*) Cambridge: MA: Printed for Samuel Green and Marmaduke Johnson, 1663. Reprint 2nd ed, 1685.

——. *Nehtuhpeh peisses ut mayut* (A Primer in the Language of the Algonquian Indians) Cambridge, 1684.

——. "A Petition from Rev. John Eliot against selling Indians for slaves." 13th of the 6th 1675. *New England Historic and Genealogical Register* 6 (July 1852).

——. trans. *The Psalter*. 1658. Appended to *Mamvsse Wunneetupanatamwe Up-Biblum God*. Cambridge, MA: Printed for Samuel Green, 1685

——. "Rev. John Eliot's Records of the First Church in Roxbury, Massachusetts." *New England Historical and Genealogical Register* 36 (1882): 291–99.

——. "Three Letters of John Eliot and a Bill of Lading of the 'Mayflower.'" Edited by J. Rendel Harris. Manchester and Aberdeen: Printed for Private Circulation, Aberdeen University Press, 1919.

——. trans. *Wusku Wuttestamentum Nullordumun Jesus Christ*. (New Testament) Cambridge: Printed for Samuel Green and Marmaduke Johnson, 1661.

Eliot, John, Richard Mather, and Thomas Weld, trans. *The Bay Psalm Book*. Cambridge, MA: n.p., 1640.

Eliot, John, and Thomas Mayhew Jr. *Tears of Repentance, Or, A further Narrative of the Progress of the Gospel Amongst the Indians in New-England.* London: Peter Cole, 1653. Reprinted in *The Eliot Tracts: With Letters from John Eliot to Thomas Thorowgood and Richard Baxter*, edited by Michael P. Clark, 249–96. London and Westport, CT: Paeger, 2003.

Elliott, John Huxtable. *The Old World and the New, 1492–1650.* Cambridge: Canto, Cambridge University Press, 1970. Reprint 1992.

Emerson, Everett, ed. *Letters from New England: The Massachusetts Bay Colony, 1629–1638.* Amherst: University of Massachusetts Press, 1976.

Faery, Rebecca Blevins. *Cartographies of Desire: Captivity, Race, and Sex in the Shaping of an American Nation.* Norman: University of Oklahoma, 1999.

Fish, Stanley. *Is there a Text in this Class? The Authority of Interpretive Communities.* London and Cambridge, MA: Harvard University Press, 1980. Reprint 2003.

Fiske, John. *The Notebook of the Reverend John Fiske, 1644–1675.* Boston: Colonial Society of Massachusetts, Anthoensen Press, 1974.

Fliegelman, Jay. *Declaring Independence: Jefferson, Natural Language & the Culture of Performance.* Stanford, CA: Stanford University Press, 1993.

Francis, Convers. *Life of John Eliot, The Apostle to the Indians.* New York: Harper, 1854, Reprint New York: Garrett Press, 1969.

Fuller, Mary C. *Voyages in Print: English Travel to America, 1576–1624.* Cambridge: Cambridge University Press, 1995

Games, Alison. *Migration and the Origins of the English Atlantic World.* Cambridge, MA: Harvard University Press, 1999.

Goddard, Ives. "Some Early Examples of American Indian Pidgin English from New England." *International Journal of American Linguistics* 43, no. 1 (January 1977): 37–41.

The Good Indian Missionary. Philadelphia: American Sunday School Union, 1857.

Gookin, Daniel. "Historical Account of the Doings and Sufferings of the Christian Indians in New England, in the Years 1675, 1676, 1677." In *Transactions and Collections of the American Antiquarian Society*, vol. 2, 423–533. Cambridge, MA: Printed for the Society at the University Press, 1836.

———. "Historical Collections of the Indians in New England, 1674." In *Collections of the Massachusetts Historical Society*, vol. 1, 1792. Boston: Munroe and Francis, 1806.

Gray, Edward G. *New World Babel: Languages and Nations in Early America.* Princeton, NJ: Princeton University Press, 1999.

Gray, Kathryn N. "'How may we come to serve God?': Spaces of Religious Utterance in John Eliot's Indian Tracts." *The Seventeenth Century* 24, no. 1 (2009): 7–96.

———. "Written and Spoken Words and Worlds: John Eliot's Algonquian Translation." *Symbiosis: A Journal of Anglo-American Literary Relations* 7, no. 2 (2003): 241–60.

Greenblatt, Stephen. *Marvellous Possessions: The Wonder of the New World.* Chicago: University of Chicago Press, 1991.

Greene, Jack P., and J. R. Pole, eds. *Colonial British America: Essays in the New History of the Early Modern Era.* London and Baltimore: Johns Hopkins University Press, 1984.

Gregerson, Linda. "The Commonwealth of the Word: New England, Old England, and the Praying Indians." In *British Identities and English Renaissance Literature*, edited by David J. Baker and Willy Maley, 178–92. Cambridge: Cambridge University Press, 2002.

Grumet, Robert Steven. "Sunksquaws, Shamans and Tradeswomen: Middle Atlantic Coastal Algonkian Women during the 17th and 18th Centuries." In *Women and Colonization: Anthropological Perspectives,* edited by Mona Etienne and Eleanor Burke Leacock, 43–62. New York: Praeger, 1980.

Guice, Stephen Andrew. "The Linguistic Work of John Eliot." PhD diss., University of Michigan, 1990.

Gura, Philip F. *A Glimpse of Sion's Glory: Puritan Radicalism in New England, 1620–1660.* Middleton, CT: Wesleyan University Press, 1984.

Gustafson, Sandra M. *Eloquence is Power: Oratory and Performance in Early America.* London and Chapel Hill: Published for the Omohundro Institute of Early American History and Culture, Williamsburg, Virginia, by the University of North Carolina Press, 2000.

Hadfield, Andrew. *Literature, Travel, and Colonial Writing in the English Renaissance 1545–1625.* New York and Oxford: Oxford University Press, 1998.

Hall, David D. "Religion and Society: Problems and Reconsiderations." In *Colonial British America: Essays in the New History of the Early Modern Era,* edited by Jack P. Greene and J. R. Pole, 317–44. London and Baltimore: Johns Hopkins University Press, 1984.

———. "Toward a History of Popular Religion in Early New England." *William and Mary Quarterly.* 41, no. 1 (1984): 49–55.

———. *Worlds of Wonder, Days of Judgement: Popular Religious Belief in Early New England.* Cambridge, MA: Harvard University Press, 1989. Reprint 1990.

Hammond, John. *Leah and Rachel, Or, The Two Fruitful Sisters Virginia and Maryland.* London: Printed by T. Mabb, 1656. Reprinted in *Narratives of Early Maryland, 1633–1684,* edited by Clayton Colman Hall. New York: Charles Scribner's Sons, 1910.

Hariot, Thomas. "A Brief and True Report of the New found Land of Virginia, 1588." In *The English Literature of America 1500–1800,* edited by Myra Jehlen and Michael Warner, 64–89. New York: Routledge, 1997.

Hill, Christopher. *The English Bible and The Seventeenth-Century Revolution.* London: Penguin Press, 1993.

Hochbruck, Wolfgang, and Beatrix Dudensing-Reichel. "'Honoratissimi Benefactors': Native American Students and Two Seventeenth Century Texts in the University Tradition." In *Early Native American Writing: New Critical Essays,* edited by Helen Jaskowski, 1–14. Cambridge: Cambridge University Press, 1996.

Holstun, James. *A Rational Millenium: Puritan Utopias of Seventeenth Century England and America.* New York: Oxford University Press, 1987.

Hubbard, William. *A Narrative of the Indian Wars in New England.* Brattleborough, VT: William Fessenden, 1814. Early American Imprints, 2nd ser., microform, 31766.

Hunter, Michael C. W., Antonio Clericuzio, and Lawrence M. Principe, eds. *The Correspondence of Robert Boyle.* 6 vols. London and Burlington, VT: Pickering and Chatto, 2001.

Jacobs, Paul Samuel. *James Printer: A Novel of Rebellion.* New York: Scholastic Press, 1997.

J. D. *A Sermon Preached at the Funeral of that incomparable lady the Honourable the Lady Mary Armyne.* London: Printed for Nevil Simmons, 1676. Reprint *Early English Books 1641–1700,* University of Michigan, microform, wing 1381:09.

Jarvis, F. Washington. *Schola Illustris: The Roxbury Latin School, 1645–1995.* Boston: D. R. Godine, 1995.

Jennings, Francis. "Goals and Functions of Puritan Missions to the Indians." *Ethnohistory* 18, no. 3 (Summer 1971): 197–212.

———. *The Invasion of America: Indians, Colonialism, and the Cant of Conquest.* Chapel Hill: University of North Carolina Press, 1975. Reprint New York: W. W. Norton & Company, 1976.

Johnson, Edward. *Johnson's Wonder-Working Providence, 1628–1651,* edited by J. Franklin Jameson. Original Narratives of Early American History Series. New York: Charles Scribner's Sons, 1910.

Jones, Katherine. "Katherine Jones, Viscountess Ranelagh to John Eliot," August 13, 1676. Royal Society Archives, London, RB/3/5/9. Previous numbers, BL 5, fols. 17–18.

Kamensky, Jane. *Governing the Tongue: The Politics of Speech in Early New England.* Oxford: Oxford University Press, 1999.

Keary, Anne. "Retelling the History of the Settlement of Providence: Speech, Writing, and Cultural Interaction on Narragansett Bay." *New England Quarterly* 69, no. 2 (June 1996): 250–86.

Keeble, N. H., and Geoffrey Nuttall, eds. *Calendar of the Correspondence of Richard Baxter, 1660–1669.* 2 vols. Oxford: Claredon Press, 1991.

Kellaway, William. "The Collection for the Indians of New England, 1649–1660." *Bulletin of the John Rylands Library* 39, no. 2 (March 1957): 444–62. Reprint Manchester: The Library, 1957.

———. *The New England Company 1649–1776: Missionary Society to the American Indians.* Westport, CT: Greenwood Press, 1961. Reprint 1975.

Kelleter, Frank. "Puritan Missionaries and the Colonization of the New World: A Reading of John Eliot's Indian Dialogues (1671)." In *Early American Re-Explored: New Readings in Colonial, Early National and Antebellum Culture,* edited by Klaus H. Schmidt and Fritz Fleischmann, 71–106. New York: Peter Lang, 2000.

Kibbey, Ann. *The Interpretation of Material Shapes in Puritanism: A Study of Rhetoric, Prejudice and Violence.* Cambridge: Cambridge University Press, 1986.

Knight, Janice. *Orthodoxies in Massachusetts: Rereading American Puritanism.* Cambridge, MA: Harvard University Press, 1994. Reprint 1997.

Kupperman, Karen Ordahl, ed. *America in European Consciousness, 1493–1750.* Chapel Hill: University of North Carolina Press, 1995.

Lane, Jill. "On Colonial Forgetting: The Conquest of New Mexico and Its Historia." In *The Ends of Performance,* edited by Peggy Phelan and Jill Lane, 52–69. New York and London: New York University Press, 1998.

Leavelle, Tracy Neale. "Geographies of Encounter: Religion and Contested Spaces in Colonial North America." *American Quarterly* 56, no. 4 (2004): 913–43.

Lechford, Thomas. *Plain Dealing, Or, News from New England.* London: Printed by W. E. & I. G. for Nath Butler, 1642.

Lefebvre, Henri. *The Production of Space.* Oxford and Cambridge, MA: Blackwell, 1991.

Lepore, Jill. "Dead Men Tell No Tales: John Sassamon and the Fatal Consequences of Literacy." *American Quarterly* 46, no. 4 (December 1994): 479–512.

———. *The Name of War: King Philip's War and the Origins of American Identity.* New York: Knopf, 1998. Reprint New York: Vintage Books, 1999.

"Letter of Pessicus and Collounicas, Naheganset May 24, 1644," *Records of the Plymouth Colony Acts of the Commissioners of the United Colonies in New England, 1643–1651.* Ed. David Pulsifer, vol. 1. New York: AMS Press, 1968.

Lochinvar. *Encouragements for New Galloway in America.* Edinburgh: Printed by John Wreittoun, 1625.

Lockridge, Kenneth A. *Literacy in Colonial New England: An Enquiry into the Social Context of Literacy in the Early Modern West.* New York: W. W. Norton, 1974.

Lowance, Mason I., Jr. "Cotton Mather's Magnalia and the Metaphors of Biblical History." In *Typology and Early American Literature,* edited by Sacvan Bercovitch, 139–62. Amherst: University of Massachusetts Press, 1972.

———. "Typology and the New England Way: Cotton Mather and the Exegesis of Biblical Types." *Early American Literature* 4, no. 1 (Spring 1969): 15–37.

MacFarlane, Alan. "History, Anthropology and the Study of Communities." *Social History* 2, no. 5 (May 1977): 637–52.

Mackenthun, Gesa. *Metaphors of Dispossession: American Beginnings and the Translation of Empire, 1492–1637.* Norman: University of Oklahoma Press, 1997.

Maclear, J. F. "New England and the Fifth Monarchy: The Quest for the Millennium in Early American Puritanism." *William and Mary Quarterly,* 3rd ser., 32, no. 2 (1975): 223–60.

Maltby, William S. *The Black Legend in England: The development of anti-Spanish sentiment, 1558–1660.* Durham, NC: Duke University Press, 1971.

Manning, Stephen. "Scriptural Exegesis and the Literary Critic." In *Typology and Early American Literature,* edited by Sacvan Bercovitch, 47–66. Amherst: University of Massachusetts Press, 1972.

Manning, Susan, and Andrew Taylor, eds. *Transatlantic Literary Studies: A Reader.* Edinburgh: Edinburgh University Press, 2007.

Mather, Cotton. *Magnalia Christi Americana, Or, the Ecclesiastical History of New-England, from the First Planting in the Year 1620 unto the Year of our Lord, 1698.* Printed for Thomas Parkhurst, London, 1702. *Eighteenth Century Collections Online* at www.jischistoricbooks.ac.uk (accessed April 8, 2013).

———. *Magnalia Christi Americana, Or, The Ecclesiastical History of New England.* Edited by Raymond J. Cunningham. New York: Frederick Ungar Publishing, 1970.

Mayhew, Experience. *Indian Converts; or Some Account of the Lives and Dying Speeches of a Considerable Number of the Christianized Indians of Martha's Vineyard in New England.*

London: Printed for Samuel Gerrish, Bookseller in Boston, 1727. Reprint Whitefish, MT: Kessinger Publishing.

———. *Observations on the Indian Language.* Boston: Press of D. Clapp & Sons, 1884.

Mayhew, Matthew. *A Brief Narrative of the Success which the Gospel hath had, among the Indians of Martha's Vineyard (and Places Adjacent) in New-England.* Boston: Printed by Bartholomew Green, 1694.

Miller, A. Richard, and Jill Miller. *1651– 2001, 350th Anniversary of Natick, Massachusetts and the Natick Praying Indians.* n.d., www.millermicro.com/natprayind.html (accessed March 30, 2013).

Miller, Perry. *Orthodoxy in Massachusetts, 1630–1650: A Genetic Study.* Cambridge, MA: Harvard University Press, 1933.

———. *The New England Mind: From Colony to Province.* Cambridge, MA: Harvard University Press, 1953.

Miller, Perry, and Thomas H. Johnson. *The Puritans.* New York: American Book Company, 1938. Reprint rev. ed. London: Harper & Row, 1963.

Milton, John. "The Ready and Easy Way to Establish a Free Commonwealth (1660)." In *The Prose Works of John Milton,* vol. 2. London: Henry G. Bohn, 1853.

Monaghan, E. Jennifer. *Learning to Read and Write in Colonial America.* American Antiquarian Society. Amherst and Boston: University of Massachusetts Press, 2005.

———. "Literacy Instruction and Gender in Colonial New England." *American Quarterly* 40, no. 1 (1988): 18–41.

Moran, Gerald F., and Maris A. Vinovskis. "The Puritan Family and Religion: A Critical Reappraisal." *William and Mary Quarterly* 39, no. 1 (January 1982): 29–63.

Morgan, Edumnd S. "The Puritans and Sex." *New England Quarterly* 15, no. 4 (December 1942): 591–607.

———. *The Puritan Family: Religion and Domestic Relations in Seventeenth Century New England.* London: Harper Perennial, 1966.

Morison, Samuel Eliot. *The Founding of Harvard College.* Cambridge, MA: Harvard University Press, 1935.

———. *Harvard College in the Seventeenth Century,* vol. 1. Cambridge, MA: Harvard University Press, 1936.

Morrison, Dane. *A Praying People: Massachusetts Acculturation and the Failure of the Puritan Missions, 1600–1690.* New York: Peter Lang, 1998.

Morrison, Kenneth M. "'That Art of Coyning Christians': John Eliot and the Praying Indians of Massachusetts." *Ethnohistory* 21, no. 1 (Winter 1974): 77–92.

Morton, Thomas. "New English Canaan (1637)." In *The Literatures of Colonial America: An Anthology,* edited by Susan Castillo and Ivy Schweitzer, 236–42. Oxford: Blackwell, 2001.

Murray, David. *Forked Tongues: Speech, Writing and Representation in North American Indian Texts.* Bloomington: Indiana University Press, 1991.

———. *Indian Giving: Economies of Power in Early Indian-white Exchanges.* Amherst: University of Massachusetts Press, 2000.

———. "Using Roger Williams' Key into America." *Symbiosis, A Journal of Anglo-American Literary Relations* 1, no. 2 (October 1997): 237–53.

Naeher, Robert James. "Dialogue in the Wilderness: John Eliot and the Indian Exploration of Puritanism as a Source of Meaning, Comfort, and Ethnic Survival." *New England Quarterly* 62, no. 3 (September 1989): 346–68.

Newcome, Henry. Henry Newcome, minister of Gawsworth, Cheshire, 1652/3. *The Autobiography of Henry Newcome.* 1st ser., vol. 26. N.p.: Chetham Society, 1852.

New England Company Archives, Bodleian Library, Oxford, Rawlinson Collection, C943, 54–73.

New England's First Fruits. London: Printed by R. O. and G. D. for Henry Overton, 1643. Reprinted in *The Eliot Tracts: With Letters from John Eliot to Thomas Thorowgood and Richard Baxter,* edited by Micheal P. Clark, 55–78. London and Westport, CT: Praeger, 2003.

Norton, Mary Beth, and Ruth M Alexander, eds. "The Trial of Sarah Ahhaton in Massachusetts, 1668." In *Major Problems in American Women's History*, 2nd ed. Lexington, MA: D. C. Heath and Co., 1996.

O'Brien, Jean M. *Dispossession by Degrees: Indian Land and Identity in Natick, 1650–1790*. Cambridge, MA: Cambridge University Press, 1997.

Pagden, Anthony. *European Encounters with the New World: From Renaissance to Romanticism*. New Haven, CT: Yale University Press, 1993.

Parker, Andrew, and Eve Kosofsky Sedgwick, eds. *Performativity and Performance*. London: Routledge, 1995.

Peters, Hugh. *A Memoir or Defence of Hugh Peters*. Boston: C. C. P. Moody, 1851. *Early English Books Online* at http://eebo.chadwyck.com/home (accessed March 26, 2013).

Pierson, Abraham. "Some Helps for the Indians, 1658." *Connecticut Historical Society Collections*, vol. 3. Hartford, CT: Published for the Society, 1895.

Pillings, James Constantine. *Bibliography of the Algonquian Languages*. Washington, DC: Government Printing Office, 1891.

Plane, Anne Marie. "Childbirth Practices among Native American Women of New England and Canada, 1600–1800." In *Medicine and Healing*, edited by Peter C. Benes, 13–24. Dublin Seminar for New England Folklife Annual Proceedings, Boston: Boston University Press, 1992.

———. "'The Examination of Sarah Ahhaton': The Politics of 'Adultery' in an Indian Town of Seventeenth-Century Massachusetts." In *Algonkians of New England: Past and Present: Dublin Seminar for New England Folklife Annual Proceedings*, 14–25. Boston: Boston University Press, 1993.

Pollock, Della. "Performing Writing." In *The Ends of Performance*, edited by Peggy Phelan and Jill Lane, 73–103. New York and London: New York University Press, 1998.

Porterfield, Amanda. "Women's Attraction to Puritanism." *Church History* 60, no. 2 (June 1991): 196–209.

Potter, Tiffany. "Writing Indigenous Femininity: Mary Rowlandson's Narrative of Captivity." *Eighteenth-Century Studies* 36, no. 2 (Winter 2003): 153–67.

Powell, Chilton L. "Marriage in Early New England." *New England Quarterly* 1, no. 3 (July 1928): 323–34.

Powicke, F. J., ed. "Some Unpublished Correspondence of the Rev. Richard Baxter and the Rev John Eliot, 'The Apostle to the American Indians,' 1656–1682." *Bulletin of the John Rylands Library* 15, no. 1 (1931): 138–76, 442–66.

Pratt, Mary Louise. *Imperial Eyes: Travel Writing and Transculturation*. London and New York: Routledge, 1992.

———. *Toward a Speech Act Theory of Literary Discourse* . London and Bloomington: Indiana University Press, 1977.

Records of the Plymouth Colony. Acts of the Commissioners of the United Colonies in New England, 1643–1651 and 1653–1678–9. ed. David Pulsifer, 2 vols. New York: AMS Press, 1968.

Roach, Joseph. "Culture and Performance in the Circum-Atlantic World." In *Performativity and Performance*, edited by Andrew Parker and Eve Kosofsky Sedgwick, 124–36. London: Routledge, 1995.

Ronda, James P. "Generations of Faith: The Christian Indians of Martha's Vineyard." *William and Mary Quarterly* 38, no. 3 (July 1981): 369–94.

———. "'We Are Well as We Are:' An Indian Critique of Seventeenth Century Christian Missions." *William and Mary Quarterly* 34, no. 1 (January 1977): 66–82.

Round, Phillip H. *By Nature and By Custom Cursed: Transatlantic Civil Discourse and New England Cultural Production, 1620–1660*. London and Hanover, NH: University Press of New England, 1999.

———. "Neither Here nor There: Transatlantic Epistolarity in Early America." In *A Companion to the Literatures of Colonial America*, edited by Ivy Schweitzer and Susan Castillo, 426–79. Oxford: Blackwell Publishing, 2005.

Rowlandson, Mary. *The Sovereignty and Goodness of God* (Samuel Green: Cambridge MA, 1682) *Early English Books Online* at http://eebo.chadwyck.com/home (accessed April 3, 2013).

Sainsbury, W. Noel, ed. *Calendar of State Papers, Colonial Series, America and the West Indies 1661–1668*. London: Her Majesty's Stationary Office, 1880. http://archive.org/stream/1964colonialrecordsc05greauoft/1964colonialrecordsc05greauoft_djvu.txt (accessed April 2, 2013).

Salisbury, Neal. "The Indians' Old World: Native Americans and the Coming of Europeans." *William and Mary Quarterly* 53, no. 3 (July 1996): 435–58.

———. *Manitou and Providence: Indians, Europeans, and the Making of New England, 1500–1643*. New York: Oxford University Press, 1982.

———. "Red Puritans: The 'Praying Indians' of Massachusetts Bay and John Eliot." *William and Mary Quarterly* 31, no. 1 (January 1974): 27–54.

Scanlan, Thomas. *Colonial Writing and the New World 1583–1671: Allegories of Desire*. Cambridge: Cambridge University Press, 1999.

Schechner, Richard. *Between Theater and Anthropology*. Philadelphia: University of Pennsylvania Press, 1985.

Schweitzer, Ivy. *The Work of Self-Representation: Lyric Poetry in Colonial New England*. Chapel Hill: University of North Carolina Press, 1991.

Schmidt, Klaus H., and Fritz Fleischmann, eds. *Early American Re-Explored: New Readings in Colonial, Early National and Antebellum Culture*. New York: Peter Lang, 2000.

Searle, Alison. "'Though I am a Stranger to You by Face, yet in Neere Bonds by Faith': A Transatlantic Republic of Letters." *Early American Literature* 43, no. 2 (June 2008): 277–308.

Sedgwick, Catherine Maria. *Hope Leslie, Or, The Early Times of the Massachusetts*. 1827. Edited by Carolyn L. Kratcher. London: Penguin Classics, 1998.

Selement, George. "The Meeting of Elite and Popular Minds at Cambridge, New England, 1638–1645." *William and Mary Quarterly* 41, no. 1 (January 1984): 32–48.

Sewall, Samuel. "The Selling of Joseph: A Memorial." In *Massachusetts Historical Society Collections*, 1878–1882, 16–21. Boston: Printed by Bartholomew Green and John Allen, 1700.

Shepard, Alexandra, and Phil Withington. *Communities in Early Modern England: Networks, Place, Rhetoric*. Manchester: Manchester University Press, 2000.

Shepard, Thomas. *The Clear Sun-shine of the Gospel* (London: J. Bellamy, 1648). Reprinted in *The Eliot Tracts: With Letters from John Eliot to Thomas Thorowgood and Richard Baxter*, edited by Michael P. Clark, 101–41. London and Westport, CT: Paeger, 2003.

———. *Confessions*. Edited by George Selement and Bruce C. Woolley, vol. 58. Boston: Publication of the Colonial Society of Massachusetts, 1981.

———. *The Day-Breaking if not The Sun-Rising of the Gospel, With the Indians in New England* (1647). Reprinted in *The Eliot Tracts: With Letters from John Eliot to Thomas Thorowgood and Richard Baxter*, edited by Micheal P. Clark, 79–101. London and Westport, CT: Praeger, 2003.

———. *God's Plot: Puritan Spirituality in Thomas Shepard's Cambridge*, edited by Michael McGiffert. Commonwealth Series, rev. ed. Amherst: University of Massachusetts Press, 1972. Reprint 1994.

———. *The Sincere Convert: Discovering the Small Number of True Believers and the Great Difficulty of Saving Conversion . . . .* Cambridge, MA: Printed by J. Flesher for Robert Home, 1689.

———. *The Sincere Convert and The Sound Believer*. Edited by John A. Albro. 3 vols. Boston: Doctrinal Tract and Book Society 1853. Reprint Ligonier, PA: Solo Deo Gloria Publications, 1991.

Sherman, William H. *Used Books: Marking Readers in Renaissance England*. Philadelphia: University of Pennsylvania Press, 2008.

Shields, David S. *Civil Tongues & Polite Letters in British America*. Chapel Hill: Published for the Institute of Early American History and Culture, Williamsburg, Virginia, by University of North Carolina Press, 1997.

Shoemaker, Nancy. *Negotiators of Change: Historical Perspectives on Native American Women.* London: Routledge, 1995.

Shurtleff, Nathaniel B., and Pulsifer, David, eds. *Records of the Bay Colony: Acts of the Commissioners of the United Colonies of New England.* 2 vols. New York: AMS Press, 1968.

Silverman, David J. "Indians, Missionaries, and Religious Translation: Creating Wampanoag Christianity in Seventeenth-Century Martha's Vineyard." *William and Mary Quarterly* 62, no. 2 (April 2005): 141–74.

Simpson, David. "Hume's Intimate Voices and the Method of Dialogue." *Texas Studies in Literature and Language* 21, no. 1 (Spring 1979): 68–92.

Smith, John. *A Description of New England . . . .* London: R. Clerke, 1616.

———. *A Map of Virginia* (London 1612). In *Narratives of Early Virginia 1606–1625*, edited by Lyon Gardiner Tyler. New York: Charles Scribner's Son, 1907.

Smits, David D. "The 'Squaw Drudge': A Prime Index of Savagism." *Ethnohistory* 29, no. 4 (Autumn 1982): 281–306.

Sosin, Jack M. *English America and the Restoration Monarchy of Charles II: Transatlantic Politics, Commerce, and Kingship.* London and Lincoln: University of Nebraska Press, 1980.

Spufford, Margaret. *Small Books and Pleasant Histories: Popular Fiction and Its Readership in Seventeenth Century England.* Cambridge: Cambridge University Press, 1985.

Stanley, Alison. "'To Speak With Other Tongues': Linguistics, Colonialism and Identity in 17th Century New England," *Comparative American Studies* 7, no. 1 (2009): 1–17.

Stearns, Raymond P. "The Weld-Peter Mission to England." *Publications of the Colonial Society of Massachusetts* 32 (1934). In *Transactions of the Colonial Society of Massachusetts, 1933–1937.* 188–246. Boston: Colonial Society of Massachusetts, 1937.

Stephen, Timothy. "Communication in the shifting Context of Intimacy: Marriage, Meaning and Modernity." *Communications Theory* 4, no. 3 (2006): 191–218.

Strong, John A. "Algonquian Women as Sunksquaws and Caretakers of the Soil: The Documentary Evidence in Seventeenth Century New England." In *Women in Native American Literature and Culture*, edited by Susan Castillo and Victor M. P. da Rosa, 191–214. Porto: Fernando Pessoa University Press, 1997.

Tanis, Norman Earl. "Education in John Eliot's Indian Utopias 1646–1675." *History of Education Quarterly* 10, no. 3 (Autumn 1970): 308–23.

Thomas, G. E. "Puritan, Indians and the Concept of Race." *New England Quarterly* 48, no. 1 (March 1975): 3–27.

Thomas, Nathaniel. "Letter From Nathaniel Thomas, on the Expedition against Philip, to Governor Winslow"; *Swanzey, 25th June, 1675.* In *Massachusetts Historical Society Collections* 1st ser., vol. 4. Boston: Massachusetts Historical Society, 1799.

Thomson, David. "The Antinomian Crisis: Prelude to Puritan Missions." *Early American Literature* 38, no. 3 (Fall 2003): 401–35.

Thorowgood, Thomas. *Jews in America, Or, Probabilities. . . .* London: H. Brome, 1660. American Culture Series, microform, 6:54.

Tinker, George E. *Missionary Conquest: The Gospel and Native American Cultural Genocide.* Minneapolis: Fortress Press, 1993.

Todorov, Tzvetan. *The Conquest of America: The Question of the Other.* Translated by Richard Howard. New York: Harper & Row, 1982. Reprint New York: HarperPerennial, 1992.

Tooker, William Wallace. *John Eliot's First Indian Teacher and Interpreter, Cockenoe-de-Long Island: and the Story of His Career from the Early Records.* New York: Francis P. Harper, 1896.

Underhill, John. *Newes From America.* London: Printed by I D. for Peter Cole, 1638.

Ulrich, Laurel Thatcher. *Good Wives: Image and Reality in the Lives of Women in Northern New England, 1650–1750.* New York: Alfred A Knopf, 1982.

———. "Vertuous Women Found: New England Ministerial Literature, 1668–1735." *American Quarterly* 28, no. 1 (Spring 1976): 20–40.

Vaughan, Alden T., ed. *The Puritan Tradition in America 1620–1730.* London: Harper & Row, 1972.

Vincent, Philip. *True Relation of the Late Battell Fought in New-England, between the English and the Pequet Salvages.* London: Printed by Thomas Harper, for Nathanael Butter and Iohn Bellamie, 1638.

Walker, Willard. "Native American Writing Systems." In *Languages of the USA*, edited by Charles A. Ferguson and Shirley Brice Heath, 145–74. Cambridge: Cambridge University Press, 1981.

Walker, Williston, ed. *The Creeds and Platforms of Congregationalism.* New York: Charles Scribner's Sons, 1893. *Internet Archive*, http://archive.org (accessed April 4, 2013).

Waterhouse, Edward. "A Declaration of the State of the Colony in Virginia (London 1622)" In *The English Literature of America 1500–1800*, edited by Myra Jehlen and Michael Warner, 129–46. New York: Routledge, 1997.

Watson, Patricia. "The 'Hidden Ones': Woman and Healing in Colonial New England." In *Medicine and Healing*, edited by Peter Burns, 25–33. Boston: Boston University Press, 1992.

Wharton, Edward. *New England's Present Sufferings, Under their Cruel Neighbouring Indians.* London, 1675. *Early English Books Online* at http://eebo.chadwyck.com/home (accessed April 3, 2013).

White, Craig. "The Praying Indians Speeches as Texts of Massachusett Oral Culture." *Early American Literature* 38, no. 3 (Fall 2003): 437–67.

White, Father Andrew. *Briefe Relation of the Voyage into Maryland* (1634). In *Narratives of Early Maryland, 1633–1684*, edited by Clayton Colman Hall. New York: Charles Scribner's Sons, 1910.

Whitfield, Henry. *The Light Appearing More and More Towards the Perfect Day,* London: J. Bartlet, 1651. Reprinted in *The Eliot Tracts: With Letters from John Eliot to Thomas Thorowgood and Richard Baxter*, edited by Michael P. Clark, 169–210. London and Westport, CT: Paeger, 2003.

———. *Strength out of Weaknesse, Or, A Glorious Manifestation of the Further Progresse of the Gospel among Indians in New England.* London: Printed by M. Simmons for John Blague and Samuel Howes, 1652. Reprinted in *The Eliot Tracts: With Letters from John Eliot to Thomas Thorowgood and Richard Baxter*, edited by Michael P. Clark, 211–48. London and Westport, CT: Paeger, 2003.

Williams, Raymond. *Keywords: A Vocabulary of Culture and Society.* London: Croom Helm, 1976.

Williams, Roger. "The Bloody Tenant of Persecution yet more Bloody. London, 1652." *American Culture Series*, 57:6. n.d.

———. "The Bloudy Tenant of Persecution. London, 1644." *Early English Books, 1641–1700,* microform, *228:E.1, no. 2.* n.d.

———. *Complete Writings.* Edited by Perry Miller. New York: Russell and Russell, 1963.

———. *A Key to the Language of America.* London: Printed by Gregory Dexter, 1643. In *Publications of the Narragansett Club*, vol. 1. Providence, RI: Providence Press Co., Printers, 1866.

Winiarski, Douglas L. "Native American Popular Religion in New England's Colony, 1670–1770." *Religion and American Culture* 15, no. 2 (2005): 147–86.

Winship, George Parker. *The Cambridge Press:1638–1692. A Reexamination of the Evidence concerning the Bay Psalm Book and the Eliot Indian Bible as well as other contemporary books and people.* Philadelphia: University of Pennsylvania Press, 1945.

———. *The Eliot Indian Tracts.* Cambridge, MA: Harvard University Press, 1925.

Winslow, Edward. *The Glorious Progress of the Gospel.* London: Printed for Hannah Allen, 1649. Reprinted in *The Eliot Tracts: With Letters from John Eliot to Thomas Thorowgood and Richard Baxter,* edited by Michael P. Clark, 141–68. London and Westport, CT: Paeger, 2003.

———. *Good News From New England* (1624). London: Printed by Matthew Simmons, 1648. Also printed in *Massachusetts Historical Society Collections.* 2nd ser., vol. 9, 1832.

Winslow, Ola Elizabeth. *John Eliot "Apostle to the Indians."* Boston: Houghton Mifflin Company, 1968.

Winthrop, John. "A Journal of the Transactions and Occurrences in the Settlement of Massachusetts and the other New England Colonies from the year 1630–1644." Hartford: Elisha Babcock, 1790. Also available online at http://archive.org/stream/journaloftransac00wint#page/n7/mode/2up (accessed October 20, 2009).

Winthrop, Robert C., ed. *Correspondence of Hartlib, Haak, Oldenburg, and Others of the Founders of The Royal Society, with Governor Winthrop of Connecticut, 1661–1672.* Boston: Press of John Wilson and Son, 1878.

Wood, William. *New England's Prospect.* London: Thomas Cotes, 1634. *Early English Books Online* at http://eebo.chadwyck.com/home (accessed April 4, 2013).

Wyss, Hilary E.. *Writing Indians: Literacy, Christianity, and Native Community in Early America.* Amherst: University of Massachusetts Press, 2000.

Ziff, Larzer. *The Career of John Cotton: Puritanism and the American Experience.* Princeton, NJ: Princeton University Press, 1962.

———, ed. *John Cotton on the Churches of New England.* Cambridge, MA: Belknap Press of Harvard University Press, 1968.

———. "The Social Bond of Church Covenant," *American Quarterly.* 10, no. 4 (Winter 1658): 454–62.

Index

Ahhaton, Sarah, 104
Ahhunnut, Dinah, 103
Algonquian bible (*Mamusse Wunneetupanatamwe Up-Biblum God*), ix, 36, 75; Charles II's response to, 20, 55n41; circulation and distribution of, 30, 55n41; dedications appended to, 37–38, 38; handwritten work and, 129–131; intentions behind, 129; linguistic assimilation in, 137; publication, 19, 124
Algonquian identity, xiii, 84; women and, 98, 115
Algonquian language, ix, 124, 136, 141; grammar development, 18, 136, 145n83, 146n87; as language of Christianity, 68, 139; speech and orthography, 131–133; texts, 16–17, 18, 128, 131, 132
Algonquian women, xv, xvi; archetypal, 109–113; attraction to Christianity, 101; as care-giver, 93; as central axis, 93–100; church membership and, 92; as civil and military leaders, 95, 101–102; colonial identity of, 98; colonial women compared to, 100–105; confessional narratives of, 91–92, 93, 98, 105; creation narratives and, 108–109; domestic violence and, 99–100; in Eliot's letters, 97, 114–115; healing and, 94–95; identity of, 115; in Natick,

91; oratory and, 105–107; religious conversion and, 92–93, 97, 108; representation of, 93; role of, 89, 93, 101, 104–105; sexuality and, 104; speech from, 97. *See also* female reception communities; femininity
Algonquians of Massachusetts, ix; creation narratives, 108–109; domestic scene of, 109–113; illness and, 74; intellectual and educational participation, 63–67; leadership, 83, 95, 101–102, 104; literacy roots, 124; living voices, 130–131; social organization, 101; space and, 61–62. *See also* children; praying Indian; *specific people and places*
Allegories of Desire (Scanlan), xi
Amos, Rachel, 98
Angier, Mary, 106
"Animadversions of Mr. Eliot's Book for Stated Counsels" (Baxter), 14
Antichrist, 11
Antony, 83
"Apostle to the American Indians" status, ix, xvin3
Armstrong, Catherine, 2
Armyne, Mary, 5, 8, 38, 54n39; Wood's dedication to, 89
Armyne, William, 89
Ashhurst, William, 5
Ashurst, Henry, 21

163

About the Author

Kathryn N. Gray is a lecturer in English Literature at Plymouth University. She has research interests in the literature and culture of seventeenth-century New England, Native American literature, and early American natural histories. Her work has been published in a number of journals, including *Symbiosis* and *The Seventeenth Century*, and in edited collections of essays, including *Blackwell's Companion to the Literatures of Colonial America*.